THE *Social Construction* OF *American Realism*

AMY KAPLAN

The University of Chicago Press
CHICAGO AND LONDON

The University of Chicago Press, Chicago 60637
The University of Chicago Press, Ltd., London

Paperback edition 1992
Printed in the United States of America

97 96 95 94 93 92   5432

Library of Congress Cataloging-in-Publication Data

Kaplan, Amy.
The social construction of American realism / Amy Kaplan.

p.   cm.
Bibliography: p.
Includes index.
ISBN 0-226-42429-4 (cloth)
ISBN 0-226-42430-8 (paperback)
1. Realism in literature. 2. American fiction—19th century—History and criticism. 3. American fiction—20th century—History and criticism. 4. Social conflict in literature. 5. Capitalism in literature. I. Title.
PS374.R37K37   1988
813′.4′0912—dc19   88-10834
CIP

♾ The paper used in this publication meets the minimum requirements of the American National Standard for Information Sciences—Permanence of Paper for Printed Library Materials, ANSI Z39.48-1984.

This book is printed on acid-free paper.

To my parents
and
the memory of Laurence B. Holland

CONTENTS

ACKNOWLEDGMENTS

I would like to thank the following friends and colleagues who have read parts of the manuscript at different stages and generously offered their advice and support: Michael Davitt Bell, Rachel Bowlby, Leo Braudy, Richard Brodhead, Sharon Cameron, Leslie Moore, Eric Sundquist, Alan Trachtenberg, Donald Weber, Christopher Wilson, and Larzer Ziff. A Morse Fellowship from Yale University provided a year's leave from teaching to work on this book. Part of the Introduction appeared in *The Yale Review* (Autumn 1984), © Yale University; an earlier version of Chapter 2 appeared in *PMLA* (1986): 69–81; and an earlier version of Chapter 3 appeared in *ELH* (Summer 1986): 433–57. I am grateful to the publishers for permission to use these materials here. Here I would like to thank Harvey Weiss.

INTRODUCTION: REALISM AND "ABSENT THINGS IN AMERICAN LIFE"

The fate of realism in American literary history has undergone dramatic reversals on theoretical, political, and historical grounds. From an objective reflection of contemporary social life, realism has become a fictional conceit, or deceit, packaging and naturalizing an official version of the ordinary. From a style valued for its plain-speaking vernacular, realism has adopted a rhetorical sophistication that now subverts its own claims to referentiality. From a progressive force exposing the conditions of industrial society, realism has turned into a conservative force whose very act of exposure reveals its complicity with structures of power. These reversals accompany changes in the historical understanding of American capitalism, from a class-based system structured by relations of production to a culture of consumption and surveillance which sweeps all social relations into a vortex of the commodity and the spectacle. Pivotal in the changing fate of realism is the enduring dominance of the romance thesis that makes realism by necessity a failure. Whereas for critics in the forties and fifties, realism failed to represent contemporary society because of the absence of a dense social fabric, for literary historians of the sixties the realists' perception of the presence of complex social changes marred their achievement of literary form. For a more recent generation of critics, realism fails because of a linguistic absence which makes referentiality impossible. Common to all these approaches is the assumption of an inadequate relation between American fiction and American society, though the blame—or credit—can be attributed to either side.

I

"One might enumerate the items of high civilization, as it exists in other countries, which are absent from the texture of American life, until it should become a wonder to know what was left."[1] So begins Henry James's famous list of the "absent things in American life" in his early book on Hawthorne. Part lament, part boast, it set the tone for the study of American fiction over half a century later, when critics sought to explain why American novelists apparently were not interested in writing about society. Whereas James points to the lack of a "complex social machinery to set a writer in motion"[2] as the major difference between Hawthorne's antebellum world and his own vastly more complicated age, literary critics of the post–World War II era turned this deficiency into the distinguishing feature of an American literary tradition. In other words, the supposedly impoverished soil of American culture has proved most fertile for the American imagination.

This view underlies the now familiar and currently disputed distinction between the European novel and the American romance, which was drawn most fully a generation ago by Richard Chase in *The American Novel and Its Tradition.*[3] In the richly textured social world of the European novel, Chase argued, characters develop in relation to entrenched institutions and the struggle between classes. The isolated hero of the American romance, in contrast, embarks on a melodramatic quest through a symbolic universe, unformed by networks of social relations and unfettered by the pressure of social restraints. As his title suggests, Chase was deliberately establishing a national alternative to F. R. Leavis's *The Great Tradition* of English novelists from Jane Austen to George Eliot, Henry James, and Joseph Conrad. Where the "great tradition" seeks order through the reconciliation of the individual and society, the American tradition, from *Wieland* to *The Sound and the Fury,* explores the open-ended states of individual alienation and cosmic disorder. Chase founds his tradition on the profoundly ahistorical thesis that, in the absence of a settled, class-bound society, Americans do not write social fiction. Despite subsequent criticism, Chase's romance thesis has in effect shaped the canon of American fiction that we still read, teach, and write about today—a canon that was initiated by Brown and Cooper, developed by Hawthorne and Melville, and reached its apotheosis in James and Faulkner, with detours through Twain, Norris, and Fitzgerald.[4]

Of course the boundary of any literary canon defines what it precludes as well as what it includes. The purpose of opening this book on

American realism with the seemingly worn-out romance thesis is not to beat a dead horse by recovering a suppressed tradition or to turn the romance/realism dichotomy on its head. Rather it is to show how the dominance of the romance in framing an American canon has done more than merely exclude realistic novels; more importantly, the assumptions underlying the romance thesis have determined the study of American realism from the forties to the present, and have limited the range of critical inquiry. The association of the romance with a uniquely American culture has displaced realism to an anomalous and distinctly un-American margin of literary criticism, which has necessarily viewed its literary mode as a failure. Reproducing James's "absent things" in different theoretical guises, studies of American realism have repeatedly reinforced the ahistorical assumption of an impossible or flawed relationship between American literature and society.[5]

Although Chase traces his theory to the "lesson of the master," James, he in fact was indebted to two contemporary trends in postwar literary criticism: the New Critics' regard for the lyric as the highest literary form and, most important, his colleague Lionel Trilling's antiliberal polemics. Even though he rejects the New Critics' myopic attention to poetic technique, Chase values the romance precisely for those poetic qualities—symbolism, for example—that raise fiction above the historical contingencies of narrative into the realm of "universal human significance." Toward a similar end but through different means, Chase codifies many of the reflections in Trilling's *The Liberal Imagination*, where to James's list of the "absent things," Trilling adds the category of "manners": "a culture's hum and buzz of implication . . . the whole evanescent context in which its explicit statements are made . . . the things that for good or bad draw the people of a culture together."[6] Turning this loss into a gain, Chase finds writers in the "New World" liberated from "the momentarily settled conditions involving contrasting classes with contrasting manners," conditions which enabled the realistic novel of the "Old World."[7]

Although the romance thesis—like the texts it privileges—seems to grow full-blown out of the American soil to define the exceptional nature of American culture, in fact it emerges victorious from an implicit political attack on alternative forms of fiction and criticism. In his influential essay "Reality in America," Trilling berates historian V. L. Parrington, whom he lumps together with critics as different as Granville Hicks and F. O. Matthiessen; he faults such critics for their deterministic view of "material reality, hard, resistant, unformed, impenetrable, and unpleasant" and for their naive expectation that literature should mechanically reflect this "reality," unrefined by the intervention of the "mind."[8] Trilling's quarrel with what might be called the aesthetics of liberalism issued in the toppling of Theodore Dreiser from the American pantheon for his crude style and lack of intellect, and the replacement of Dreiser by Henry James for the latter's belief in the creative power of the mind to shape its own reality within the limits of moral ambiguity rather than the field of social relations. While the need to value James over Dreiser may sound ludicrous today, for Trilling this exchange amounted to a political choice: "Dreiser and James: with that juxtaposition we are immediately at the dark bloody crossroads where literature and politics meet."[9] The liberal praise of Dreiser's realism for its "great brooding pity" for the victims of capitalism, ran the risk, in Trilling's eyes, of endorsing Stalinism, for, according to another essay, "some paradox of our natures leads us, when once we have made our fellow men the objects of our enlightened interest, to go on to make them the objects of our pity, then of our wisdom, ultimately of our coercion."[10] To represent class difference in America, implies Trilling, is to impose a politically dangerous and aesthetically disingenous literary mode. The only stand against these threats, for Trilling, is "moral realism which is the product of the free play of the moral imagination," i.e., the qualities for which he valued James.[11]

Thus Trilling's and Chase's vision of the American novel must be understood in the context of their times. They were recasting a literary tradition to echo their own generation's disillusionment with oppositional politics and their disbelief in the efficacy of human agency in what Trilling called the "social field," the province of the novel itself. This tradition contributed to the broader intellectual consensus which held that America was a classless society without internal ideological conflicts. Yet the legacy of these critics extended beyond their own time to frame an American canon which equates the romance with the exceptional nature of American culture and which makes realism an anomaly in American fiction; as an inherently flawed imitation of a European convention, realism is, in effect, un-American. If the "thinness" of American culture cannot nurture social fiction, then those novelists who do confront contemporary social issues must be imaginatively handicapped, inorganically related to that culture.

In the 1960s critics reclaimed what Larzer Ziff called "the lost generation" of American realists, writers never lost to literary historians, such as Alfred Kazin.[12] This rediscovery, however, reproduced Trilling's distinction between "mind" and "reality" in the form of two distinct critical approaches: the definition of realism primarily on formalist grounds and the use of realism to designate a literary historical period between the Civil War and World War I. Critics such as Donald Pizer, Harold Kolb, and Charles Walcutt delineated the formal characteristics, the recurring imagery, and the philosophical dimensions that could define realism and naturalism as coherent and serious literary genres.[13] But by and large these critics divorced the texts they analyzed from the social context embedded in those forms. The second set of critics, in contrast, grouped diverse texts together according to an extra-literary category, the historical background of social change—an approach reflected in the titles of such works as Warner Berthoff's *The Ferment of Realism* and Jay Martin's *Harvests of Change*.[14] Although these critics viewed realistic writing as a response to the upheavals of urban-industrial capitalism, they judged texts either by their mimetic accuracy, which usually missed the mark, or by New Critical measures, which found them lacking in organic form and narrative unity. The treatment of texts as responses to social change implicitly situates literature outside the arena of social history, looking down and commenting upon it, and thereby reinforces the rigid split between social structures and literary structures. Reproducing Trilling's distinction between "mind" and "reality," those critics who valued the realists for their commitment to the representation of contemporary American social life often devalued the realists as unsophisticated literary craftsmen. Stylistic inconsistencies and problematic endings were usually treated as internal formal flaws rather than as narrative articulations of ideological problems. The period from *The Adventures of Huckleberry Finn* to *Sister Carrie* is rich in examples of that peculiarly American category, the failed masterpiece.

Contemporary literary theory has effectively broken down the dichotomy between social context and literary form implicit in the concept of realism as empirical reflection and in the assumption that American novelists who turn their gaze on society write flawed prose. The influence of theory can be found in Eric Sundquist's *American Realism: New Essays*, an anthology which reflects two distinct trends in literary criticism: poststructuralism and the renewed interest in history.[15] The antimimetic assumption of postructuralist theory which holds that reality is not reflected by language but that language in fact produces the reality we know has opened the realistic narrative to sophisticated interpretive scrutiny. These approaches, however, tend to locate the power of realistic texts precisely in their ability to deconstruct their own claims to referentiality. Through the lenses of contemporary theories, those characteristics once considered realistic are revalued for exposing their own fictionality. The spokesman for American realism, William

Dean Howells, for example, operates under the anxiety of Hawthorne's influence, a pressure which at key points disrupts the realistic trajectory of his novels, swerving them into the realm of romance.[16] Edith Wharton, once considered the rare American novelist of manners, writes a "romance of identity" in *The House of Mirth*, whose heroine's magnetic appeal is explained by the psychoanalytic theory of narcissism.[17] Thus new theories tend to support an old thesis—that American novelists escape from or fail to represent their society; the concept of realism disappears in the current critical discourse as the romance continues to subvert realistic representation.[18]

In his introduction to *American Realism*, Sundquist revoices Chase's thesis in arguing that American realism "did not achieve a certain and stable force, exhaust that force and perish; rather it failed case by case by refusing to renounce romance completely and by levelling the barriers of aesthetic freedom too completely."[19] On the one hand, Trilling's contest between the free mind and obdurate reality returns in Sundquist's conclusion, which privileges James and Crane both for the "continued presence of the romance" in their writing and for their modernity, "because they demonstrate the increasing discrepancy between the figurative life of the mind and the literal life of the material."[20] On the other hand, Sundquist revives the literary-historical approach to realism which ties together the diversity of literary forms generated by writers between the Civil War and World War I in response to the bewildering social transformations of industrial capitalism. Yet instead of trying to confront or represent those changes, American writers "returned ever more feverishly to the imagination."[21] Thus the history of realism in America is once again the history of failure.

Yet the perceived failure or impossibility of mimesis has led recent critics to chart a more dynamic relation between social and literary structures, one that does not place the text outside society as an imaginative escape, a static window for observation, or a reflecting mirror. Historical perspectives hold that the textual production of reality does not occur in a linguistic vacuum; neither is it politically innocent, of course, but always charged by ideology—those unspoken collective understandings, conventions, stories, and cultural practices that uphold systems of social power. These approaches situate realistic texts within a wider field of what has been called "discursive practices." Thus we now understand, for example, the strange amalgam of romance and realism in Dreiser and Norris, not as a failure of form, but in relation to the unstable language of financial speculation which informs both the content and the narrative strategies of their novels.[22] We see realism in the

Princess Casamassima not as the free play of the moral imagination but as the enactment and exposure of the discourse of surveillance which polices the urban social system.[23] June Howard has recently reinterpreted the genre of naturalism as a literary form with an "immanent ideology" that "struggles to accommodate that sense of discomfort and danger" of its period.[24] As they begin to treat literary form as a social practice, these historical approaches reclaim the American novelist's engagement with society. Realists do more than passively record the world outside; they actively create and criticize the meanings, representations, and ideologies of their own changing culture.

The renewed interest in history, however, has reconstructed a new social context for realism as well. Realism is now related primarily to the rise of consumer culture in the late nineteenth century, in which the process of commodification makes all forms of the quotidian perform in what Guy Debord has called the "society of the spectacle." In this context, the novelist's attempt to represent everyday life is understood either as a way of staging a "series of acts of exhibition"[25] for public consumption, or as a means of engaging in one of the most common activities of modern urban life: "just looking."[26] Realism is similarly related to the culture of surveillance, in which the realist participates in the panoptic forces which both control and produce the real world by seeing it without being seen in turn.[27] In these historical revisions everyone is either a performer or a spectator, an inspector or a specimen. These studies have succeeded in resituating the realistic project as cultural practice within society rather than placing the realist outside society as a neutral observer. Yet by viewing realism as the staging of spectacles or the enforcement of power, these approaches do not view the production of the real as an arena in which the novelist struggles to represent reality against contradictory representations. By treating realism as an expression of consumer culture or a form of social incorporation, these studies tend to overlook the profound social disturbances that inform realistic narratives.[28]

Changes in the historical understanding of realism have accompanied the reevaluation of realism's political stance, from a progressive force exposing social conditions to a conservative force complicit with capitalist relations. This change is once more dramatized by the critical stature of Theodore Dreiser.[29] No longer notorious for their exposure of a brutal, class-ridden urban society, his novels heroically enact the ceaseless theatricality of modern urban life and the externalization of the self onto evanescent social roles. No longer valued or scorned for his depiction of social facts, he is lauded for his sentimentalism, which embraces rather than criticizes the logic of capitalism.[30] Freed from the strictures of both Parrington and Trilling, Dreiser has been reinstalled in the literary pantheon to embody the romance of American capitalism.

II

If, as successive generations of literary critics have asserted, realism repeatedly fails in its claims to represent American society, then the realistic enterprise must be redefined to ask *what* realistic novels do accomplish and *how* they work as a cultural practice. My project is not to rewrite the history of American realism as a history of success but to move beyond that dichotomous judgment to explore the dynamic relationship between changing fictional and social forms in realistic representation. If realism is a fiction, we can root this fiction in its historical context to examine its ideological force. Why does the fiction of the referent become a powerful rallying cry for some, a point of contention for others, and an assumption taken for granted by still other writers at the particular historical juncture of the 1880s and 1890s? How do literary texts produce a social reality that can be recognized as "the way things are"? And what counterforces threaten to disrupt this process of recognition? How does "reality" come to be associated with depictions of brutality, sordidness, and lower-class life, and how are the same realms often cordoned off as "unreal"? Is realism part of a broader cultural effort to fix and control a coherent representation of a social reality that seems increasingly inaccessible, fragmented, and beyond control?

This book explores these questions by reexamining realism's relation to three interrelated contexts which have remained central to the study of realism but whose complexity has been obscured by the dominance of the romance thesis: realism's relation to social change, to the representation of class difference, and to the emergence of a mass culture. These broad contexts are given historical specificity through close analysis of the theory and practice of realism in the works of William Dean Howells, Edith Wharton, and Theodore Dreiser, authors who, each in a different way, have become critical touchstones in the debate about the viability of realism in American fiction.

This study opens with the premise that the urban-industrial transformation of nineteenth-century society did not provide a ready-made setting which the realistic novel reflects, but that these changes radically challenged the accessibility of an emergent modern world to literary representation. Realism simultaneously becomes an imperative and a problem in American fiction. It neither compensates for the absence of a complex social fabric nor records a naive belief in the correspondence between language and the intractable material world; rather it explores and bridges the perceived gap between the social world and literary representation. Realists show a surprising lack of confidence in the capacity of fiction to reflect a solid world "out there," not because of the inherent slipperiness of signification but because of their distrust in the significance of the social. They often assume a world which lacks solidity, and the weightiness of descriptive detail—one of the most common characteristics of the realistic text—often appears in inverse proportion to a sense of insubstantiality, as though description could pin down the objects of an unfamiliar world to make it real. The realists inhabit a world in which, according to historian Jackson Lears, "reality itself began to seem problematic, something to be sought rather than merely lived."[31] Realistic narratives enact this search not by fleeing into the imagination or into nostalgia for a lost past but by actively constructing the coherent social world they represent; and they do this not in a vacuum of fictionality but in direct confrontation with the elusive process of social change.

This realism that develops in American fiction in the 1880s and 1890s is not a seamless package of a triumphant bourgeois mythology but an anxious and contradictory mode which both articulates and combats the growing sense of unreality at the heart of middle-class life. This unreal quality comes from two major sources for the novelists in this study: intense and often violent class conflicts which produced fragmented and competing social realities, and the simultaneous development of a mass culture which dictated an equally threatening homogeneous reality. Attempting to steer a precarious course between these two developments, realists contribute to the construction of a cohesive public sphere while they at once resist and participate in the domination of a mass market as the arbiter of America's national idiom.

This study attempts to recuperate realism's relation to social change not as a static background which novels either naively record or heroically evade, but as the foreground of the narrative structure of each novel. For it is the sense of the world changing under the realists' pens that makes the social world so elusive to representation. Henry James articulates this dual sense of urgency and evasiveness when he writes of his return to New York in *The American Scene* in 1904. The enigma of the tall buildings supplants the "absent things" with the "terrible things in America," terrible by virtue of being "impudently new and still more impudently 'novel.'"[32] Restating the impossibility of realism in America, James notes the lack of a New York Zola, with "his love of the human aggregation" and more importantly the "huge reflector" of his novelistic tradition.[33] In contrast to James's earlier view of Hawthorne's New England, however, here it is not the absence of a complex social machine but the sense he has, while watching the skyscrapers dwarf Trinity Church, that the enormity of this machine and the rapidity of its changes had outstripped the literary forms available for representing it: "the monstrous phenomena themselves, meanwhile, strike me as having, with their immense momentum, got the start, got ahead of, in proper parlance, any possibility of poetic, of dramatic capture."[34] James articulates both a fear and a challenge underlying many realistic novels, that social "material" as he calls it is not an absence but something monstrous and threatening, and that the novelist is not in the role of reflecting but of capturing, wrestling, and controlling a process of change which seems to defy representation.

Thus realism will be examined as a strategy for imagining and managing the threats of social change—not just to assert a dominant power but often to assuage fears of powerlessness. The threats of social change surface double-faced in the realistic novel: they appear as the potential for revolutionary upheaval, which the narrative of *A Hazard of New Fortunes*, for example, works to quell; or as the corporate imposition of novelty as the status quo, the "impudently new" which *The House of Mirth* both counters and enacts in its narrative structure. In *Sister Carrie* the threat of and desire for revolutionary change are pitted against the monotony of change as the quotidian, in an unresolved conflict. American realism will be treated in these analyses in part as what Fredric Jameson has called a "strategy of containment," but realism does not totally repudiate revolutionary change by seeking to "fold everything which is not-being, desire, hope and transformational praxis, back into the status of nature."[35] The realists do not naturalize the social world to make it seem immutable and organic, but, like contemporary social reformers, they engage in an enormous act of construction to organize, re-form, and control the social world. This act of construction makes the social world at once mechanical and improvised, locked in place and tentative. Furthermore, by containing the threats of social change, realistic narratives also register those desires which undermine the closure of that containment.[36]

For realists, the problem of representing social change is inseparable from the problem of representing social classes, a link made by James in his own use of the word "alien" in *The American Scene*. There he labels as "monstrous," like the skyscrapers, the working-class immigrants crowding the steets in New York City. The immigrants' "monstrous presumptuous interest" does not just impose itself from without, it makes the narrator's "most intimate relation" to society seem alien and threatening: "the idea of the country itself underwent some profane overhauling through which it appears to suffer the indignity of change."[37] Class difference and class conflict have long been viewed as the social medium which either enables or cripples the realistic novel. Whereas for some the apparent absence of a class-based society in America makes realism impossible, for others the proliferation of classes in urban industrial society produces the raw material for realism. While critics have continually faulted realists for their "inaccurate" portrayal of working-class and immigrant life, Howard has more productively analyzed this "inaccuracy" as an ideological strategy for imposing class hierarchies through representation.[38]

Class difference struck the realists less as a problem of social justice than as a problem of representation. They were less concerned with the accuracy of portraying "the other half" than with the problem of representing an interdependent society composed of competing and seemingly mutually exclusive realities. The novels in this study are filled with crowds and mobs which must be "sifted and strained" into what James calls the "germ of a public" and what Howells calls a "vision of solidarity." The novels construct a vision of a social whole, not just as nostalgia for lost unity or as a report of new social diversity, but as an attempt to mediate and negotiate competing claims to social reality by making alternative realities visible while managing their explosive qualities. In contrast to Howard's argument that the main naturalist strategy is to reinscribe class power-relations as formal narrative divisions between the spectator and the brute, I will argue that realistic strategies tend less to regulate conflict by formalizing otherness than to negotiate conflict in the narrative construction of common ground among classes both to efface and reinscribe social hierarchies.

Both Howells and Wharton have been criticized for their lack of realism, for their inability to portray those classes outside their immediate purview. One, however, portrays middle-class life and the other upper-class society in relation to the pressure of other classes lurking at their boundaries. In fact the realist participates in drawing such boundaries in a way that exposes their tenuous yet ideological necessity. To present a coherent view of a society as a whole, realists draw boundaries and explore their limits. The social world of each novel is constituted as much by those outside the immediate range of representation as by those at the center. In *A Hazard of New Fortunes*, the claims of a shadowy urban working class continually threaten to explode into the middle-class community, whose representation is shaped by this pressure. In *The House of Mirth*, viewed as one of the few American novels of manners to portray the claustrophobic setting of the upper class, the representation of high society depends as much on attracting the spectatorship of crowds as it does on excluding those crowds. Dreiser's novels, alternately praised for their depiction of working-class life and their spectacle of consumer culture, construct a world in which consumption is offered as a problematic solution to the power relations of a class society. All three authors focus on class difference to forge the bonds of a public world that subsumes those differences. Where Howells imagines a community based on work and character, Wharton seeks community in the exchange of intimacy and Dreiser posits a community of anonymous consumers and spectators with shared desires. Realistic novels often share an impulse with their utopian counterparts to project into the narrative present a harmonic vision of community that can paradoxically put an end to social change. Realistic novels have utopian moments that imagine resolutions to contemporary social conflicts by reconstructing society as it might be.

Those urban spaces often treated as the unproblematic setting of the realistic novel prove, on closer scrutiny, to be a threatening repository of the unreal which must be brought into the realm of representation and tamed: the streets of *A Hazard of New Fortunes*, the ballrooms of *The House of Mirth*, the work-places of *Sister Carrie*. Not only does the social space populated by these novels extend to the crowded city streets, but this expansion of representation renders domestic space a conflicted and problematic realm for representation. The realists are preoccupied with the problem of inhabiting and representing rented space, from the middle-class apartment of the Marches, to Lily Bart's boardinghouse and Hurstwood's rented beds, to the hotel rooms of Norma Hatch and Carrie. Rented spaces constitute a world filled with things neither known nor valued through well-worn contact, but cluttered instead with mass-produced furnishings and the unknown lives of strangers and their abandoned possessions, and valued through the measure of time and space as money. The project of the realistic novels is to make these rented spaces inhabitable and representable. While realistic narratives chart the homelessness of their characters, they thereby construct a world in which their readers can feel at home.

In constructing a cohesive social world to contain the threats of social change, realists had to draw from and compete with other cultural practices that had the same goal. If class conflict posed fragmented realities that challenged the cohesion of any public sphere, the growing dominance of a mass culture—in the form of newspapers, magazines, advertising, and book publishing—created a national market which constructed for consumers a shared reality of both information and desire. The new media promised a coherent and a cohesive world in place of older forms of cultural authority. In asserting their own authority to represent reality, novelists wrote out of this newly developing mass culture against which they attempted to define their work. Realism cannot be understood only in relation to the world it represents; it is also a debate, within the novel form, with competing modes of representation. Howells, both in his criticism and his novels, asserts realism's truth value not only in its fidelity to real life but in its contest with popular fiction and mass journalism. Wharton, who wrote best-sellers in an age that coined this term, defined her own writing against the popular women's fiction that preceded her and the society novelist, with whom she was often identified. Dreiser, whose apprenticeship included journalism and the editorship of a short-lived ladies magazine, both incorporated these popular modes and dissociated his realism from them.

To understand realism's struggle with other modes of representation is to restore to realism its dynamic literary qualities. The development of realism has traditionally been explained in terms of its parody of older conventions of the romance, as in the case of *Don Quixote.* Alfred Habegger has shown how realism in the fiction of Howells and James engages in an internalized polemic against the early maternal tradition of the sentimental novel.[39] Yet realism can also be understood as an argument, not only with older residual conventions, but with emergent forms of mass media from which it gains its power and against which it asserts itself. Realistic novels do more than juggle competing visions of social reality; they encompass conflicting forms and narratives which shape that reality.

In this competition with other cultural practices, realism also becomes a strategy for defining the social position of the author. To call oneself a realist means to make a claim not only for the cognitive value of fiction but for one's own cultural authority both to possess and to dispense access to the real. Indeed realists implicitly upheld the contradictory claim that they had the expertise to represent the commonplace and the ordinary, at a time when such knowledge no longer seemed available to common sense. If the realists engaged in the construction of a new kind of public sphere, they were also formulating a new public role for the author in the mass market. Realists are often seen to take the self-effacing stance of the neutral observer. Yet by writing so often about writers, realists explore both the social construction of their own roles and their implication in constructing the reality their novels represent.

Chapters 1, 3, and 5 of this book explore how the concept of realism evolves in the early writing career of Howells, Wharton, and Dreiser, both to articulate a theory of representation and to position the social role of the author. Through a close analysis of *A Hazard of New Fortunes*, *The House of Mirth*, and *Sister Carrie*, chapters 2, 4, and 6 focus not on the question of whether realism fails or succeeds but on narrative process, on how realism works to construct a social world out of the raw materials of unreality, conflict, and change.

1

THE MASS-MEDIATED REALISM OF WILLIAM DEAN HOWELLS

American realism emerges in literary history in bellicose terms—as a war, a struggle, a campaign—and William Dean Howells appears as the leader of the charge. This rhetoric originated with Howells and his contemporaries, who represented their espousal of realism as a belligerent act; while Howells bragged about "banging the babes of romance," his allies praised his "frank and fearless attacks . . . upon worn-out romantic ideals."[1] A formidable foe must have reared its head for Howells to persist in his increasingly combative style throughout his influential literary criticism of the 1880s and 1890s. His position as editor of the *Atlantic Monthly* and then as critic for *Harper's Monthly* gave him the opportunity to fight this battle through his editorial decisions. Yet despite the vehemence with which Howells launched his attacks, the opponents of realism remain as elusive and hydra-headed as the concept of realism itself.

The persistence of Howells's bellicose rhetoric throughout twentieth-century criticism should alert us to a method for exploring his theory and practice of realism. Rather than as a monolithic and fully formed theory, realism can be examined as a multifaceted and unfinished debate reenacted in the arena of each novel and essay. The dynamic of the argument between realism and its opponents may tell us more about realism than would a taxonomy of its characteristics. Although on the surface, Howells's criticism often triumphantly takes the offensive against outmoded literary conventions, his writing also reveals an embattled undertone, as a defense against newer and more threatening alternatives. Realism can therefore be understood as both an aggressive and a defensive literary stance, which while pitting itself most obviously against the residual forms of the romance, more anxiously asserts itself against emerging forms of mass culture. While it is well known that Howells repeatedly condemns the popular fiction of the mass market, it is less noted that he was equally wary of the modes of representation embodied in the modern newspaper, a subject he explores at length in his novel *A Modern Instance* and returns to in *The Rise of Silas Lapham*. This chapter will argue that Howells formulates his theory and practice of realism in an uneasy debate with the development of the mass media in the late nineteenth century.[2]

I

Realism's favorite whipping boy is the romance, a protean category which encompasses subjects as diverse as classical art, the Romantic movement, and popular fiction. To Howells the romance represents more than the sum of its aesthetic failings; his critique of its enslavement to past conventions, its idealization of subject matter, and its aristocratic pretensions is part of a political debate about the nature of American culture. In an essay which dubs realism "democracy in literature," Howells accuses the opponents of realism of harboring "the last refuges of the aristocratic spirit which is disappearing from politics and society, and is now seeking to shelter itself in aesthetics."[3] Romance becomes a catchword in his lexicon for an elitist conception of culture as the inherited and well-guarded property of the upper classes. Howells criticizes the Arnoldian defense of high art, in the name of the whole social order, against what some see as anarchy and the realists view as a democratizing society. A partner in this political process, realism extends literary representation to ordinary people whom artists have either neglected or idealized. If the romance chains literature to outdated artistic conventions, realism frees it to represent contemporary life and thereby expands the range of culture beyond the traditionally "cultured classes."

The political import of realism for Howells lies not only in the literary enfranchisement of its subject matter but also in its revaluation of the activity of reading and writing. By repeatedly referring to the romance as a form of idleness, he associates it with the leisured gentleman of letters, who treats art either as a treasured possession or a dilettante's pursuit. Howells validates realism, in contrast, as productive work for both readers and writers, and thereby locates it within the producer's ethos of the middle class. Shunning both economic and creative privilege, the realist serves as a producer among equals and takes his inspiration "from wherever men are at work, from wherever they are truly living."[4] True life—reality—is here equated with work, which is viewed not simply as an occupation but more importantly as a system of value which privileges industriousness and self-discipline as the basis of communal life. As a cultural force, realism turns reading into work, an act which unites its practitioners not through the worship of high art or the transport to imaginary worlds but through the mutual recognition of a common identity rooted in the productive sphere.

Howells's obsessive antagonism to the romance contradicts his own concept of literary evolution, adopted from Hippolyte Taine, in which realism develops organically to express a democratic society and to replace the outdated romance, itself an appropriate outgrowth of an earlier period. If social evolution determines the predominance of a particular literary mode, why attack the loser so fiercely? The loser in Howells's criticism—the last vestiges of an "aristocratic spirit"—often serves as a scapegoat for a more contemporary threat: the rise of the mass media and the restructuring of popular culture in the form of mass-circulation newspapers and magazines, national advertising, and the book publishing industry. Howells's most scathing reviews attack not aristocratic culture but popular fiction, whether the dime novels and story magazines of the working class or the best-sellers read by the middle class, such as *Ben Hur* and *Trilby.* He characterizes this literature for the "unthinking multitude" as a coarse form of amusement, akin to the circus, the burlesque, card-playing, and horse-racing.[5] Opposed to the work ethic of realism, the popular romance turns literature into a consumer item and reading into an act of consumption. By characterizing the romance as an "idle lie," Howells conflates elite culture, as a form of upper-class leisure, with popular culture, as a form of mass consumption.

Although he declaims against the falsehood of the popular romance, Howells finds it threatening not only because it diverges from mimetic norms but also because it performs a social function that directly competes with his view of realism's goals. The power of popular fiction feared by Howells lies less in its encouragement of antisocial tendencies, as Alan Trachtenberg has argued, than in its enormous socializing potential.[6] The 1880s and 1890s saw an unprecedented boom in the output of novels, leading Howells to claim that they "really form the whole intellectual life of such immense numbers of people, without question of their influence, good or bad."[7] By force of numbers and accessibility alone, popular fiction could construct a shared world for masses of readers. Facing this new social power of fiction with ambivalence, Howells hoped to harness it for his own program of "democracy in literature," but feared the bond it could forge among readers as consumers at play rather than as producers "wherever men are at work."

The mass production of fiction in the late nineteenth century challenged not only the social mission of realism but also the parallel goals Howells set for the magazine editor. Although Howells is often viewed as a spokesman for genteel culture, he can be understood more accurately as a transitional figure between the gentleman literary editors of the major nineteenth-century journals, *The Century, North American Review,* and *Atlantic Monthly,* and a younger generation of professional businessmen who edited magazines such as *McClure's, Cosmopolitan,* and *Ladies' Home Journal.*[8] Like his genteel predecessors, Howells saw himself as the guardian of tradition, upholding and nurturing the values shared by his readers. Yet in the role of educator and enlightened guide, he also tried to expand the horizons of his cultivated readers to more democratic vistas. He put this vision into effect cautiously at the *Atlantic* by introducing to his New England readership authors from the West and the South, such as Mark Twain and Bret Harte, and more aggressively at *Harper's* by throwing his weight behind younger writers such as Stephen Crane, Abraham Cahan, and Hamlin Garland.

Howells left his position as editor of the *Atlantic* at a time when the growth and the rationalization of the publishing industry were limiting the cultural authority of the genteel editor, who found less leeway to follow the guidelines of taste and enlightenment as he became more bound to commercial demands. Rather than converse with a known community of "gentle readers," new editors of cheaper magazines actively created both their product and audience through aggressive managerial and marketing techniques.[9] Upon leaving his editorial position, Howells still tried to keep a foot in both publishing worlds. An excellent businessman, he successfully marketed his novels and criticism by negotiating unusually lucrative contracts with Harper's publishing house. Part of this contract included writing a regular column for *Harper's Monthly* from 1886 to 1892 entitled "Editor's Study." The first column describes "the study" as a gentleman's library, a retreat from the exigencies of the business world—"the Grub Street traditions of literature."[10] Howells envisions the activity of criticism as polite conversation with a reader invited "to sit at fine ease, and talk over . . . such matters of literary interest as may come up from time to time." This conversation, however, becomes a monologue, as the reader is not "allowed to interrupt" and "is reduced to silence."[11] From the "Editor's Study," Howells could thus project the authoritative voice of the enlightened editor, whom he calls the "unreal editor," without confronting the limits or power of "the real editor" who must manage his authors and market his product to an audience.

In the "Editor's Study" the desire for an intimate yet silenced reader attests to Howells's fears of losing control over a recognizable audience. As literacy increased at the end of the nineteenth century and the publishing industry was further rationalized, the reading public became ever more stratified and did not conform to Howells's notion of a common culture uniting a public of different classes, regions, and backgrounds. On two accounts Howells feared the outpouring of popular writing molded by the mass market. On the one hand, the mass-produced romance competed with his aspirations for realism as a democratizing force by projecting a shared fantasy-world to its readers; on the other hand, the institutionalization of a reading public divided by class and education not only challenged the democratizing potential of literature as a common cultural bond, it also removed a large class of readers from the control of the enlightened editor. The editor's role seemed more circumscribed by his own economic considerations and by the existence of a large body of texts and readers impervious to his cultural guidance. When Howells criticizes the popular romance for the escape it provides from reality into "flights of fancy," he is also expressing discomfort with its escape from the control of the authoritative formulators of American culture, a discomfort he implicitly admits in his desire for a silenced reader.[12]

If the loss of power on the part of the editor bothered Howells, he was equally concerned by what he saw as the concomitant ascendancy of the novelist as a voice of cultural authority and by the power of fiction to shape reality. "The modern human being," he paraphrases Vernon Lee as claiming, "has been largely fashioned by those who have written about him, and most of all by the novelist." Modernity is defined here by fiction, which, through its "indefinitely vast and subtle influence on modern character," has the power to form the human figure.[13] As the word "fashioned" suggests, this formation changes rapidly and erratically, according to the dictates of the market. Fictionality itself—rather than the particular form of the romance—seems to be the underlying enemy of realism, and its danger lies not in its deviance from a normative reality but in the way in which modern life has become indistinguishable from fiction. Such anxiety about the power of fiction can be understood as part of what Jackson Lears has called the general fear of "unreality" and "weightlessness" at the heart of middle-class life in the late nineteenth century. According to Lears, this sense of unreality—manifest psychically in the increase in nervous disorders—stems from the breakdown of traditional centers of cultural authority—the community, the home, the church—which had once guaranteed an optimistic belief in the harmony of moral and material progress.[14]

Although Howells's novels provide a richly detailed account of this breakdown, his fear of unreality stems from slightly different sources. Unreality was not an absence for Howells, nor merely a loss of social cohesion and inner certitude. Instead, it was institutionalized in modern social structures such as the city and in modern cultural forms such as popular novels and mass-circulation newspapers. These institutions both mediated and constructed the reality of everyday life to make it less immediately accessible and more fictionalized to ordinary people. In 1895, Howells wrote that, during a period of psychic turmoil in his own life fifteen years earlier, he was unable to bear the excitement of reading fiction and felt an "impossible stress from the Sunday newspaper . . . which with its scare-headings, and artfully-wrought sensations, had the effect of fiction, as in fact it largely was."[15] To counter this "effect of fiction" that makes the everyday seem unreal, Howells calls for a mimetic fiction to represent faithfully ordinary life. Realism is not to reflect passively a solid reality; it is to face the paradoxical imperative to use fiction to combat the fictionality of everyday life; unable to anchor itself in a stable referent, it must restore or construct a new sense of the real.

As the 1880s progressed, another source of the unreal quality of modern life for Howells was his growing awareness of conflicting social groups in America that lived competing social realities. The period of Howells's most engaged struggle for realism saw escalating labor violence which to some observers threatened to develop into all-out class warfare. While class conflict was dramatized by major events, such as the railroad strikes of 1877 and the Haymarket riot of 1886, it more subtly infused all forms of social interaction to challenge the belief in a unified national identity which culture could embody. As editor and critic, Howells brought the issues of class conflict and social justice before his readers through his reviews of works by novelists such as Tolstoy and Zola, and social reformers and economists such as Henry George, Laurence Gronlund, and Richard Ely. It is well known that Howells, in the aftermath of the Haymarket riot, took the unpopular position of defending the right of the anarchists to a fair trial. Yet class conflict for Howells posed more than a problem of social justice; it questioned the existence of a cohesive and coherent social reality, posing a problem of social cognition, of knowing others. Thus the unreality of bourgeois life for Howells stemmed not merely from inner ennui and the lack of moral authority, but from radically competing claims on the part of outsiders, whether the provincial social climber, Silas Lapham, or the unknown masses in the streets of New York City in *A Hazard of New Fortunes*.

We can now begin to define Howells's conception of realism through the argument with the opponents he posits for it. As "democracy in literature," realism contests, in the name of the social whole, the elitist maintenance of an insular and exalted culture. Yet realism equally opposes the rise of a popular mass culture which unites people as consumers through the medium of the market. By dismissing both notions of culture as forms of leisure or idleness, Howells defines realism as productive work. As work rather than entertainment, realism produces knowledge, the knowledge of oneself and others joined together in a social whole. The major work of the realistic narrative is to construct a homogeneous and coherent social reality by conquering the fictional qualities of middle-class life and by controlling the specter of class conflict which threatens to puncture this vision of a unified social totality.

In a well-known review of Howells's works, Henry James wrote that Howells was "animated by a love of the common, the immediate, the familiar and vulgar elements of life."[16] But James failed to understand that Howells was animated less by an appreciation of these ever more evasive qualities of modern life, and more by anxiety about the lack of confidence in the existence of a common, familiar, immediate reality to which language can refer. This anxiety is suggested by the urgency of his critical tone, which often neither describes nor prescribes, but instead exhorts, pleads, and proclaims the need to construct a familiar reality in fiction as though it could provide not a battering ram against the elite bastion of culture but a bulwark against an unnamed threat. Thus Howells's realism is animated by the desire to construct the quotidian out of and against the forces which make it inaccessible.

To counter the opponents of realism, Howells develops what can be called an "aesthetic of the common." A pivotal term in his critical vocabulary, "the common" refers at different times to distinct and often contradictory entities: to the lower classes—"common men and laborers"; to a shared human identity—"our common humanity"; and to ordinary life—"the commonplace." To resolve the tensions between these meanings, realism works to ensure that social difference can be ultimately effaced by a vision of a common humanity, which mirrors the readers' own commonplace, or everyday life.

According to the first of Howells's definitions, realism extends literary representation to social groups formerly neglected or idealized in literature: the mountain folk of Mary Murfee, the New England villagers of Mary Wilkins Freeman, Hamlin Garland's midwestern farmers, Stephen Crane's prostitutes, and Abraham Cahan's immigrant workers. Howells endorses these writers not simply for their inclusion of lower-class characters, but more importantly for freeing them from their "conventional and artificial guise of fancy and tradition" which make them "palatable for the literary elect." This liberation requires the use of devices such as dialect to portray people "as they are" rather than to romanticize their "poor, hard, dull narrow lives."[17] The political and cognitive goal of Howells's aesthetic of the common is to further the democratization process by introducing people of different classes and regions to one another to make them "know one another better, that they may be all humbled and strengthened with a sense of their fraternity."[18]

The successful portrayal of the "common people" in literature depends on the second definition of "common" as a shared human identity. Persons of different social groups belong together in fiction because "men are more like than unlike one another."[19] Howells transforms Matthew Arnold's criticism of America's lack of "distinction" into a compliment by arguing that "the idea that we call America has realized itself so far that we already have identification rather than distinction as the fact which strikes the foreign critic." He explains "identification" further: "Such beauty and such grandeur as we have is common beauty, common grandeur, or the beauty and grandeur in which the quality of solidarity so prevails that neither distinguishes itself to the disadvantage of anything else."[20] The goal of realism suggested by this definition is to create "solidarity," to pave a common ground between diverse social groups through the recognition of the essential likeness of individuals in all social classes.

Howells anticipates Erich Auerbach's well-known definition of nineteenth-century realism as the breakdown of neoclassical styles in favor of "the serious treatment of everyday reality, the rise of the more extensive and socially inferior human groups to the position of subject matter for problematical-existential representation."[21] Yet, for Howells, the democratization of literary representation was less the triumphant revolution that Auerbach suggests than a contradictory struggle to forge bonds between members of antagonistic social classes. A tension emerges in Howells's criticism between two meanings of the common, tension in the most abstract sense between identity and difference. This conflict can be seen in Howells's praise for Mary Murfee's portrait of Tennessee mountain folk: "the perfect portrayal of what passes even in a soul whose body smokes a cob-pipe or dips snuff, and dwells in a log hut on a mountain-side, would be worth more than all the fancies ever feigned."[22] Howells implies that we should read about such characters to penetrate the details of their concrete existence—which make them different from us—so that we may reach their essential identity with us in an abstract sense of the "soul." Realistic portrayal takes a curiously idealistic shift here to undermine its own mimetic tenet of fidelity to lives "as they are." Furthermore, realism reveals an aggressive impulse in this example of the portrait of a "common" man whose representation strips away and alienates his material existence to reveal his soul.

Despite the stated goal of realism to represent social diversity, Howells shows discomfort with evidence of social difference, which often appears indistinguishable from social conflict. He attempts to resolve the conflict between the common as social difference, and the common as essential identity, in a third sense of the word—as the commonplace, or ordinary. "Let fiction cease to lie about life," exhorts Howells in *Harper's*, "let it portray men and women as they are, actuated by the motives and the passions in the measure we all know. . . . let it speak the dialect, the language, that most Americans know—the language of unaffected people everywhere."[23] The truth value of realism lies not in empirical accuracy but in adherence to common sense, to a communal consensus about the way things are—"the measure we all know." Yet in a society of immigrants in which many Americans did not speak the same dialect, let alone the same language, a common language had to be constructed against the counterforces of foreign tongues and social fragmentation. Realism may strive to make known to middle-class, "cultivated" readers people, culture, and ways of life that are foreign to them; realism does not jar readers with the shock of otherness, it provides a recognizable mirror of their own world. Realism has the imperative of bolstering that world to insure that social difference can be transcended in the medium of the commonplace. Howells thus envisioned realism as a strategy for containing social difference and controlling social conflict within a cohesive common ground.

A key weapon in this critical strategy is Howells's emphasis on the centrality of character portrayal in fiction.[24] He repeatedly calls for a uniquely American literature to base itself on the episode which concentrates on small groups of individuals rather than on the broad survey of an expansive social network found in a Balzac or a Tolstoy. This focus on character resolves the contradiction embedded in Howells's aesthetic by providing a common denominator within which to represent diversity in an unthreatening shape. He praises Mary Wilkins Freeman, for example, for the "community of character" that "abounds" in her sketches, which are not linked by "community of action." Defending this view from the charge of narrowness, he argues that "each man is a microcosm," and that "this depth is more desireable than horizontal expansion in a civilization like ours, where the differences are not of class, but of types, and not of types either so much as character."[25] "Character-painting" of the individual human figure has the function of scaling down an increasingly interdependent society to a manageable size. The episode replaces complex relations between conflicting social groups with the more intimate and knowable range of character.

Character for Howells and his contemporaries implied more than a neutral descriptive term for a structural element in a novel; it carried the moral connotations of personal integrity—"to have character." As Warren Susman has shown, to the nineteenth-century producer-oriented society, "character" implied a distinct concept of the self directly linked to the work ethic.[26] Delineating selfhood by thrift, restraint, and responsibility, the culture of character presumed the existence of an inner core of an essential self that could be consolidated and expressed through actions. If the self is continuous with its actions, work is the major vehicle for making character known to others. The knowledge of character is inseparable from the communal judgment of character as morally good or bad. Thus Howells implicitly associates character with his conception of writing as production and opposes it to the fanciful nature of fiction as idle consumption.

Yet by defining character in the novel against its antithesis, the story, Howells implicitly undermines the assumption that character manifests itself morally through action. "Character-painting," not "story-telling," is the hallmark of realism; Howells rarely advocates the former without denigrating the latter. He associates stories not only with the "old trade of make-believe" but with the popular fiction of mass culture. As the staple of the romance, stories are subject to the same scorn as entertainment, idleness, and lying. This connection may have been reinforced by the fact that inexpensive all-fiction magazines circulating at the time were themselves called "story papers." More importantly, through the narration of conflict, stories assume that social relations can be represented through action. While Howells dismisses stories for their contrived and artificial nature, he may have been more concerned about their open-ended quality. To base a novel on plotting means to acknowledge that conflicting and incompatible stories can constitute the social reality which the novelist represents. The force of Howells's belief in character thus must be understood as a bulwark against the disruptive potential of the story.[27]

Ideologically, the delineation of character marks off the serious from the popular while formally it offers a way of controlling and ordering the potentially fragmentary and conflicting consequences of plotting. Elaborate plots in the hands of Dickens or Eliot provide the means for representing social connectedness between diverse social classes with no visible relations. Howells chooses the unifying qualities of character to play this role. It is a critical commonplace that American writers have not produced great realistic novels because of the lack of class distinctions in America. Yet fear of the explosive nature of those distinctions may have led Howells to privilege character as the unifying bond of American realism.

If Howells developed his theory of realism in part as a response to anxiety over social collapse, he did not simply express nostalgia for a lost wholeness in preindustrial forms of social life. In his advocacy of regional literature, he acknowledges that social coherence cannot be reconstituted in a preindustrial community but has to be reconceived on a national scale. Rather than simply chart the breakdown of traditional community, realism seeks to construct new forms of social cohesiveness. Realism thus has a utopian impulse that strives to contribute to the formation of a new kind of public sphere, controlled neither by the traditions of an elite nor the dictates of the marketplace. Realism, in Howells's view, builds a framework to unite this public sphere by offering the knowledge of others bound together in a social whole. It attempts to represent a broad and complex society by dissolving the threats of otherness—whether from individual strangers or organized classes—into the common denominator of the ordinary. Realism attempts to pave a common ground among classes and individuals by managing and controlling conflict between them. The common thus has an expansive and exclusive function; it breaks down the old barriers of literary representation while it imposes new limits to delineate a common realm.

II

The realist's project to construct a public sphere faced serious competition from the development of the mass media in the 1870s and 1880s. Indeed Howells's utopian vision of a "common reality" was already being put into effect by the press, which also claimed to purvey ordinary life in the daily newspaper through new categories of reporting such as the "human interest" story. Although the daily newspaper had been circulating on a mass scale since the 1830s, only in the 1880s did the press begin to mold a national audience for which it could present a homogeneous reality. As papers grew dependent on the wire services and syndication, and reporters as a group formulated standardized professional goals, the press began to serve up a common world for a diverse readership to consume on a daily basis. The concomitant growth of national advertising contributed to this production of a homogeneous reality by shifting from the promotion of local businesses to the coordination of national markets. Newspapers thus constructed for their readers both common knowledge about the world around them and common desires which could be fulfilled by the goods the newspapers advertised.[28]

The rise of the modern newspaper is often seen as a popular counterpart to the genesis of literary realism.[29] Indeed, Howells himself started his career as a country journalist and wrote in 1916 that "the newspaper was a school for reality."[30] When he turned to writing novels, however, the newspaper proved a disconcerting competitor to the realistic novel. Although the generation that followed Howells may have drawn on journalism as the model for their fiction, Howells's contemporaries, such as Twain and James, shared his wariness of the newspaper business, from which they tried to differentiate their own literary production through their satirical portrayals of journalists. In 1882, Howells explored the ramifications of the newspaper business for the realist in what is often considered his first major realistic novel, *A Modern Instance*.

The modernity of *A Modern Instance* is commonly located in the story of a divorce that represents the breakdown of the traditional basis of private and public life.[31] Yet equally modern and less noted by critics is the novel's tale of the career of a city newspaperman, who heralds the rise of the mass media and its formation of a new kind of public.[32] Bartley Hubbard stands at the intersection of these two intertwined narratives, as each stage of his failing marriage accompanies a new development in his morally dubious career. The first use of the word "modern" in the novel refers to Hubbard's initial attempt to reorganize the country newspaper along the "modern conception."[33] Thus Hubbard can be read as Howells's figure for modernity, not only in his unscrupulous attitude toward the sanctity of marriage, but just as importantly in the shape of his career as a writer.

The extremes of moral condemnation and personal identification with which Howells treats Hubbard have long been explained in terms of Howells's projection of a troubling side of his psyche.[34] Yet Howells wrote *A Modern Instance* not only during a period of psychic turmoil but also at a major turning point in his career, when he relinquished the security of editorship of the *Atlantic* and "threw himself upon the market" as a novelist.[35] Through the narrative of Hubbard's career, Howells grapples with systemic changes in the social production of modern writing, changes which both enabled and threatened Howells's theory and practice of realism. In his portrayal of Hubbard as a writer, Howells works toward a conception of realism that he was to articulate more fully in his criticism in the latter half of the decade. Hubbard emerges as a demonic realist, from whom Howells attempts to distance his own writing while exploring its limits.

As a newspaperman, Hubbard's most blatant offense lies in his commercialism and opportunism. He reduces all writing to the cash nexus, his sole criterion for writing or publishing any piece, regardless of its style or content, being its selling power. Yet Hubbard's business interests alone do not explain the moral condemnation to which Howells subjects him. Hubbard's "modern conception" of the newspaper threatens to debase the value of writing, but it also raises important questions about the constitution of a reading public and about its relationship to writers and editors.

Starting his career as "a practical printer" of a "village newspaper," Hubbard reorganizes the Free Press in Equity on "a paying basis," an enterprise that prepares him for the profession of journalist he later adopts in Boston (p. 21). When he moves from the Maine countryside to the city, he happily works for the publisher, Witherby, who openly subordinates his editorial policy to the dictates of his advertisers. Run from the "counting room," his paper, the *Daily Events*, refuses to publish any article or editorial which opposes the interests of its major advertisers (p. 156). Although the novel subjects Witherby and Hubbard to moral condemnation for their policies, they represent a wider trend in the newspaper business in the 1880s. With the growth of the department store and the nationwide marketing of manufactured goods, the demand for advertising space accelerated so rapidly that income from advertising rose from 44 percent to 55 percent of total newspaper revenue between 1880 and 1890.[36] According to Schudson, "circulation became less a private matter of pride and income and more a public and audited indicator of the newspaper's worth as an advertising medium."[37] This change meant that the newspaper had to become a kind of advertisement for itself; if the paper's primary goal was to increase circulation in order to sell more products for its advertisers, it had to present the news in such a way as to advertise itself as a desirable product. "Spice" is Hubbard's term for the news which advertises itself through sensationalism and entertainment, and his own career devolves into a story of unalloyed spice (p. 136).

Howells represents an opposing view of the newspaper through the character Ricker, an older journalist with personal integrity who befriends Hubbard upon his arrival in Boston. That Hubbard takes the position on the *Events* only after it is turned down by Ricker attests to the shady nature of this move. In an argument with Ricker, Hubbard defends his conception of the newspaper as a "private enterprise" which must be run in the interests of its owner. Ricker argues on the contrary that the newspaper may be "private property, but it isn't a private enterprise, and in its very nature can't be" (p. 209). Instead, he considers it "a public enterprise, with certain distinct duties to the public" (p. 209). Echoing Howells's conception of the magazine editor, Ricker sees the newspaper editor as "sacredly bound not to do anything to deprave or debauch [his] readers" and also as "sacredly bound not to mislead or betray them, not merely as to questions of morals and politics, but as to questions of what we may lump as 'advertising'" (p. 210). Implicit in Ricker's notion of the truthfulness of the press is a conception of the public as a polis, a group of citizens bound by shared political and ethical concerns. Ricker's audience is a known community, a body already in place which can be led and elevated by enlightened writers and editors.

Although Hubbard views the newspaper as a form of private enterprise, his description of his ideal paper does imply a definite conception of its public role. His newspaper can only succeed financially by appealing to a broad public audience. Yet in contrast to Ricker, Hubbard envisions a paper which must construct its own public by soliciting readers from different levels of society. Hubbard describes his ideal paper this way:

> I should make it pay by making it such a thorough newspaper that every class of people *must* have it. I should cater to the lowest class first, and as long as I was poor I would have the fullest and best reports of every local accident and crime; that would take *all* the rabble. Then, as I could afford it, I'd rise a little, and give first-class non-partisan reports of local political affairs; that would fetch the next largest class, the ward politicians of all parties. I'd lay for the local religious world, after that;—religion comes right after politics in the popular mind, and it interests the women like murder: I'd give the minutest religious intelligence, and not only that, but the religious gossip, and the religious scandal. Then I'd go in for fashion and society,—that comes next. I'd have the most reliable and

thorough-going financial reports that money could buy. When I'd got my local ground perfectly covered, I'd begin to ramify. Every fellow that could spell, in any part of the country, should understand that, if he sent me an account of a suicide, or an elopement, or a murder, or an accident, he should be well paid for it; and I'd rise on the same scale through all the departments. I'd add art criticisms, dramatic and sporting news, and book reviews, more for the looks of the thing than for anything else; they don't any of 'em appeal to a large class. I'd get my paper into such a shape that people of every kind and degree would have to say, no matter what particular objection was made to it, 'Yes, that's so; but it's the best *news*paper in the world, *and we can't get along without it*. (p. 210)

Hubbard's ideal paper brings together a diversified public of readers and writers clearly stratified by class and gender. The newspaper transcends and neutralizes these divisions by institutionalizing social differences in distinct journalistic departments. Like the realist, Hubbard forges a unified reading public that can see its own image in a social totality reflected in print; yet this unity has no other political or cultural aim than to fuel the private profit of the paper's owners. Hubbard conceives of a public sphere bound by the shared roles of consumer and audience viewing themselves as the object of consumption. The journalistic concept of the public, which Howells represents through Hubbard, is indistinguishable from publicity.

In contrast to Ricker, Hubbard divorces the public from an active political body. This separation can be seen in his initial reorganization of the country paper "upon the modern conception, through which the country press must cease to have any influence in public affairs, and each paper become little more than an open letter of neighborhood gossip." Yet in place of this withdrawal from political activity, Hubbard "continued to make spicy hits at the enemies of Equity in the late struggle and kept the public spirit of the town alive. He had lately undertaken to make known its advantages as a summer resort" (p. 22). Hubbard transforms the function of the village newspaper from the expression of public opinion to the advertisement of "public spirit." On the Boston *Events* he similarly advocates the practice of "independent journalism," which involves the separation of journalism from party allegiances. While historians of journalism have interpreted the dissociation of the news from partisan politics as part of the democratization process, Howells points to another effect of this development. When Hubbard does not allow the *Events* to take sides in the elections, he himself instead starts betting on the elections as though they were a sporting event (pp. 261ff.). His notion of independent journalism transforms readers from political participants into passive spectators, and the public sphere of politics into a new source of entertainment.

Thus if Ricker sees the market as the debasement of the traditional public sphere, Hubbard views the market as constituting a new public. Howells may take Ricker's side by highlighting Hubbard's immorality against Ricker's integrity, and by representing Hubbard and Witherby as moral deviants rather as symptoms of broader change. Yet the narrative also attests to Hubbard's power by allowing him to supplant Ricker in the market. Furthermore, Howells concedes to Hubbard's prescience in his later novels, in which the *Events* resurfaces with Hubbard's signature.[38]

The journalism espoused by Hubbard can be seen as a direct threat to Howells's conception of realism, threatening by virtue of its very similarity to that realism. Both strive to construct a public sphere, one through knowledge and common work, and the other through publicity and consumption. As realism does, the newspaper represents a wide range of social classes, uniting them through the medium of the market rather than through mutual recognition of a community. The newspaper also resolves a source of tension for the realist: on the one hand it has a democratic leveling effect by equally including all strata of society as subject matter. On the other hand it reinforces and controls the threat of social difference through a fixed hierarchy of representation, as each class assumes a particular department and style—the working classes are criminalized in the crime story, for example, while the upper classes are glamorized on the society page. The newspaper in a sense reintroduces in a modern context the classical levels of style which realism strives to break down; it more thoroughly executes the project of realism to manage social difference through representation.

In addition to his conception of the reading public, Hubbard's career represents a new brand of professionalism, which Howells treats with great ambivalence. Hubbard's journalism becomes more heinous in the novel as he adopts it as a career goal rather than as a means to the end of becoming a lawyer. Originally working on the village newspaper as a stepping-stone to the law, Hubbard realizes in Boston that journalism offers a vocation which can provide a much quicker route to success for the newcomer to the city. Howells wrote *A Modern Instance* at a time when reporters were indeed defining themselves as professionals with more visibility than the formerly well-known city editors. According to Howells the journalist was beginning to see himself as a "sovereign character" rather than as a lowly country editor who was the despised vassal of "local notables who used him" (p. 143). While Howells could be expected to applaud the emerging autonomy of a writing profession, he was disturbed by the sense that the profession existed to perpetuate itself, with no higher duties to the broader public, just as the writing in newspapers existed to sell itself, with no commitment to the education of its audience.

A Modern Instance opposes Hubbard's journalism to the older profession of the lawyer, represented by the country practitioner, Squire Gaylord, and the Boston attorney, Atherton. Both act less as legal specialists than as gentlemen of letters who articulate public opinion and whose profession is only a means of serving the community as a voice of moral authority. In fact we never see either of the lawyers practicing law, except when Gaylord turns his daughter's divorce trial into a vehicle for a personal vendetta and moral crusade. Instead, the two lawyers, in different capacities, serve as scholars, confidants, personal and financial advisors, community leaders, and general spokesmen for social order; each is a kind of moral policeman, whether in small-town Maine or the patrician community of Boston. Instead of serving the public, as lawyers do, journalists are represented as serving only themselves and their employers. In the eyes of Marcia Hubbard, the newer profession of the journalist does not compare to the law in dignity. In Marcia's conflict between her allegiance to her father and to Hubbard, Howells represents the conflict between two very different conceptions of professionalism. Like Marcia torn between her father and husband, Howells placed himself somewhere in between: he welcomed the benefits of professionalization, the political and financial autonomy that it allowed. But he questioned how then to reconnect the writer to a larger public, through a channel other than the marketplace.

If Hubbard's journalism is threatening to Howells because of the new brand of professionalism and the relationship to the public it entails, Hubbard appears all the more problematic as a figure for the realist. He continually deploys one major realistic strategy in his use of parody to undermine sentimental illusions. In the opening courtship scene, for example, he mocks the romantic expectations of Marcia, who serves as a figure for the sentimental novel, in her blind self-sacrifice to love. The subject matter of Hubbard's articles also matches that of the realist: life in a logging camp, housing in Boston, the life of the self-made man, the charity functions of the middle class. Indeed one of Hubbard's first articles, about searching for an apartment in Boston, was to be rewritten by Howells eight years later in the beginning of *A Hazard of New*

Fortunes. In *A Modern Instance*, however, Howells emphasizes that Hubbard, with his "true newspaper instinct," worked on the article with a motive that was "as different as possible from the literary motive." This difference lies in his writing "for the effect which he was to make, and not from any artistic pleasure in the treatment." Such a treatment would involve giving the story "form," by entering the lives of the characters and their response to the city. Instead of showing the "poetry of their ignorance and their poverty," Hubbard is concerned with the "bottom facts" of housing rents. "Upon these bottom facts, as he called them, he based a 'spicy' sketch, which had also largely the character of the *exposé*. There is nothing the public enjoys so much as an *exposé:* it seems to be made in the reader's own interest; it somehow constitutes him a party to the attack upon the abuse and its effectiveness redounds to the credit of all the newspaper's subscribers" (p. 136). Howells depicts Hubbard as having more concern with the reader's emotional response than with the relation of the writing to its subject matter. The exposé, according to Howells, epitomizes the newspaper's self-referential effect. Although it claims to uncover the facts of the external world, it advertises the newspaper's leadership in public crusades, and it mirrors the readers' complacency.

Why does Howells point to the exposé as the chief difference between the newsman's instinct and the literary motive, since the exposé shares so much with realism's imperative to uncover the hidden truth of contemporary life? In attributing to Hubbard's piece an essential cheapness, despite its being "thoroughly readable," Howells may express resentment against the newspaper's power to mobilize a mass audience. More significantly, Howells disapproves of the aggressive nature of the exposé, which embodies the writer's violence toward his subject matter. News-gathering for Hubbard is a kind of invasion, a violation of the boundaries between the public and the private, whether through the interview or the secret investigation. Hubbard's transformation of the country paper from a participant in public affairs to an "open letter of neighborhood gossip" participates in this larger trend to reveal private life to public view. The newspaper no longer represents only the traditional public sphere of politics or its violation in the crime story, instead it mines the traditional private sphere of domesticity, through stories about domestic disputes, elopements, and the personal life of the successful businessman. Indeed these are topics which Howells, perhaps uneasily, advocates for realistic representation and writes about as well.

In *A Modern Instance* the newspaper contributes to the breakdown of social order usually attributed to the scandal of divorce, for both equally violate the boundary between private and public realms. Throughout the novel, characters complain about the exposure of private domestic life in the public arena of representation. In speaking against divorce, Atherton voices the genteel belief in the private life of the home as the bedrock of a public morality. For the newspaperman, the two realms are also inseparable. The private realm is exposed to the public view, however, not as a moral paradigm but as an item of consumption, as "spice." For Atherton, one realm supports the other as they reinforce their separateness; for Hubbard, one preys on the other.

Nowhere is the aggressive nature of journalism made more vivid than in Hubbard's theft of his friend's story in an article entitled "Confessions of an Average American." The title itself makes the story almost a parody of Howells's realism, by combining the kind of material he advocated (the "Average American") with the style of the sensationalist exposé ("Confessions"). The American, Kinney, is a vernacular Whitmanian figure, a backwoodsman and a cook, virile and domestic, a man of nature and a homespun intellectual, a type appearing in the kind of regional literature supported by Howells. When Kinney entertains the Hubbards and Ricker after dinner with his life history, the reporters ask about using it for an article. Kinney politely yet adamantly refuses, insisting that he intends to write his own story some day. Recognizing the market value of such a tale, Bartley writes the article the next evening, an act he justifies by claiming that Kinney could not have written it for himself. "There's no theft about it," he argues, "Kinney would never write it out, and if he did, I've put the material in better shape for him here than he could ever have given it" (p. 254). After reading the story in a newspaper out West, Kinney mistakenly accuses Ricker of its authorship in a letter to Hubbard. Finding the letter "amusingly characteristic, so helplessly ill-spelled and ill-constructed," Hubbard shows it to Ricker as proof that Kinney could in fact never have written his own story (pp. 258–59). Rather than accept Hubbard's self-justification, Ricker cuts off their friendship to protest Hubbard's not correcting Kinney's mistaken assumption about the authorship of the article.

Howells's condemnation of Hubbard's act can be measured by the act's severe consequences: the article eventually loses Hubbard his friends, his job, his professional credibility, and the faith of his wife. Indeed, the only time Marcia stands up to Hubbard in the novel is in response to hearing about his authorship of the story. The severity of Hubbard's punishment reflects the dilemma the article posed for Howells about his own role as realist. His need to punish and thereby dissociate himself from Hubbard speaks to the uncomfortable resemblance between his theory of realism and Hubbard's practice. When Kinney sees the article, he is furious at Ricker for breaking a "gentleman's agreement." Howells thereby poses the question of whether the modern writer can indeed act the role of gentleman, or whether as a professional he must subordinate all such allegiances to the dictates of the market.

Hubbard's article expresses Howells's fear not only of the market but also of the aggression informing his "aesthetic of the common." As the average man, Kinney represents just that type of ordinary "ungrammatical" character which Howells advocates as the subject of realistic representation.[39] Yet Hubbard's treatment of his subject poses questions about the relationship between the writer and his less than grammatical material. Howells claims that the realist must represent the average person, who cannot tell his or her own tale. The realist thus plays the role of translator and mediator to make such persons known to the grammatical classes. Hubbard's outright theft of Kinney's story suggests an anxiety about the posture that informs all realistic writing. Like the journalism practiced by Hubbard, realism may be a form of appropriation. In representing formerly invisible classes, realism may deprive them of their own tales and turn them from subjects into objects. How is the realist's goal of knowledge and mediation to be distinguished from the journalist's intrusion into the lives of others? How is the realist to avoid doing similar violence to his subject matter? If realism strives to alleviate class conflict by opening a common ground of representation to all groups, Hubbard's article shows that realism, like journalism, also reproduces those class distinctions within the ground of representation as a hierarchy of style separating the grammatical from the ungrammatical. If journalism on the one hand expands the arena of representation to a more democratic public, it dispossesses readers of their own lives to return those lives to them as consumable items, as "spice." Does realistic representation demand a similar act of dispossession? In representing the unrepresented, does it practice a new form of disenfranchisement?

Howells attempts to answer these questions in chapter 31 of his novel by banishing Hubbard from his own realm of realistic representation and finally, at the end, by killing him off. He thereby blames Hubbard for his individual excess and sets the realistic novel above Hubbard's journalism. Hubbard is killed by putting into practice his own theory of spicy journalism. He oversteps the boundary between public and private when he prints the gossip about the domestic life of an important member of a western town, who in response promptly kills him. Hubbard in effect is buried as a story in a newspaper, as we appropriately read about the last stage of his career in a newspaper article. Howells's need to punish Hubbard for his individual transgression stems from the fear that Howells's own writing is indeed trapped in the same systemic changes which Hubbard's career represents. The novel after all is about a divorce, the very subject of gossip which Ricker continually criticizes the press for cannibalizing. Howells, too, participates in breaking down the boundary between private and public spheres by bringing the story of domestic degeneration into the public realm of realistic representation, rather than leaving it in the confiding whispers of Atherton's study or his fianceé's drawing room. Howells's attempt to dissociate himself from Hubbard's journalistic realism can thus only remain incomplete. As most critics have noted, the novel indeed retreats from realistic representation after it banishes Hubbard; after chapter 31, it withdraws into the genteel world of polite conversation as Atherton's commentary presides over the narrative. The realism of *A Modern Instance* undermines itself when it exorcizes its own demon, Hubbard, an act which demonstrates how uncomfortably close realism lies to Hubbard's transgressions.

The scandal of Bartley Hubbard lies not only in his journalism and in his disregard of the marriage vows, but also in his affront to Howells's notion of "character," the foundation of the realistic edifice. Throughout the novel, Hubbard undermines the nineteenth-century culture of character to supplant it with a more modern concept of the self as "personality," which according to Susman depends on displaying an external image to an audience, rather than on controlling an inner essence through work.[40] In the opening courtship scene Hubbard lectures Marcia on the "formation of character" and ends by mockingly praising her "influence as ennobling and elevating" (p. 10). He here parodies an aspect of the culture of character not mentioned by Susman, which locates the moral influence of women in the domestic sphere as a major mold of character. Thus Hubbard opens the novel by undermining the concept of character as a moral, developmental self nurtured by a domestic self-sacrificing woman.

If Hubbard's speech mocks the notion of character, he contests it more profoundly as a character in a novel. He challenges the link between character and the work ethic, which assumes that the essential morality of a person can be known through his actions. Squire Gaylord hires Hubbard originally for his hard work and his self-made Franklinesque qualities. Even a cynic like Gaylord cannot see through Hubbard immediately, because of an implicit social code which assumes that character is legible from work. Hubbard similarly deludes the rest of the villagers, who, after Marcia breaks off the engagement, are so impressed with the "spectacle of his diligence" that the minister's sermon on "the beauty of lilies" reminds them of Hubbard as the "Heroic Worker" (p. 68). Yet the narrator informs us that work for Hubbard did not signify repentance, but that he threw himself into work to avoid confronting any moral issues. "He discovered in himself," explains the narrator, "that dual life of which everyone who sins or sorrows is sooner or later aware: the strange separation of the intellectual activity from the suffering of the soul, by which the mind toils on in a sort of ironical indifference to the pangs that wring the heart; the realization, that in some ways, his brain can get on perfectly well without his conscience" (p. 67). Although, like the realist, Hubbard treats writing as work, his writing fosters a "dual life" which directly opposes the unitary nature of writing and work posited by the nineteenth-century producer ethos and upheld by Howells's theory of realism.

Ben Halleck, the son of a patrician Boston family, criticizes Hubbard as "a fellow that assimilated everything to a certain extent, and nothing thoroughly" (p. 170). What Halleck can see only as the lack of depth is in fact Hubbard's cultivation of the modern art of personality. Personality depends on making an impression in the eyes of others, rather than on cultivating an internal essence which constitutes character and which is manifest through work. In contrast to character, personality is not a moral category, but one suitable to mass society, in which the key evaluation of selfhood is not whether one is good or bad but whether one is known or unknown, a somebody or a nobody.[41] The realization of personality depends on both standing out in a crowd and appealing to it by charisma; personality depends not on work but on performance and showmanship. Personality is not a quality attributed to an inner self, but a projection of an image to others. Hubbard, in contrast to the other characters in the novel, prefigures the full-blown culture of personality. Unlike the others, Hubbard lacks a known history that accumulates to form his self. An orphan of undesignated class or social situation, he was educated with the sons of the upper class among whom he acts at home, yet finds himself equally comfortable at the city desk and in beer halls. Chameleon-like, he adopts the colors of his surroundings and seems to have no solid inner self. A measure of his success is that he fools so many people by mirroring their expectations: the Squire believes he is a hard worker; the town is taken in by his charm; Ben Halleck befriends him in college; Ricker brings him into the newspaper fraternity; the natural man, Kinney, admires and looks up to him; the small-town girl, Marcia, never fully loses her infatuation with him.

As befits his mobile and rootless background, Hubbard adapts remarkably well to city life, the modern milieu in which social interaction depends on seeing and being seen by strangers. Squire Gaylord, in contrast, finds during his visit to Boston that "the city cramps me; it's too tight a fit; and yet I can't seem to find myself in it" (p. 192). In his culture of character, Gaylord assumes that the self does have definable dimensions. Hubbard in contrast finds the city comfortable not because it conforms to the limits of the self but because without such limits he can find himself everywhere in the expansive space of urban life. As a journalist, he successfully fulfills his occupation to be everywhere and to see everything, and to be seen in turn.

Hubbard's definition of success is to stand out in the crowd, whether this consists of going to every church in town to impress the inhabitants or writing an exposé of the housing market. Indeed, Hubbard is completely taken up with self-display. In contrast to his wife, Marcia, who is concerned with saving money for the future, he is obsessed with clothes and loves to spend money. Whereas she would like him to work hard in order to become a lawyer in the future, he only wants to make an immediate impression in the present. When he returns to Maine, for example, he insists on parading through the streets in his finery, arm in arm with the Squire, to display his success and his control over the Squire, even though he has no desire for a true reconciliation. Hubbard's expanding physical corpulence manifests his desire to be seen for its own sake.

In his portrayal of Hubbard, Howells charts a major social transition from the culture of character to the culture of personality. Yet because his theory of realism was dependent on the centrality of character, Howells could not totally treat his characters as personalities, as would a later writer like Dreiser. When Hubbard loses his job and leaves his wife, he abandons the moorings of character and is banished from the novel, from the direct realm of realistic representation. Howells cannot make this suddenly anonymous figure, divorced from the institutions of domesticity and work, the focus for his representation, as Dreiser does with Hurstwood. Like Huck Finn when he tears up his letter to Miss Watson, Bartley's decision to leave his wife takes him outside the structures of character and beyond the pale of representation. With the same initials as Bartley Hubbard, as many critics note, Ben Halleck magically appears at the beginning of the next chapter, just as Tom Sawyer surfaces to supplant Huck Finn.

Critics often see this last section of *A Modern Instance* as they do the end of *The Adventures of Huckleberry Finn,* as a failure, a retreat into comfortable genteel values.[42] Howells, on the contrary, leads us to the threshold of a cultural transition which he can neither cross nor abandon. If, in Hubbard, Howells demonstrates the breakdown of character and its transformation into personality, from which would emerge a figure like Dreiser's Carrie with her endless surface identities, in Ben Halleck he demonstrates the impossibility of returning to an older conception of character. While Hubbard defies the sanctity of character, Ben Halleck clings to it at the cost of total self-sacrifice and self-denial. "Character is a superstitution," he complains, "a wretched fetish" (p. 288). Halleck worships this fetish, and maintains his character only by denying, to the point of sickliness, his desire and his capacity to act. Both Hubbard's crass desire to be seen and Halleck's decision to disappear, lest he act on his desire for Marcia, manifest the same lack of faith in the integrity of character. If one abandons all self-control, the mainstay of character building, the other takes self-control to the absurd extreme. If Howells cannot represent Hubbard in his pursuit of personality outside the bounds of work and domesticity, neither can Halleck's extreme self-denial offer the substance for realistic representation.

Thus Bartley Hubbard represents two opposing tendencies in Howells's realism. As a character, Hubbard leads the narrative of *A Modern Instance* to the limit of Howells's theory of realism, which is rooted in the work ethic and the related centrality of character portrayal. As a journalist, Hubbard enacts the demonically violent urge lurking in Howells's "aesthetic of the common." Howells turns this violence against Hubbard himself to protect realism from its own aggression, but the substitution of Halleck for Hubbard only attests to the latter's centrality to the realistic enterprise. And Howells never quite lays Hubbard to rest.

III

Two years after the publication of *A Modern Instance,* Howells resurrects Bartley Hubbard to introduce *The Rise of Silas Lapham.* In one of his few titles which bears the name of a character, Howells follows his theory of realism to build a novel around the knowledge of character, but what he reveals instead is the unknowability of character in the social world he constructs. The novel opens with Bartley Hubbard interviewing Silas Lapham, a recently successful "self-made" businessman, for "The Solid Men of Boston" series in the newspaper *The Daily Events.*

While Howells simply uses the format of the interview to present Lapham's history before the opening of the novel, he makes it uncomfortably dependent on Hubbard's journalistic method. Yet this format also sets up Hubbard as an implicit rival to the novel that follows, as though Howells were putting into practice his claim in *A Modern Instance* that the "literary motive" is more powerful than the journalistic. Howells introduces Hubbard only to dismiss him and to distinguish realism from the journalistic interview. Although Hubbard disappears from the novel with no explanation after one more short scene, Howells cannot totally differentiate his own writing from Hubbard's, and he exposes realism to be complicit in the same network of cultural practices that makes the interview a necessary mode of communication.

Hubbard starts out his interview with a joke—"your money or your life"—and concludes that he wants both—that Lapham is interesting as a character because of his financial success (p. 3). This joke brands Hubbard's interview as a form of robbery, and Hubbard does aggressively bully Lapham throughout their discussion. The reporter mocks his subject while goading him to expose himself, which makes Lapham vaguely uncomfortable with the "use of him as material." Hubbard prides himself on understanding more than Lapham does about his own life, and he brags to his wife that Lapham "regularly turned himself inside out to me" but complains that he could not let himself "loose on him the way I wanted to. Confound the limits of decency" (p. 20). Hubbard would prefer to turn the interview into an exposé.

When he records the spoken interview, Hubbard renders Lapham's revelations in "sincere reporter's rhetoric" to make his life sound like a parody of the rags-to-riches story. Hubbard's interview turns the man inside out not to reveal his true character, but to mold him to a conventional story. Howells, however, shows the power of this rhetoric by making Lapham himself use the same clichéd style to tell his own tale of his self-sacrificing mother and hard-working father. We later learn that Lapham is an avid reader of the newspapers as his major source of knowledge and entertainment. Thus Howells does not set up an opposition between the natural speech of his character and the rhetoric of the newspaper, for the two are indistinguishable. Instead he distinguishes his own realistic novel from Hubbard's interview. The novel implicitly claims interest in Lapham not because of, but despite, his success. Realism's goal is to reveal the man beneath the money, the "character" behind the crass, wealthy capitalist. During the interview, Lapham shows Hubbard a family photograph which looks like "the standard family-group photograph in which most Americans have figured at some time or the other" (p. 8). Despite the conventionality and awkwardness of the pose, the photograph "had not been able to conceal the fact that they were all decent, honest-looking, sensible people." This description uses photography as a model for realism, not for its accurate and life-like qualities, but for its capacity to unveil the common decency of characters beneath artificial conventions. While Hubbard decries decency as setting artificial limits on his bottom-line facts, Howells claims decency as the bottom-line of realism, a claim which the narrative proceeds to invalidate.

The interview is a crucial form for introducing the novel, because it raises the essential question for realism, the problem of knowing and representing others. This problem does not occur in the insular circle of elite society represented by Atherton in *A Modern Instance,* where everyone is known and those outside are not worth knowing. Nor is it a problem in the small-town life of Equity, Maine, or the Vermont home of the Laphams. The knowledge of others does become a problem in the modern city, whose primary social milieu is the aggregation of strangers. On the ferry from Boston to Nahant, Lapham raises this question of knowing strangers. Lapham exclaims that he does not recognize faces after seven years of riding the same boat because the town is full of strangers, and that, furthermore, he cannot interpret the faces he sees to learn about the lives behind them. "The astonishing thing to me," he states, "is not what the face tells, but what it don't tell" (p. 70). But he concludes that he is better-off not being able to read the inner life from the surface appearance, because his life would be vulnerable to be read as well, which "would take a man out of his own hands." The narrator, at this point, interjects to contradict Lapham, to claim that "the greater part of the crowd on board—and, of course, the boat was crowded—looked as if they might not only be easily but safely known. . . . In face they were commonplace, with nothing but the American poetry of vivid purpose to light them up, where they did not wholly lack fire. But they were nearly all shrewd and friendly-looking, with an apparent readiness for the humorous intimacy native to us all." This scene on the ferry can be read as a revision of Whitman's "Crossing Brooklyn Ferry," a poem that also addresses the problem of knowing others. The poet starts by invoking the natural environment which he sees face-to-face only to turn to the surrounding crowd with bewilderment. To the crowd on the ferry and to that of the future, he asks "what is it then between us?" While the poet finds the crowd enigmatic and threatening, he comes to celebrate the crowd in harmony with the self. In contrast, Howells's ferry to Nahant offers two opposing stances. On the one hand Lapham finds nothing between himself and the crowd; the crowd remains illegible to him, and he prefers to remain inscrutable to protect his private self. On the other hand, the narrator finds the crowd to be an open book, easily, safely, and monotonously known. The realistic narrator rides neither in harmony nor in conflict with the crowd; he stands above it and sees through it to make it familiar and unthreatening, "native to us all."

Although Silas Lapham prefers to keep himself in "his own hands," he proves incapable of making himself known by telling his own tale to the upper-class members of patrician Boston. As a "nongrammatical" character, he cannot address the grammatical class he is attempting to join. In the pivotal dinner scene at the Coreys' he can narrate his tale as long as he remains in the common historical yet distant arena of the Civil War. As soon as he proceeds to tell the same story of his financial rise that he told to Hubbard, he humiliates himself. His speech does not have the effect of forging a connection with the strangers of another class but has the contrary effect of distancing them. This scene launches his downward social and financial spiral, which culminates in his moral rise—the irony of the title. The realistic writer, then, has the role of revealing the character, which Lapham cannot tell himself, and of forging a common bond. Yet if the realist has this democratizing function of making people known to one another, of mediating their differences, this function depends upon his maintaining and regulating the boundaries between them.

The interview allows the writer to enact this mediation: it provides a format for gaining knowledge of strangers which the writer controls, while it attests to the elusive nature of the connections between people. The interview as a routine means of news-gathering was a relatively new form in late-nineteenth-century journalism; it had previously been used only for major political figures.[43] Members of the upper class and practitioners of a traditional journalism at first resisted the interview because it violated the boundaries between the public and the private. The interview can be seen as part of a genre of class tourism, as segments of society were simultaneously brought closer together by the urbanization process yet further segregated by the spatialization of class within modern cities. In the late nineteenth century, "the house beautiful" movement, which offered voyeuristic glimpses into model homes of the rich, shared the same cultural preoccupation as did investigations of slum life; both introduced the environments of foreign classes to middle-class readers. These explorations assume what the interview assumes: that classes have become inaccessible to one another and that individuals cannot know one another face-to-face through direct contact or conversation. In this context the writer as guide and translator becomes the necessary mediator.

The Rise of Silas Lapham appropriately ends with an interview as it begins with one, to frame the entire novel with this one-way dialogue. Hubbard, however, is replaced by the Reverend Sewell, who is often viewed as the spokesman for Howells's realism, as the sane, moderate voice of commonsense morality. This view can be supported by the fact that he supplants Hubbard at the end of the novel, when Lapham demonstrates his moral "rise" by returning to his original rural way of life. Sewell, however, shares some revealing concerns with Hubbard. Sewell's interest in Lapham is described in terms suggesting some of the voyeurism of the newspaper interview: "He was intensely interested in the moral spectacle which Lapham presented under his changed conditions," and he had a "burning desire to know exactly how, at the bottom of his heart, Lapham still felt" (pp. 319, 321). While one represents Lapham through "sincere reporter's rhetoric," the other can be said to do the same with sincere clergyman's rhetoric. Howells may pose Sewell as an alternative to Hubbard to link his own narrative with the older cultural authority of the minister rather than with the modern authority of the newspaper. He shows, however, that both figures mirror one another and are implicated in the same cultural practice as his own realism, which often dominates and silences the very subject it represents.

At the end of the novel, Silas Lapham may have the last word in response to Sewell's questions, but he is rendered more ungrammatical and inarticulate than ever, doomed to undo his tale and doomed to repeat it. Just as the narrative returns him to his origins in a kind of wish-fulfillment to undo his entire life story, Sewell reveals Lapham's essential decency by laying bare his real self. Throughout the novel, the Laphams are searching for a moral anchor or center of individual responsibility, only to find their search undermined by the decentered conditions of the world around them, represented by the Civil War and the rise of corporations, which impose forces beyond their control. The narrative enacts a similar search to posit character as a moral anchor in a world in which "small things are no more." If the Laphams try to grasp a standard of value based on individual autonomy, Howells has us grasping a standard of character. The ending, however, reveals an aggression in this standard of character that requires unraveling the narrative, stripping the character of his story and returning him to a mythical origin, which we first learn about through Hubbard's "sincere reporter's rhetoric."

The interviews that frame *The Rise of Silas Lapham* represent only one kind of practice in a larger system in which impersonal forms of mass media provide the major channels of communication between people. In *A Modern Instance* an interview first provides Hubbard with his opportunity to renew his contact with the Hallecks. The syndicate system reprints Hubbard's story, which Kinney reads out West. An advertisement in a local gazette informs the Gaylords of the divorce proceedings. In *The Rise of Silas Lapham* the Coreys learn about the Laphams through their paint advertisements which splatter the landscape. In each example, knowledge of others circulates in the media through the national marketplace. The media seem to be doing realism's job of creating a nationwide readership and paving a common ground between diverse social groups. Realism for Howells depends on the democratizing force of the market, which allows a woodsman like Kinney to be known in Boston, and the Laphams to be known through their ads. Realism participates in this exchange of the knowledge of persons from different regions and classes. Howells attempts to harness this power of the media while he tries to purge it of total dependence on the market and independence of any other values. Realism thus participates in constructing a society which appears more interdependent and interconnected than ever before while the connections between people appear more invisible and elusive. Although Howells tries to construct a community based on character, on mutual recognition, his narratives depend upon the media to bring together characters in spite of their diverse worlds. His novels enact what he later laments in "The Man of Letters as a Man of Business," that "at present business is the only human solidarity, we are all bound together by that chain."[44]

2

THE UNREAL CITY IN *A Hazard of New Fortunes*

The city has long been viewed as both the setting and the subject of American realistic fiction at the turn of the century. In fact, we curiously treat the seamy side of urban life as the touchstone of "the real" itself; thus the more slums, poverty, crime, and corruption, the more realistic the novel. Late nineteenth-century writing, however, suggests a more problematic relation between urban life and realistic representation. In both fiction and nonfiction, "the city" often signifies "the unreal," the alien, or that which has not yet been realized. Represented by what it might become—by its potential, its threat, its promise—"the city" figures as a spatial metonymy for the elusive process of social change. To realize the city as a subject for representation means to combat its otherness and to fix its protean changes within a coherent narrative form. This confrontation with the "unreal city" as the site and sign of change informs the realism of William Dean Howells's *A Hazard of New Fortunes* (1890), one of the first major novels about New York City.

I

By the 1880s *the city* had become a shorthand term for everything threatening in American society. "The city is the nerve center of our civilization. It is also its storm center," begins a chapter, "Perils—The City," in Josiah Strong's 1885 best-seller, *Our Country: Its Possible Future and Its Present Crisis* (1885).[1] That "the city has become a serious menace to our civilization" he attributes to the following litany of dangers associated with its "largely foreign" lower-class inhabitants:

> Here is heaped the social dynamite; here roughs, gamblers, thieves, robbers, lawless and desperate men of all sorts, congregate; men who are ready on any pretext to raise riots for the purpose of destruction and plunder; here gather foreigners and wage workers; here skepticism and irreligion abound; here inequality is the greatest and most obvious, and the contrast between opulence and penury the most striking; here is suffering the sorest. As the greatest wickedness in the world is to be found not among the cannibals of some far off coast, but in Christian lands where the light of truth is diffused and rejected, so the utmost depth of wretchedness exists not among savages, who have few wants, but in great cities, where, in the presence of plenty and of every luxury men starve. (p. 132)

Although Strong echoes denunciations of city mobs and urban depravity voiced since the eighteenth century, he also articulates a specific fear that emerged in response to the railroad strikes of 1877.[2] When labor violence erupted in several cities at the same time, Americans saw the once disorganized "insolent rabble" transformed into a specter of organized social revolt. By 1886, Strong's prophecy of urban apocalypse seemed fulfilled by the Haymarket Riot in Chicago, when at a rally culminating weeks of labor unrest someone in the crowd threw a bomb at advancing police.[3] The nationwide hysteria that ensued expressed the middle-class terror of being swallowed up by the outbreak of violence from below, by what Strong calls "volcanic fires of a deep discontent" (p. 133). As social historians have shown, this perception of the urban menace increased in proportion to middle-class withdrawal from urban centers into new suburbs and segregated neighborhoods, "little islands of propriety," in Dreiser's words.[4] The "unreality" of urban life was magnified as vast metropolitan tracts became off-limits to seasoned city-dwellers as well as to outside observers. Onto this geographic and social terra incognita the middle classes projected anxieties about the lack of cohesiveness within their own families and communities. Violent events, such as the Haymarket Riot, crystallized the fear of internal instability and change in the external threat of class warfare.

Strong's comparison of the working classes to "cannibals in some far off coast" both articulates the unreal and menacing qualities of urban life and implies a solution. Journalists, reformers, and pulp novelists depicted the city as a new frontier or foreign territory to settle and explore and regarded its inhabitants—usually immigrants—as natives to civilize and control. The notion of settlement, a way of conceptualizing urban class differences, has two related meanings: to make the city knowable and inhabitable by the middle classes and to subdue the city's unsettling foreign forces. This dual goal informs the influential exposé of slum life published the same year as *Hazard,* Jacob Riis's *How the Other Half Lives.*[5] After introducing the central problem of knowledge, that "one half does not know how the other half lives," Riis starts his inquiry at the "boundary line of the Other Half [that] lies through the tenements" (pp. 1–2). With camera in hand, Riis crosses this line to enter the murky realms of lower-class life. Although his book aims to improve the living conditions of the poor, it appeals more immediately to the hearts and minds of his readers—the other "other half." Playing on fears of urban violence, Riis highlights the alien features of the immigrants to fix the foreign-born as "other" in the eyes of his readers. Yet his mission of reform suggests that proper housing could transform the world of the alien immigrant into a vision of middle-class domesticity. The home, he implies, can make the boundary line disappear by turning it into a mirror. The settlement-house movement, made famous by Jane Addams, based itself on a similar principle, that middle-class missionaries living in the slums could remodel the poor in their own image and neutralize their unsettling difference.[6] For these reformers, to settle the city meant to map a threatening terrain as manageable landscape.

In *A Hazard of New Fortunes,* Howells wrote his own narrative of urban settlement. Neither a prophet of doom, like Strong, nor a social reformer, like Riis, Howells did share their anxiety about social unrest, which he addressed in his influential theory of literary realism. Realism, as we have seen, strives to pave a common ground for diverse social classes by extending literary representation to "the other half" while reassuring middle-class readers that social difference can be effaced in the mirror of the commonplace. This social goal has an aesthetic correlative in Howells's emphasis on proportion between descriptive details and formal unity. "Realism," he warns, "becomes false to itself, when it heaps up facts merely, and maps life instead of picturing it."[7] In Howells's literary criticism, realism emerges as an elaborate balancing act: it reconciles social diversity within an overarching community, assimilates disparate facts to a commonsense morality, and frames a plenitude of details within a coherent form.

Howells found such balances shaken, however, by the very events that led him to write *Hazard:* his support of the Haymarket anarchists in 1886 and his move from Boston to New York two years later. The "civic murder" of the anarchists for their incendiary speech made Howells doubt the existence of a shared justice system for all American citizens, and the polygot streets of New York City taxed his faith in a common American idiom—let alone a shared dialect.[8] Howells's first novel about the modern metropolis both undercuts the common ground of his theory of realism and strives to reconstitute it. As a narrative of settlement, *Hazard* forges an urban community out of the debris of social conflict, and molds a common language from "a veritable Babel of confusion."[9] On the "largest canvas" he had "yet allowed" himself, Howells struggles to contain the centrifugal force of his urban materials within a coherent narrative frame.[10]

To settle the city—in both senses of the word—*Hazard* works to master the "unreal city" and overcome its otherness. Howells constructs a real city in fiction by populating it with what Raymond Williams has called a "knowable community"—a network of mutual social recognition that unites diverse members.[11] Eschewing his earlier practice of focusing on one character or family, Howells builds a plot that centers on a wide range of middle-class characters who have just moved to New York City and who together form a tenuous colony around the production of a literary magazine. To make themselves at home in this foreign territory, the newcomers must subdue the shadowy but intrusive presence of the city's native inhabitants. Howells has long been unfairly criticized for his lack of lower-class characters—and therefore for his lack of "realism." *Hazard,* in fact, explores the way the urban community defines itself in an ongoing, if repressed, relation to the city's absent "other half."[12] Like any knowable community, this one is delimited by what it excludes or fails to assimilate. The specter of class conflict that so haunted Howells's contemporaries puts pressure on the course of his narrative to tell a countertale of the city's unsettling force. Realism in *Hazard* is a process of imagining and managing the threats of social change inscribed in the "unreal city."

II

Howells introduces the city through the traditional trope in urban literature that identifies the writer with the figure walking through the streets.[13] Adding a twist to this convention, he has a married couple, the Marches, explore the city in search of an apartment to rent. He thereby tests the viability of domesticity as a touchstone of the real. Once again, Howells implicitly competes with Bartley Hubbard by rewriting, in effect, his first city-article while giving it the "form" of the "literary motive." Since the publication of *Hazard,* the apartment-hunting scene has been criticized for its lack of literary form, its excessive detail, and its aimlessness, points underscored by the fact that the Boston couple does, after all, take one of the first flats they see.[14] Howells himself conceded that this section "incorporated long stretches of carpentry where [it] arrived at little or nothing of the real edifice."[15] The importance of this scene, however, lies in its very excess: the lack of subordination to a unified plot or theme calls attention to the "carpentry," to the construction of the narrative itself. At the outset, the city disrupts narrative continuity as something unwieldy that must be brought under control. Deploying the Marches as scouts in this foreign territory, the narrative struggles to chart a domesticated and unthreatening terrain. A close analysis of the apartment-hunting scene will show how it generates the major strategies for settling the city and making it real.

Encountering a city that resists representation, Basil complains to his wife about "the acquisition of useless information in a degree unequaled in their experience," a complaint that curiously foreshadows later criticism of the scene itself.[16] But this search does prove more valuable than the Marches can acknowledge:

> They came to excel in the sad knowledge of the line at which respectability distinguishes itself from shabbiness. . . . There was an east and west line beyond which they could not go if they wished to keep their self-respect, and within that region to which they had restricted themselves there was a choice of streets. At first all the New York streets looked to them ill-paved, dirty and repulsive; the general infamy imparted itself in their casual impression to the streets in no wise guilty. But they began to notice that some of the streets were quiet and clean . . . that they wore an air of encouraging reform and suggested a future of greater and greater domesticity. Whole blocks of these downtown cross streets seemed to have been redeemed from decay. (p. 58)

The "line," rather than the city, is the object of knowledge here. Contrary to our conventional expectation of realistic description, the Marches do not come to know the city streets by accumulating detailed observations. Instead, the "knowledge of the line" makes the city visible in greater detail by limiting their sight to particular neighborhoods. Starting with a general sense of the city as other, threatening and repellent, they soon assimilate social conventions that steer them through the streets. Guided by the line, they can distinguish an unthreatening domestic space by excluding large segments of the city in the generalized perception of "decay." The "knowledge of the line" has a double function: it frames a coherent picture of the city and relegates unassimilable fragments to the peripheral category of "useless information." It is the limiting power of the line that brings the city into vision and allows the Marches to inscribe themselves within it.

The Marches' settlement of the city can be read as a continual struggle to renegotiate their "knowledge of the line" against the barrage of "useless information." This is a social, geographic, and cognitive conflict that pits a cohesive domestic enclave against the fragmented space of the streets. The Marches seek a home—both a physical space and a locus of value—to provide a refuge from the city as well as a lens for viewing it. When they arrive in New York, they do not find a blank space upon which to transcribe their fantasy of domesticity—an image that coheres only within the confines of their hotel suite; instead, they find a cityscape already cluttered with prior inhabitants and strewn with their history. The apartments they examine have been furnished by earlier occupants, and several have been carved out of formerly grand mansions. The entire city appears overcrowded with the ubiquitous tenements of the poor, who spill out into the streets in discomfiting proximity to the Marches.

In their dual struggle to inhabit and represent the city, the Marches employ a variety of strategies to domesticate the threatening urban terrain. While walking through Washington Square, for example, they convince themselves that they have "met the familiar picturesque raggedness of southern Europe with the old kindly illusion that somehow it existed for their appreciation and that it found adequate compensation for poverty in this" (p. 55). Paradoxically, by viewing New York as a foreign country, the Marches can experience it as familiar. The role of tourist places them in a known relationship to the city and allows them to distance themselves from the surrounding poverty by framing it within the secure lines of the "picturesque." In the course of their search, however, the "purely aesthetic view of the facts" is undercut by the sensory assault of the streets. When they ride past a block of tenements, the stench from the garbage heaps offends them so much that they angrily turn away and cannot reassure themselves "with saying that it was as picturesque as a street in Naples or Florence and with wondering why nobody came to paint it" (p. 65). More than an olfactory offense, the garbage heap challenges the Marches' secure "knowledge of the line" and breaks down the boundaries upon which their representations depend. A type of "useless information," the odor cannot be contained within the lines of the "picturesque." The stench seeps through the window of the coupe, which, like the home, both separates the Marches from the streets and frames their view of it. Furthermore, the sense of smell undermines the primacy of sight, the sense that maintains the distance between the Marches as observers and the street as an object of observation, and the sense identified with "picturing," with Howells's mode of realistic representation.

The "knowledge of the line" does more than passively distance the Marches from the tumultuous city streets; it aggressively composes the fragments of urban life into a spectacle for observation. To this end, the newly constructed elevated railroad replaces the horse-drawn coupe as an updated lens for viewing and controlling this urban spectacle. Traveling above the threatening crowds, the train offers vivid glimpses into the homes of the poor; it reminded Basil of a kind of theater,

> to see those people through their windows: a family party of workfolk late at tea, some of the men in their shirt-sleeves; a woman sewing by a lamp; a mother laying her child in its cradle; a man with his head fallen on his hands upon a table; a girl and her lover leaning over the windowsill together. What suggestion! What drama! What infinite interest! (p. 76)

Adopting the reassuring stance of the spectator, Basil can outline individual human figures against the city crowds and transform the bewildering anonymity of the tenements into homey tableaux. The moving lens of the L masters the city's rapid pace by framing the spectacle of working-class life in a series of domestic still lifes. From this perspective, Isabel finds that

> the fleeting intimacy you formed with people in the second- and third-floor interiors, while all the usual street life went on underneath, had a domestic intensity mixed with a perfect repose that was the last effect of good society with its security and exclusiveness. (p. 76)

Such one-way intimacy derives from the power to violate the domesticity of others. Voyeuristic intrusions into the homes of the poor allow the Marches to externalize these "interiors" as mirrors of their own genteel values. Observed through these windows, "the other half, " in effect, disappears.

As vehicle for the Marches' line of vision, the L has a double-edged effect: it expands their perspective to otherwise inaccessible corners of urban life, and it violently dislocates what they see. To convince themselves that "there is no misery" among the inhabitants of New York, who are "so gay about it all," the Marches "celebrated a satisfaction they both had in the L roads":

> "They kill the streets and the avenues; but at least they partially hide them, and that is some comfort; and they do triumph over their prostrate forms with a savage exultation that is intoxicating. Those bends in the L . . . they're the gayest things in the world. Perfectly atrocious of course, but incomparably picturesque! And the whole city is so," said March, "or else the L would never have got built here. New York may be splendidly gay or squalidly gay, but prince or pauper, it's gay always." (p. 66)

March's strategy for representing the city here replicates the violent exhilaration he ascribes to the L. His obsessive repetition of the word "gay" levels all distinctions in meaning and refers to nothing but itself. Just as the L destroys the street it supplants and simultaneously hides the debris, "gay" represses its own referent. Throughout the search for a home, "the line" similarly represses the knowledge of "useless information" to produce coherent pictures of the city. Although the Marches seek a domestic refuge from the city's assaults, their own representations of the city often aggressively subdue its otherness. The L can be read as a metaphor for the violence implicit in *not seeing* in order to make the city visible and real.

The violence with which the Marches reinscribe "the line" reflects as much anxiety about their own place in the city as about the poor. Like many middle-class families in the 1880s, the Marches are renting an apartment in an urban center for the first time in their lives. As yet, no clear legal or semantic differences even separated the "tenement" from the "apartment."[17] This collapse of class boundaries may have proved even more threatening than the gulf between classes that Riis condemns. The close sight of the tenements unmediated by the L makes Basil March declare that all flats inherently oppose domesticity, motherhood, and family, the foundations of his own social identity. The only difference Basil can delineate between poor and middle-class renters stems from a genteel sense of character: "those poor people can't give character to their habitations. They have to take what they can get. But people like us—that is, of our means—do give character to the average flat" (p. 69). Basil insists on this contrast precisely because his search for an apartment thrusts him into a position of relative powerlessness and anonymity uncomfortably close to those characterless masses.

Any encroachment upon this distinction destabilizes the Marches' construction of reality, as attested to by Isabel:

> "I'm beginning to *feel* crazy. . . . I don't believe there's any *real* suffering—not real *suffering*—among those people; that is, it would be suffering from our point of view, but they've been used to it all their lives and they don't feel their discomfort so much." (p. 69)

The fear of being like "those people" threatens Isabel's sanity because it blurs the boundaries of her self-image. To reinforce her own sense of reality, she draws a line between "our point of view" and "their point of view," between an intelligible human response and the natural results of poverty. This line not only denies the social reality of the poor; it also effaces any conflicting perspective. It secures the Marches' self-representation by universalizing their response in the category of "the real" and "the human," and by relegating "those people" to the unintelligible margins.

The narrative, however, immediately undermines Isabel's distinction between "real" and "unreal" suffering through the sudden appearance alongside the Marches of a "decently dressed person" rummaging through the garbage heap (p. 70). This beggar emerges from nowhere, like the return of the repressed, to deny their denial of "real" misery. The repeated emphasis on his respectable appearance suggests that it is his likeness to the Marches, as much as his poverty, that shocks and upsets them. The fact that he speaks French enhances this bond and thwarts their strategy of making New York familiarly foreign. Just as the smell of garbage seeps through the protective lining of "the picturesque," contact with this "decent-looking" scavenger oversteps the dividing line between "us" and "them," between "real suffering" and natural poverty. The unsettling appearance of the beggar shifts the course of the narrative and brings the Marches' search to an unresolved halt. Yet the beggar's intrusion is never laid to rest; suddenly recalling him at the end of the novel, Basil speculates that he was probably a confidence man, and thereby negates his reality.

Howells's narrative strategies for representing the city parallel the Marches' strategies for settling it. Even though his irony exposes the limits of their vision, he reinscribes similar boundaries within the broader representation of New York. The entire novel can be read as an escalating struggle between the "knowledge of the line" and the "acquisition of useless information." This struggle takes the form of drawing and redrawing the boundary line between the background and the foreground of the novel. Just as the Marches cordon off a domestic space against the teeming streets, the narrative distinguishes a colony of interrelated characters in the foreground against a background of fragmented objects and characterless masses. The background is carefully composed of catalogue-like descriptions that yoke together inanimate details and fragments of lower-class inhabitants, and frame them together in a naturalized cityscape.

The following description, for example, of the street that so offends the Marches, makes no distinction between things and persons, who are signified synecdochically by parts of their bodies or the sounds of their voices:

They drove accidentally through one street that seemed gayer in perspective than an L road. The fire escapes, with their light iron balconies and ladders of

> iron, decorated the lofty house fronts; the roadway and sidewalks and doorsteps swarmed with children; women's heads seemed to show at every window. In the basements, over which the flights of high stone steps led to the tenements, were greengrocers' shops abounding in cabbage, and provision stores running chiefly to bacon and sausages, and cobblers' and tinners' shops, and the like in proportion to the small needs of a poor neighborhood. Ash barrels lined the sidewalks and garbage heaps filled the gutters; teams of all trades stood idly about; a peddler of cheap fruit urged his cart through the street and mixed his cry with the joyous screams and shouts of the children and the scolding and gossiping voices of the women; and the burly blue bulk of a policeman defined itself at the corner; a drunkard zigzagged down the sidewalk toward him. (pp. 64–65)

This panorama of contiguous objects absorbs the poor into a naturalized cityscape overflowing with sights and noises but devoid of full human figures or speech. Its effect is summarized by the narrative comment that follows it:

> It was not the abode of the extremest poverty, but of a poverty as hopeless as any in the world, transmitting itself from generation to generation and establishing conditions of permanency to which human life adjusts itself as it does to those of some incurable disease, like leprosy. (p. 65)

The placement of this commentary has the same effect as its content; it frames the fragmented background in the natural, unchanging order of things. All social interaction takes place outside this realm in the foreground, in the domesticated sphere of the characters.

Critics have long treated the city in *Hazard* as the setting of the novel, evaluating it in terms of its fidelity to the historical New York City.[18] I am suggesting that background and foreground are neither external historical categories nor purely formal demarcations within the text. Navigating the course between these two realms becomes a major strategy for settling the city and making it real. The drawing of boundaries offers a narrative solution to the ideological question of how to represent and control social difference and conflict. "The line" divides the city into two separate but unequal camps and veils the antagonism between them so that the social nature of this division fades from view. What comes into view as background, as cityscape, becomes invisible as an arena for social agency. Against this setting, the foregrounded colony of characters stands out as a metonymy for the whole city—the knowable urban community.

Howells's major realistic novel reveals the tension inherent in his "aesthetic of the common": a sense of the city as a shared, or common, reality depends upon continually banishing the "other half," the common people, into the tamed cityscape. In the following passage, for

example, in the middle of the novel, we can see the narrative processing the immigrants into the background of the text while the Marches watch the government agency process them to enter the country:

> The Marches paid the charming prospect a willing duty and rejoiced in it as generously as if it had been their own. Perhaps it was, they decided. He said people owned more things in common than they were apt to think; and they drew the consolations of proprietorship from the excellent management of Castle Garden, which they penetrated for a moment's glimpse of the huge rotunda, where the emigrants first set foot on our continent. It warmed their hearts so easily moved to any cheap sympathy, to see the friendly care the nation took of these humble guests. . . . The government seemed to manage their welcome as well as a private company or corporation could have done. In fact, it was after the simple strangers had left the government care that March feared their woes might begin, and he would have liked the government to follow each of them to his home, wherever he meant to fix it within our borders. (p. 303)

Identifying with the power of the state, the Marches achieve a sense of common ownership not by including the immigrants but by excluding them from the definition of commonality and, in effect, dispossessing them. Although the narrator takes a highly ironic stance toward the Marches and accuses them of "cheap sympathy," the references to "our continent" and "our borders" tacitly align the reader and the narrator with the Marches and government agency. This passage, then, exemplifies an important tendency in Howells's realism. It rejects an older representation of class difference through the genteel extension of "sympathy," and replaces it with the language of common ownership based on control and modern management. *Hazard* builds a foreground that can be treated as common property among the narrator, reader, and characters, by managing the city's lower-class immigrants in the background.

Although Howells's theory of realism depends upon balance and proportion—on "picturing" rather than "mapping"—his practice is fraught with tension. Realism in *Hazard* continually contests its own drive to contain conflict and "minimize excess."[19] Throughout the novel, narrative excess strains the boundaries of the urban representation and forces their realignment. Fragments threaten to intrude into the foreground, and the background threatens to engulf the characters. When such a crossing does occur, as in the appearance of the beggar or in the strike at the end of the novel, it disrupts the continuity of the narrative. The power of Howells's novel lies in demonstrating the constant readjustment of vision necessary to renegotiate the "knowledge of the line" against the intrusion of "useless information." If we reread *How the Other Half Lives* through Howells's shifting lines, we may find that Riis crosses over the line not to abolish it but to make "the other half" known in the form of *useful information;* by so doing he conceptually reinforces the hierarchy between classes. Through the relentless pressure of "useless information," *Hazard,* in contrast, makes "the line" itself knowable to readers as the necessary yet tenuous strategy for the middle-class settlement of the city.

III

While the search for a home stakes out the perimeter of the foreground, the production of middle-class culture—in the form of a literary magazine—provides the framework that binds this sphere. Both the urban-settlement theme and the plot of the novel revolve around the magazine *Every Other Week,* which offers the only point of intersection for all the characters in the novel and, for many, their only social and economic tie to New York City. As a cultural enterprise, the magazine puts into effect the common bond of realistic representation: it forges disparate urban settlers into a knowable community, only to expose the fragility of that bond. If Howells uses the March family to inscribe and explore the boundaries of the real city, he turns to Fulkerson, the syndicate man, to uphold and reinforce them, and to Lindau, the German socialist, to violate them. As figures of the author, these characters embody conflicting trajectories in Howells's practice of realism.

As the magazine's founder, manager, and motor force, Fulkerson orchestrates the community of characters. A figure for the novelist, he "exists to make connections, to keep the action flowing smoothly, to lubricate the flow of narrative illusions."[20] Fulkerson appears as a somewhat refined or domesticated version of Hubbard; animated solely by the profit motive, which dictates his management of the magazine, Fulkerson does very little harm to himself or others in this pursuit. Language is Fulkerson's most powerful tool for managing both the magazine and the foreground of the story. The novel opens in the middle of Fulkerson's speech persuading March to move to New York to edit the magazine. A "pure advertising essence," Fulkerson enlists the other characters in his schemes by manipulating their fantasies of a new life in the city. He promotes the magazine, for example, as a cooperative venture among contributors, as "something in literature as radical as the American Revolution in politics: it was the idea of self-government in the arts" (p. 213). His rhetoric of cooperation represses the fundamental social structure of the magazine and the community: Dryfoos owns the magazine and therefore wields power over all his employees.

The smooth operation of the magazine depends as much on Fulkerson's rhetoric of unity as it does on the relations of property and power that his language cloaks. When these relations are made known, they threaten to tear apart the knowable community. Fulkerson's authority over the magazine reaches its limit during the banquet he organizes to celebrate the publication of the first issue. Although he plans to turn the Dryfoos household into an advertisement, Dryfoos himself transforms the party into a bald display of wealth and power. When the fragile community of characters discovers that the relations between them are controlled by money, Fulkerson's rhetorical agility loses its sway. His disastrous banquet shatters the cohesiveness of the foreground, exposing the traces of the conflicts relegated to the background.

In the figure of Fulkerson, Howells explores the tendency of realism to privilege the foreground as the totality of urban social relations, and he pushes this tendency to its unstable limits. Fulkerson reduces the meaning of "New York" to the critics who review his magazine, and he devours the outlying city as raw material for articles or advertisements. To Fulkerson, the city simply "belongs to the whole country" (p. 12). In part, Howells's realism shares Fulkerson's goal of representing New York as a common possession, and the novelist runs the risk of colonizing this common ground as a mirror of middle-class culture. Just as Fulkerson's rhetoric of cooperation denies the underlying property relations of the magazine, the representation of New York as a common possession represses the knowledge of dispossession that it enacts. The knowable urban community maintains its identity by displacing "the other half" from the social geography of the city. Yet Fulkerson's loss of control exposes the instability of a realism that achieves social cohesiveness and narrative coherence by containing conflict in a smoldering background. During the failed celebration of cooperation, these conflicts erupt, not in the margins, but within the foreground itself, threatening to unravel the bonds of the knowable community.

Fulkerson's rhetorical control over the foreground is first challenged at the banquet by Lindau's outburst against the capitalist, Dryfoos. As translator for the magazine, Lindau embodies the countermovement in realism that voices the conflicts silenced in the background. While Fulkerson's language levels all otherness, Lindau forces "the other half" into the line of vision of the urban settlement. Lindau himself is represented as a translation, an amphibious figure who speaks both English and German and who acts equally at home in his tenement and in the Marches' new apartment. His accent calls attention to his immigrant origins, while his missing hand, a casualty of the Civil War, makes him a genuine American. Unlike the other characters, Lindau can merge into the anonymity of the street. We first see him as an unnamed portrait in a crowd, and we last hear him as an unidentified voice emerging from the crowd of strikers. His hybrid presence bridges the background and the foreground, undermining the reassuring distinctions between them.

In contrast to Fulkerson's palliative rhetoric of advertising, Lindau's language is often labeled "violent"—not simply because Lindau advocates revolution but because he subverts the conventional meanings of such basic concepts as "freedom," "liberty," "the Civil War," "common reality," and "America." When he first meets March, for example, he immediately challenges the convention of saying "our country," explaining that during the Civil War he sacrificed his hand to "your country." "What country," he asks, "has a poor man got?" In contrast to what happens in *Silas Lapham*, the Civil War in *Hazard* cannot be summoned from the past as a common ground to alleviate present class differences. Lindau refuses to see the war itself as a struggle to free the slaves and unify the nation:

"Do you think I knowingly gave my hand to save this oligarchy of traders and tricksters, this aristocracy of railroad wreckers and stock gamblers and mine slave drivers and mill serf owners? No; I gave it to the slave; the slave—Ha! Ha! Ha!—whom I helped to unshackle to the common liberty of hunger and cold." (p. 193)

The violence done by Lindau's language can be summarized in one short statement that resonates throughout the novel: "der *iss* no Ameriga anymore!" Instead of viewing the country as a common possession, a "United" States, Lindau represents the entire nation as a battlefield. He violently displaces "the line" between a communal foreground and its naturalized setting with the line between social classes—between property owners and the dispossessed.

While Lindau voices the centrifugal force of realism, the representation of his speech quells the threat of fragmentation that he thrusts into the foreground. Although the written signs of his German accent make him sound more "realistic," they have the contradictory effect of muting the force of his speech. On the one hand, his foreign pronunciation of English words underscores his critique of the meaning of those words;

on the other hand, the rather comic misspellings that represent his accent detract attention from his subversive content. Branded so blatantly on the page as "alien," Lindau often sounds like a caricature of himself. His accent separates him from the other characters, who presumably, like the narrator and readers, all speak standard English. Thus the realistic representation of Lindau's speech turns against itself: by bracketing his language as "other" and "unreal," it contains the unsettling effect of his words.[21]

March's defense of Lindau against Dryfoos has the similarly paradoxical effect of silencing Lindau's disruptive voice. March's protest signifies neither his political conversion nor the moral awakening that critics have applauded.[22] Instead, it keeps him from acknowledging Lindau's claim that March is as powerless as the urban working class. When Dryfoos, for example, orders March to fire Lindau, March realizes "as every hireling must, no matter how skillfully or gracefully the tie is contrived for his wearing, that he belongs to another, whose will is his law" (p. 353). This recognition connects March to the other inhabitants of the city through their common dispossession instead of through a communal sense of ownership. By refusing to fire Lindau, March recuperates his own self-image and dissociates himself from the identity of a worker. "I'm not used to being spoken to as if I were the foreman of the shop," he explains, "and told to discharge a sensitive and cultivated man like Lindau as if he were a drunken mechanic" (p. 351). In supporting Lindau, March reinforces his own "knowledge of the line" and absorbs Lindau into the foreground as a "cultivated man," as "one of us." March's threatened resignation ultimately defends his own heroic fantasy of total autonomy in which he "became a free lance and fought in whatever cause he thought just; he had no ties, no chains" (p. 359). But March immediately finds his act preempted and made meaningless by Lindau's prior resignation; he does not even have the freedom to choose to quit and make his moral mark (just as he did not have the choice to move to New York). Lindau has the last silent word in this dispute.

In the figure of Lindau, Howells questions one of his own fundamental assumptions about realism: that all Americans speak a common language—the language "we all know"—which stems from and refers to a shared social reality. He kills off Lindau at the end of the novel to uphold this assumption, to protect the unifying goal of realism from conflict and fragmentation. At the same time, he shows that the necessary expulsion of this threatening foreign force blocks the achievement of unity.

IV

In the climactic strike near the end of *Hazard* the threat posed by Lindau is dramatized on the streets of the city. The strike wipes out the boundary lines so carefully mapped during the opening apartment-hunting scene: between foreground and background, between observer and spectacle, and between the home and the street. In the strike scene, the background suddenly crashes into the foreground and kills off two of its members. This collapse of boundaries yokes the colony of characters to the rest of the city through a network of violence and thereby shatters the vision of the city as a possession shared by a community of inhabitants.

As the indispensable lifeline of the modern city, the transportation system interlocks individuals, neighborhoods, and activities that otherwise remain isolated and unrelated. Transportation strikes have a special visibility because they can bring the everyday operations of the city to a halt, and their violence encroaches on the public arena of the streets, unhidden by the walls of the factory. The centralizing function of the streetcars parallels the role of the narrative, which connects the novel's disparate stories and characters and the different elements of urban life. The eruption of the strike in *Hazard* thus threatens both the social cohesion of the city and the ongoing coherence of the narrative.

The strike first erupts as an external catastrophe that eludes representation—an explosion of "useless information" from an unknowable source. Both the narrative and the characters struggle to bring the strike into focus and to control its unsettling force. March, for example, frames the strike within the known coordinates of medieval history:

> the roads have rights and the strikers have rights, but the public has no rights at all. The roads and the strikers are allowed to fight out a private war in our midst—as thoroughly and precisely a private war as any we despise the Middle Ages for having tolerated—as any street war in Florence or Verona—and to fight it out at our pains and expense. (p. 407)

In addition to distancing the strike historically, this representation displaces the contestants in the dispute: here it is not capital versus labor but "the public" versus capital and labor. The roads and the strikers become rival families who together oppose the public realm of the city as a whole. To allay his own fear of powerlessness, March identifies with "the public," the idealized common good that transcends the petty interests of the workers and the employers. March's representation turns the strike into an external disruption that imposes itself on the community, "the public," rather than an articulation of the fundamental social relations of that community.[23]

March's depiction of the strike makes it invisible to him; when he finally goes into the streets to see it in person, he actually cannot find what he is looking for. He wanders through the streets, searching for the violence he has read about in the newspapers, but all he sees are "decent-looking people," like himself, who do not match his image of the foreign and monstrous invasion. Because March cannot see the violence inherent in a system that subordinates these ordinary people, he does not find the strike until he literally bumps into it. Seduced by the apparent calm, he hops a crosstown car that is suddenly stopped by a group of strikers trying to prevent scabs from running the cars.

At the moment at which March's car stops, the narrative also comes to an unusual and abrupt halt. Instead of proceeding directly to the riot, the narration backtracks in time to the Dryfoos household that morning. At no other moment in the novel is narrative time suspended in this way. While on the level of the story, the riot stops March's car, on the level of narrative sequence, it is Dryfoos's argument with his children that interrupts the ride. This splicing of scenes forces the reader to experience the confrontation between Dryfoos and his children in the midst of the violence on the city streets. The two stories converge when Conrad Dryfoos, dazed by his father's slap and spurred by the encounter with a fellow Christian socialist, decides to play the quixotic role of peacemaker for the strikers. But Conrad, like March, cannot find the strike he is searching for, until it hits him with a fatal bullet that pierces all romantic fantasies. The shot that kills Conrad is the culmination of two separate yet interwoven stories: the streetcar strike and "the fall of the house of Dryfoos."[24] Conrad's death deals the final blow to the family's failed effort to settle in New York after selling their farm in Indiana. By forcing Conrad to become a businessman like himself, Dryfoos tries to compensate for the uprootedness that he and his wife experience in the city. Conrad's death displays the violence and the failure of his paternal authority.

Hazard opens with the establishment of one home in New York and ends with the destruction of another. For both the Marches and the Dryfoos family, domestic insecurity is projected onto the unsettling presence of the urban lower classes. In the opening scene, "the line" carves out a domestic space for the Marches by subduing the poor in a naturalized cityscape or turning them into a mirror. During the strike, the sudden eruption of violence from below crosses that line and destroys the Dryfoos home. A shot from an unknown source in the background kills Conrad as an innocent bystander. But the narrative indirectly attributes Conrad's death to the less innocent outbreak of violence within the foreground itself—in the relationship between father and son. The narrative juxtaposition of these two stories collapses the opening boundary between the safe shelter of the home and the foreign threats of the city streets. By simultaneously representing the confrontations between Dryfoos and his children and between strikers and police, the narrative refuses to isolate or repress this violence in the background. Although the strike first appears as the external source of urban violence, it exposes the violence at the core of the urban social system. It pervades the domestic relations of the characters and shatters the fragile urban settlement in the foreground of the novel. If the familiar values of domesticity turn the settlement into a knowable community, the strike suddenly defamiliarizes the family unit, and renders it as alien and threatening as the surrounding unreal city. As an antidenouement, the strike scene exposes the violent course that the narrative itself must take to articulate and control the conflicts that inform the representation of the city.

The representation of the streetcar strike in *Hazard* strains the conflicting forces of Howells's realism to the limit. At the moment when the narrative threatens to shatter, it musters its strategies to control the centrifugal pull of total fragmentation. As soon as Conrad is shot, the narrative abruptly draws away from the strike into the shelter of the foreground. It then searches desperately for closure, for a unifying conclusion that can heal the scars left by violent disruptions. But the search for an ending in *Hazard* only arrives at the impossibility of closure by reenacting the narrative fragmentation it strives to contain. The problem with *Hazard*'s ending is neither the absence of a conclusion nor the infinite openness that critics have noted, but the presence of too many different finite and limited conclusions.[25] The last one hundred pages can be read as a discussion about how realistic novels might end; the narrative meanders through a dress shop of conventional endings, trying on and discarding one after another. We are offered a potpourri of conclusions: the reconciliation of enemies in death, marriage, nonmarriage, a move to Europe, and the Christian scheme of atonement and sacrifice. Each one of these endings does provide a kind of resolution, a resting place on its own ground, but each is undermined by pressure from conflicting grounds.

With the dismissal of the background, the narrative clings stubbornly to the foreground. It moves from one character to the next, bestowing an ending on each one, just as Dryfoos approaches each character in search of a rapprochement that can justify the death of his son. But he always arrives too late to overcome the rifts, which he does not fully understand. Dryfoos's final insistence on holding Lindau's funeral at his own home reconsolidates the foreground in a ritual that parodies reunion. Despite Basil's delight in the poetry of the situation, this reconciliation in death only underlines the impossibility of reconciling these two characters in life.

While Dryfoos tries through his feeble actions to compensate for his son's death, March uses language to impose meaning on the events he has witnessed. If Dryfoos weaves the final plot, March offers thematic unity, "the moral of the story" that can pull together its scattered pieces. Yet March's moralizing at the end of the novel, whether his theme is Christian or economic, also achieves only partial closure. Right after his long disquisition on "this economic chance world," which has often been read as the central theme of the novel, Isabel responds to something else she hears him saying: "Do you mean to say, Basil, that you are really uneasy about your place? That you are afraid Dr. Dryfoos may give up being an angel and Mr. Fulkerson may play you false?" (p. 438). Isabel's question deflates Basil's universal reflections that compensate for his own fear of powerlessness. In Basil's thwarted gesture toward thematic closure, Howells undercuts the strategy of framing narrative excess within the lines of moral commentary. Long accused of an "obtrusive moralism" himself, Howells at the end of *Hazard* exposes the drive toward moral unity in realism as a dream of mastery to compensate for the lack of control.[26]

In the search for closure, the narrative does toy with fulfilling the fantasy of total mastery. When Dryfoos leaves the city after Lindau's funeral, March and Fulkerson magically have the chance to purchase their own magazine at a very cheap price. As independent owners, Fulkerson can realize his rhetoric of cooperation and March can pursue his business as a man of letters, without there being any conflict between the two aims. But even this resolution of independent ownership does not free them completely from "trembling before Dryfooses." As soon as they assume ownership, they are forced to subordinate artistic decisions to the restrictions of the market, which punctures their dream of independence and cooperation.

The domestic conflicts of the novel are also partially resolved in the marriage of Fulkerson and Miss Woodburn, the modern manager and the daughter of the Old South. Their marriage affirms the perpetuation of domesticity in the city after the collapse of the Dryfoos family. Fulkerson's marriage, however, is represented as one more of his advertisements—this time, for romantic love and nuptial bliss. Fulkerson falls in love according to all the rules in the book, and his marriage has neither a history nor a context. Juxtaposed with Alma's refusal to marry Beaton after the only extended courtship in the book, Fulkerson's marriage seems to occur solely because of the need for a wedding at the end of a novel. It both fulfills the convention and undermines it by exposing its pure conventionality.

At the end of *Hazard,* the narrative aggressively reinstates the boundary line separating the background from the foreground and tries to neutralize the tension between them. The characters cannot retreat from the city to their rural homes, as they do in Howells's earlier Boston novels, such as *The Rise of Silas Lapham* and *The Minister's Charge.* Instead, the "unreal city" recedes into the background, withdrawing the extremes of labor and capital and leaving behind a small-town community. United by the bonds of domesticity and ownership, this community no longer borders on a wider cityscape. The street scenes have disappeared. Yet this glimpse of a middle-class utopia as a fantasy of pure foreground makes only one more incomplete gesture toward closure. A trace of the street resurfaces in Basil's recollection of the French beggar, who once again emerges out of nowhere like the return of something repressed (p. 439). Basil's insistence that the beggar must have been an imposter reminds us of the unsettling pressure of city streets in the opening scenes. The ending of *Hazard* returns to the beginning only to perpetuate its tensions between the "knowledge of the line" that contains fragments in a coherent frame, and the bombardment of "useless information" that shatters the line. In the concluding scenes, these fragments have grown as large and unwieldy as the city itself.

Howells's narrative of settlement leads to the edge of the "unreal city"—to an abyss of conflict and fragmentation that it can neither enter nor bridge. *Hazard* both fulfills and exhausts the project of realism to embrace social diversity within the outlines of a broader community, and to assimilate a plethora of facts and details into a unified narrative form. By the end of the novel, the paint threatens to fly off the surface of Howells's largest novelistic canvas. After the publication of *Hazard* in 1890, Howells stops exploring the dangerously shifting boundary lines of his urban representation, and turns to domestic and utopian fictions that remain within the untested perimeter of the foreground. His domestic fiction inscribes a social space richly infused with internal conflicts, but no longer defined in relation to otherness, to the threatening encroachment of social change. In contrast, the utopian *A Traveller from Altruria* (1894) directly faces the issues of change and conflict raised by *Hazard,* while it contains them in the protected rural setting of a New England hotel. *A Traveller from Altruria* does not wrestle with the conflicted social terrain of *Hazard;* it ingests the background of conflict as subject for conversation rather than as a problem for realistic representation. In his utopian writing, Howells displaces the unreal city—which exerts such a powerful force in *A Hazard of New Fortunes*—with the ideal landscape of Altruria.

3

EDITH WHARTON'S PROFESSION OF AUTHORSHIP

Absent from the roll call of American realists, Edith Wharton has traditionally been relegated to the margins of literary history as a novelist of manners or an aloof aristocrat clinging to outmoded values. In spite of her portrayal of the society of her time, critics have deemed her too narrowly confined to chronicling upper-class life with no "conception of America as a unified and dynamic economy, or even as a single culture."[1] In addition to her supposedly circumscribed subject matter, Wharton's conception of authorship has excluded her from the ranks of the realists; critics commonly view her as an aristocratic "lady" who, holding herself apart from the changing society around her, criticizes the crass consumerism of the nouveau riche from the perspective of the stalwart antimodernist. Feminist criticism has recuperated a sense of Wharton's modernity by calling attention to her critique of the commodification and exploitation of women at the turn of the century.[2] Not only have feminist critics widened the social space of her novels to show how they touch the pulse of contemporary social change, but they also have revised Wharton's conception of authorship to show how she struggled to become an active "maker of art" both against a male tradition which objectifies women as passive, beautiful objects and against the limited role of "the lady novelist." An important corrective to earlier views of Wharton, this approach, however, often isolates her in a separate sphere of women's literature as "one of our American precursors of a literary history of female mastery and growth."[3]

In this chapter I reassess Wharton's place in American literary history not as an antimodernist or a woman writer alone, but as a professional author who wrote at the intersection of the mass market of popular fiction, the tradition of women's literature, and a realistic movement which developed in an uneasy dialogue with twentieth-century modernism. Wharton's treatment of women cannot be separated from her engagement in a pervasive system of exchange that transforms the production of literature and the nature of authorship as well as the meaning of gender at the turn of the century. Through her participation in the changing profession of authorship, Wharton's enmeshment in the consumer society she so ruthlessly depicts may have contributed to her often overlooked influence on a younger generation of writers in the twenties, such as Sinclair Lewis and F. Scott Fitzgerald, who rejected their male precursors for what they saw as a stifling Victorian realism.

By studying Wharton as a realist, I situate her writing at the complex intersection of class and gender, without reducing her career to a simple expression of either category. As we have seen in the first chapter, realism does more than describe a literary product, it also provides a strategy for defining the nature of the producer and her work. Realism refers not only to the relation of the literary text to the world it represents, but also to the representation of the author to that world. If realism articulates anxiety about the accessibility of the social world to representation, it also expresses anxiety about the author's social position, which never occupies the complacent stance of the outside observer. Although Wharton did not espouse realism as a cause, as Howells did, writing realistically was implicit in her more pronounced struggle to define the nature of professional authorship. Like Howells, she viewed writing as work rather than leisure and treated realism as a tenuous balancing act negating the idealism of genteel culture while resisting the sentimentalism of mass culture. Yet Wharton's evolving sense of realism and professionalism involved a complex relation to the changing contours of "woman's place."

I

In her autobiography, *A Backward Glance*, Edith Wharton wrote that the publication of *The House of Mirth* in 1905 had transformed her at the age of forty-three from a "drifting amateur into a professional" author.[4] Wharton's long and tortuous apprenticeship has been charted by her biographers as a narrative of personal growth and psychological integration, achieved in rebellion against the social confinement of women to passive domestic roles.[5] In her autobiography, however, Wharton maps out a different route toward professionalism, one which does not treat the writing process as a dyadic one—primarily between the author's self and the object she creates—but instead emphasizes the mediating social context in which art is produced. Until the publication of her first book of short stories in 1899, writes Wharton, she had no "real personality" of her own. She does not describe this discovery as an inner revelation; rather, she imagines her name on a book cover when Scribner's first proposes the collection:

> *I* had written short stories that were thought worthy of preservation! Was it the same insignificant *I* that I had always known? Anyone walking along the streets might go into any bookshop, and say: "Please give me Edith Wharton's book," and the clerk, without bursting into incredulous laughter, would produce it, and be paid for it, and the purchaser would walk home with it and read it, and talk of it, and pass it on to other people to read! (p. 113)

According to this passage, professional identity evolves not simply from becoming a whole person but from learning to construct a separate "personality" in the public eye and to externalize one's name on a book that can circulate in the marketplace.

The following discussion of Wharton's apprenticeship examines her strategies for producing both a literary work and a professional self for the market at the turn of the century. Focusing on the recurring spatial metaphors in her early fiction, her book on interior design, and one of her early reviews, I shall trace Wharton's effort to write herself out of the private domestic sphere and to inscribe a public identity in the marketplace. In examining this process, I shall contest both the traditional view of Wharton as an antimodernist and the recent feminist criticism which too often equates the dilemma of her women characters, entrapped in the domestic realm, with that of the writer herself. The case of Wharton's apprenticeship challenges, in addition, the paradigm of feminist criticism which locates women's writing in a "separate sphere," whether at the subversive margins of a male-defined tradition or within a subculture of their own. Wharton's profession of authorship is more complicated than this paradigm allows, for her writing undermines those boundaries between feminine and masculine, private and public, home and business, boundaries which both arise from and collapse into the medium of the market. Yet Wharton's apprenticeship does not leave her at rest in either sphere: as we shall see, she rejects the domestic tradition of the novel by embracing the apparent freedom of the literary marketplace, but there she confronts threatening limits which lead her to revalue a privatized feminine sphere ultimately in conflict with her model of professional authority. This dynamic and unresolved conflict shapes the trajectory of Wharton's transformation from a "drifting amateur into a professional."

For Wharton and her contemporaries, professionalization involved the rejection and revision of older genteel models of authorship, which treated writing as the leisurely activity of the man of letters rather than as disciplined work.[6] In her early search for intellectual mentors, Wharton belittled her male peers, who, no matter how well-read, merely channeled their scholarly pursuits into "dilettantish leisure" (p. 95). As evidence of her own achievement of professionalism, she notes her "daily systematic effort of writing." Like Howells, Wharton conceived of writing as productive work as a protest against the wastefulness of upper-class idleness. To define writing as a profession, however, rather than as an amateur's hobby, Wharton had to confront her own class's disdain for and fear of work, which was treated as a dirty word—akin to sex or money. The New York old guard imagined their affluence to grow naturally and mysteriously from inherited real estate, and anyone openly involved in making money—even buying and selling stocks—was spoken of in a whisper, as if he were committing adultery.[7] Writing books for sale was an equally distasteful activity, viewed as a distinctly vulgar form of business. "In the eyes of our provincial society," writes Wharton, "authorship was still regarded as something between a black art and a form of manual labor" (p. 69). The distrust of the business of writing thus embodied a deeper fear of its association with the lower classes. This fear of intellectual work in Wharton's own class reflected anxiety about the claims of others; both the nouveau riche and the working class were perceived as pressuring and threatening an insular social world whose economic base and social power were becoming more and more insecure.[8] In the late nineteenth century, the idea of authorship as a profession enabled writers to steer clear of the stigma of the ineffectual dilettante, without reducing them to the level of the common worker.

As a woman, Wharton defined the profession of authorship not only against the gentleman of letters but even more urgently against the role she inherited as a "lady of leisure," whose work was described by some as pure idleness and by others as conspicuous consumption. Although she claims that, because none of them worked, the men and women of the "old set" inhabited similar social spheres, she still sought refuge as a child in her father's library from the even more claustrophobic atmosphere of her mother's drawing room. Social critics, such as Charlotte Perkins Gilman, decried the idleness of the well-bred woman as the cause of the nervous disorders that she suffered, as did Wharton.[9] Both women were treated by the famous rest cures of Dr. Weir Mitchell, which prescribed more idleness as medicine.[10] Although Wharton was anything but idle her entire life, she can be seen to adopt and subvert the social image of the lady of leisure by writing diligently and routinely in bed every morning for much of her life.[11]

Yet as Thorstein Veblen argued, the upper-class woman did more than indulge in mere idleness, she engaged in the activity of "conspicuous consumption," the artful composition of the display of leisure.[12] In his terms, the lady of leisure must work hard to adorn herself as the "chief ornament" to "beautify the household" (or in Lily Bart's case, as a commodity on the marriage market that will win her this privileged place).[13] Through conspicuous consumption, the lady becomes a narcissistic artist who produces herself as an object of art.[14] Paradoxically this self-display is self-effacing because it functions as a sign of her husband's wealth and status. Although the lady of leisure is both producer and product, her status as sign requires that she erase any trace of the productive labor that makes her existence possible. As "chief ornament of the household," the woman of leisure appears along with her home as a completely finished product, with no seams exposed.

In *A Backward Glance*, Wharton suggests how debilitating this definition of woman's work was for an aspiring writer. She recalls showing her mother the opening of her first novel when she was eleven years old:

> "Oh, How do you do, Mrs. Brown?" said Mrs. Thompkins. "If only I had known you were going to call I should have tidied up the drawing room." Timorously I submitted this to my mother, and never shall I forget the sudden drop of my creative frenzy when she returned it with the icy comment: "Drawing rooms are always tidy." (p. 73)

The young Wharton here received a chilling double message: first, that woman's work is never done—in the less than ordinary sense that it should never be performed in public; and second, that nice girls do not write novels. The work of writing embarrasses Wharton's mother as much as the exposure of a drawing room that needs to be cleaned. Against this inheritance, Wharton defines the role of professional author to legitimate writing as respectable work. She rejects the definition of the lady of leisure as a finished product, as a self-enclosed yet self-effacing sign in a tidy drawing room. As a writer, she subverts this role by producing signs for a market outside the home. Writing becomes a strategy for untidying her mother's oppressively neat drawing room.

In her critique of the lady of leisure she implicitly forms a conception of realism by contrast. Whereas domesticity anchors the real for Howells in the midst of the chaotic city streets, upper-class domesticity epitomizes unreality. If the lady of leisure adorns the unreal hothouse of the drawing room, the professional author exposes the reality of its underlying untidyness and the concealed work that produces it. The professional realist then takes her own product out of the home and the drawing room to the streets of the market.

By pitting professional authorship against domesticity, Wharton defines herself against an earlier generation of American women novelists, known as the sentimental or domestic novelists, who in fact paved a way for women into the literary marketplace. As recent scholarship has shown, popular women novelists of the mid-nineteenth century viewed their writing as an extension of woman's work at home. Through the power of moral influence, they aimed to expand the feminine values of the domestic sphere, which they opposed ideologically to the male ethos of the public marketplace.[15] These women represented themselves as writing from the heart to sway other sympathetic hearts, rather than writing for the anonymous market or judgmental critics, and they located their audience at the hearth rather than the library—as Fanny Fern wrote, "mine is a story for the table and arm-chair under the reading lamp in the living room, and not for the library shelves."[16] Even though many were successful businesswomen in an open and expanding field, they did not consider their work as authors to be primarily self-defining.[17] Catherine Sedgwick, for example, wrote that "her *author's* existence had always seemed something accidental," and Harriet Beecher Stowe later claimed that "God wrote" *Uncle Tom's Cabin.*[18] In denying their own public agency, these novelists, according to historian Mary Kelley, tried to absorb their writing into their domestic roles.[19] Authorship for these women demanded both self-assertion and self-effacement, much like the self-display through conspicuous consumption practiced by the lady of leisure.

Despite their self-denial, these novelists left a powerful legacy for the continuing production of the novel in nineteenth-century America. By the time Wharton was growing up in the 1870s, popular fiction had become synonymous with women's fiction among middle-class readers, and novel writing was viewed as women's work.[20] In 1871, for example, 71 percent of all the novels published in the United States were written by women,[21] and by 1894 Thomas Higginson could write in Scribner's almanac, *The Woman's Book,* that "women were the originators of the modern novel."[22] For many, these origins devalued a genre already made suspect by the Puritan hostility toward fiction and the elitist fear of the novel's genuinely popular appeal.[23] Thus Wharton's mother forbade her to read novels as a child, an order which Wharton found "singularly ungrateful" when she considered "the stacks of novels which [her mother], [her] aunts, and [her] grandmother annually devoured" (p. 68). The double taint of novel writing as both a commercial and a feminine endeavor came together in society's condemnation of Mrs. Beecher Stowe for being "so 'common' yet so successful" (p. 68). For a member of Wharton's class, one who wrote for money risked being identified with common workers and being dependent on vulgar opinion. To become a woman novelist involved the further risk of being devoured as well as rejected, of being trivialized and absorbed into the category of the forbidden yet the consumable. If the upper-class lady was treated as a conspicuous commodity—a unique objet d'art, the sentimentalist produced inconspicuous commodities—mass-produced novels. Wharton was to adopt the role of professional author to distinguish her own writing as much from the devalued sentimental novelist as from the idle lady of leisure and the impotent genteel dilettante.

In discussions of women's literature, it has become a critical commonplace to note that "women writers inevitably engage a literary history and system of conventions shaped primarily by men," which have the effect of silencing women's voices.[24] To achieve an autonomous voice, women writers must therefore wrestle with the power of male influence and seek female predecessors to contribute to their own submerged countertradition. While such a pattern of rebellion and revision undeniably informs the work of many women writers, it ignores the historical evidence which suggests that the genre of the novel was not shaped primarily by men and that women have from its inception participated in its formation and development. Furthermore, if women writers have indeed contributed to establishing the conventions of the novel, as Higginson claimed at the end of the nineteenth century and literary historians have since verified, it stands to reason that women as well as men might have to struggle as much against female as male forms of influence. Alfred Habegger, for example, has revised our understanding of the origins of realism in the hands of Howells and James as a debate within the novel form against the "maternal tradition of Anglo-American women's fiction."[25] This debate changes the contours of the genre as it explores and rethinks changing gender roles. Yet Habegger, interestingly, does not mention Wharton, who as a woman struggled against the domestic legacy of the American female novelists to define her notion of professional authorship, and who rejected their sentimental product to define her notion of realism. Thus, to shape a role for herself as author, Wharton confronted not the silence and exclusion of women from literary production but the volubility and commercial success of the domestic tradition of American women novelists. To write herself out of the domestic sphere into an alternative realm of professional authorship, Wharton had to grapple with the precedent of women novelists who ventured into the market only to reinforce their place at home.

Several of Wharton's early stories enact this struggle against the female influence of sentimentalism. "The Pelican" (1899) rejects the domestic tradition of American fiction through a devastatingly ironic portrayal of the thirty-year career of a woman lecturer.[26] As a young widow with a baby to support, Mrs. Amyot starts delivering "drawing room lectures" on timely topics from the appreciation of Greek art to "Homes and Haunts of the Poets" (pp. 88, 90). Long after her child grows up, she continues to lecture to public audiences, using the same rationale of doing it "for the baby" (p. 91). While her intimate tone of voice and her motherly courage initially contribute to her popularity, as she ages her currency dwindles to leave her haunting the hotel lecture circuit for the wealthy, who only come to hear her out of charity. As the topics of the day move beyond her grasp to the wider spheres of scientific and literary scholarship, audiences lose interest in hearing about familiar subjects that a lecturer can master by reading in the Athenaeum or the public library; "it was the fashion to be interested in things one hadn't always known" (p. 94). The story ends with a humiliating confrontation between the mother and her thirty-year-old son, who held the illusion that his mother only lectured because of popular demand, and whose masculinity is wounded to find that, on the contrary, she uses him as an excuse for her paltry career. The last line of the story leaves Mrs. Amyot crying, "I sent his wife a sealskin coat for Christmas," as her son walks away (p. 103).

A death knell for the domestic tradition, this story satirizes both Mrs. Amyot's sentimental style—"the art of transposing second-hand ideas into first-hand emotions that so endeared her to her feminine listeners" (p. 91)—and her social role—lecturing for "the baby." Her untrained mind cannot comprehend a new definition of knowledge as the specialized province of experts acquiring new ideas, rather than as the common property of amateurs sentimentalizing received truths. Her justification for speaking in public—to fulfill her duties of motherhood—is also exposed as a sham. When in the final line her motherhood is expressed through a consumer item, the domestic tradition has descended into that commercial world of the market it set out to oppose.

Our response to Mrs. Amyot in "The Pelican" is mediated by the narrator, a learned gentleman who plays the role of her confidant and patronizing adviser. We define her silliness and anti-intellectualism from the perspective of his wide-ranging knowledge, and we share in his condescension and sympathy toward her. The narrator's authority totters, however, when at the end he suddenly finds that watching Mrs. Amyot ascend to the lectern "was like looking at one's self early in the morning in a cracked mirror. I had no idea I had grown so old" (p. 99). Through this cracked mirror, we see that the genteel dilettante maintains his own self-image by patronizing Mrs. Amyot, and that his style is as outdated as hers. Wharton here points to the collusion between the genteel man of letters and the sentimental and domestic woman artist.

A definition of the professional author as an expert with the authority to represent social reality depends on drawing a sharp contrast with the former two types, who must be devalued as merely amateur and popular. For Wharton, this demarcation provides an important strategy for keeping her own writing from being consumed by the same tradition of women's fiction that her aunts and grandmother devoured. From her earliest attempts at writing, Wharton feared being identified with this tradition. When she wrote her first novella, "Fast and Loose," at the age of fifteen, she accompanied it with mock reviews that accused her of sounding like a "sick sentimental schoolgirl,"[27] which her biographers have understandably read as evidence of her self-deprecation. Yet these reviews also indicate her sense of audience: the literary marketplace and the institution of criticism, rather than the heart or the hearth. It is interesting that Wharton returns to this novella twice during her apprenticeship, as a private joke which reveals her attitude toward her own writing. One of her earliest published stories, "April Showers," starts with a quotation from her own novella as the final lines from a manuscript by a schoolgirl who has her book "April Showers" accepted by mistake, because the publisher of *Home Circle* misplaced her letter and thought the manuscript belonged to a famous "society novelist," Kathryn Kyd (pp. 189–96). This self-reference shows Wharton's concern about being "mistaken" for a "society novelist," one of the popular descendants of the domestic novelists after their decline in the 1870s. Indeed reviewers often did treat Wharton as just that.

In a later story, "The Expiation," Wharton again uses "Fast and Loose" as the title of a novel written by a young woman in a conventional and boring marriage, who hopes the daring qualities of the novel will make it a "*succès de scandale*" (pp. 438–56). Disappointed when the critics praise it for its sweetness and conventionality, only promptly to ignore it, she makes a deal with her uncle, an Anglican bishop, who also has failed to sell his homiletic tracts with titles such as "Through a Glass

Brightly." He denounces her book from the pulpit for its immorality, which immediately makes the book a bestseller and her a celebrity, and she secretly donates the proceeds to her uncle's church to install a new chantry window. If in "The Pelican" Wharton relegates the domestic and genteel traditions to the status of amateur, here she exposes their commercial pandering to a mass culture, a culture in which the scandalous and daring only reinforce the conventional status quo. In a sense, she anticipates the argument of Ann Douglas in *The Feminization of American Culture* and extends it to the post–Civil War period; in the alliance of sentimental culture and genteel culture, both groups, out of a sense of powerlessness, set themselves above the incipient consumer culture around them only to contribute to its development.[28]

In these satires of sentimental women artists, Wharton delineates her own writing as professional and realistic by contrast. The ethos of professionalism serves a double purpose: it posits a creative realm outside of and antagonistic to the domestic domain, and it imagines a way of entering a cluttered literary marketplace while transcending its vagaries and dependence upon popular taste. Professionals claim to have a specialized product—in this case, expert knowledge of reality—which is neither available to the untrained amateur through common sense nor dictated by demands of the market. But although her professional sense permitted Wharton to claim that her novels possess more realistic and enduring qualities than the mere sentimental commodities produced by "society novelists," still, throughout her career, she felt the need to keep differentiating her own writing from these popular genres, to protect herself from a discomfiting sense of closeness. To have a professional identity and produce realistic work meant to dissociate herself from her female precursors.

II

Although Wharton defined professional authorship against the sentimental tradition, she did not thereby identify herself solely with a male-dominated tradition; she also actively sought out other female precursors such as George Sand, George Eliot, and Anna de Noailles. In the example of their lives and works, she found both inspiration and warnings about the dangers a woman writer faced in attempting to enter a professional community. If professionalism could distinguish the serious writer from her trivialized competitors, it could also be deployed by the custodians of that profession, the critics, to exclude her. Wharton expressed the fear of such exclusivity in her review of Leslie Stephen's biography of George Eliot in 1902.[29] In this, her fullest discussion of a woman writer, Wharton praises Eliot for her realism, for "the direct grasp of reality that was to be a distinguishing mark of her matured talent." Eliot emerges here as an antithesis to the domestic novelists (whom she too criticized in her review of "Silly Novels by Lady Novelists").

Wharton attributes Eliot's waning reputation to the hostile reception of her scientific metaphors and vocabulary. According to Wharton, male critics complained that Eliot had "sterilised her imagination and deformed her style by the study of metaphysics and biology" (p. 247). In her defense, Wharton argues that science has always provided inspiration and vocabulary for great writers from Milton to Goethe. "Is it because these were men," she asks, "while George Eliot was a woman, that she is reproved for venturing on ground they did not fear to tread? Dr. Johnson is known to have pronounced portrait painting 'indelicate in a female'; and indications are not wanting that the woman who ventures on scientific studies still does so at the risk of such an epithet" (p. 248).

"Science" here has an important resonance for Wharton's contemporaries, beyond its specific meaning in Eliot's work. Appeals to "the scientific spirit" were commonplace among realists as diverse as Zola and Howells. Science conferred the authority to represent social reality in the late nineteenth century, much as portraiture had entailed the authority to represent the individual in an earlier period. In general, scientific knowledge became the major source of legitimation for most professions in the late nineteenth century; such knowledge distinguished the expertise of the specialist from the common sense of the lay person, the amateur knowledge of the dilettante, and the commercialism of the quack.[30] Within several professions, this expertise was used to supplant and exclude the untrained and uneducated female practitioner, who often became the recipient of advice or the object of scientific investigation. Just as women had been objectified in portrait painting, they were now equally objectified by scientific knowledge.[31] In the process of excluding women practitioners in the late nineteenth century, for example, the medical profession held the scientific consensus that intellectual effort decreased women's reproductive power and thereby deformed them as women.[32] In this context, Wharton's choice of the words "sterilised" and "deformed" to describe the male critics' view of Eliot's imagination implies that to write with professional authority, to use scientific language, as Eliot did, was to run the risk of being scientifically condemned as unwomanly. In her review, Wharton commends Eliot for appropriating a male discourse in her writing rather than accommodating writing to a feminine sphere and tradition; at the same time, she acknowledges that such an attempt to seize professional authority may lead to rejection and exclusion.

In the second part of the review, Wharton discusses the price Eliot paid for venturing onto scientific and professional ground. She claims that Eliot's later works sacrificed their realistic portrayal of characters in moral crises to her "cumbersome construction." Eliot could not accommodate internal reality to the external demand for plot: "the fusion of the external and the emotional was peculiarly unsuccessful; her plots are as easily detachable from her books as dead branches from a living tree" (p. 250). Wharton traces Eliot's reliance on artificial, stock plots to the male adventure novel, which Eliot used to appeal to popular taste. Despite this acquiescence, Wharton concludes, what "her later books lost in structural unity they gained in penetration, irony and poignancy of emotion: an exchange almost purely advantageous in the case of an author whose psychological insight so far surpassed her constructive talent" (p. 250). Wharton, however, judges Eliot's accomplishment as an exchange: a relinquishment of the male act of construction for the female quality of psychological insight. Wharton attributes this disjuncture to Eliot's life, to her attempt to compensate for her own moral deviation from social laws with a strict adherence to the laws of fiction. In the logic of Wharton's essay, Eliot's violation of the moral code of marriage through her relationship with G. H. Lewes parallels her trespassing on gender boundaries through her appropriation of scientific language. To pay for both transgressions, Eliot retreated further into the feminine sphere, not of domesticity, but of the emotional, psychological, and private life. Just as her own public image as a celebrity became severed from her inner self, according to Wharton, her construction of plots became separated from her realistic depiction of characters.[33]

Thus Wharton presents Eliot as an alternative to the domestic novelists, only to find her trapped in a similarly unreal feminized interior. Eliot's career, therefore, presented the crucial dilemma that Wharton faced during her own apprenticeship: how could a woman writer fuse plots and character, structure and feeling, exterior and interior, the public discourse and the private sensibility that were split in Eliot's novels? How could she extend the realism of the interior to the construction of a novel that represents society as a whole? Could a woman writer achieve professional authority without rebounding into a privatized feminine sphere? In the larger scheme, would the profession of authorship accommodate women; or, like other professions in the late nineteenth century, would it usurp their traditions only to entrench them more firmly in their domestic place?

III

These questions are already indirectly posed in Wharton's first full-length book, *The Decoration of Houses*, the product with which she entered the literary marketplace in 1897.[34] Written in collaboration with interior decorator Ogden Codman, the book is considered one of the first statements of modern principles of interior design. By writing a manual on interior decoration which uses for its examples the sumptuous villas of France and Italy, Wharton appears to have accepted her class's definition of woman's work as conspicuous consumption. A close reading of this document, however, suggests just the opposite: *The Decoration of Houses* represents a step out of her mother's drawing room. Wharton later explained the need for such a book on the grounds that interior decoration was a trivialized form of woman's work, a mere "branch of dressmaking."[35] Like novel writing, it remained in the province of female amateurs. *The Decoration of Houses* thus served a double purpose: it contributed to the professionalization of interior design, one of the new fields open to women at the turn of the century, and its language served as a metaphor for Wharton's developing views of professional authorship.

As a polemic, *Decoration* exposes the mess inside the fashionable Victorian house by criticizing the popular treatment of interior design as a haphazard collage of bric-a-brac, the "superficial application of ornament." "Tyrannized over by the wants of others," most women, the authors claim, tend "to want things because other people have them, rather than to have things because they are wanted" (pp. 18, 17). They settle for the latest fad, for cheap forms of mass-produced "originality," as a feeble display of the personal touch. If we imagine this text as a retort to her mother, we see Wharton arguing that the typical drawing room is in fact an untidy and unstable place; the chief ornament, the lady, does not preside, but she yields herself to a commercial stereotype of the woman of the house only to find her identity dwarfed and effaced by the objects around her. The unreality of domestic space lies not in its insulation from the marketplace, but in its unacknowledged enslavement to that realm whose disorderly clutter is reproduced in the home.

The authors argue that interior decoration should not entrap the self but should express the individuality of the occupant by externalizing the self onto surrounding objects. To achieve control over their domestic space, women must adopt the role of planners, rather than the planned for, by adhering to classical principles of architectural design. The main argument of *The Decoration of Houses* is that interior decoration must be treated as a branch of architecture. In fact, Wharton and Codman claim that no distinction should be made between the architectural structure of the house and the design and decoration of its interior space. The internal structure of each room should be organized according to the same principle of architectural proportion as governs the external form. In their words, "all good architecture and good decoration (which, it must never be forgotten, *is only interior architecture*) must be based on rhythm and logic" (p. 10).

Edmund Wilson once called Wharton "the poet of interior decoration,"[36] an epithet that might be more accurately replaced with "the poet of interior architecture." This concept transforms the definition of woman's work from that of conspicuous consumption into the activity of construction. Rather than simply reject the traditionally female realm of domesticity, Wharton appropriates the traditionally male discourse of architecture and brings it into the interior space which had consigned women to decorating themselves as one among many ornaments. She thereby attempts to break down the dichotomy between the private space of the interior, which requires an invitation to enter, and the external structure of the building, which confronts the public gaze. For Wharton, breaking down these dichotomies involves a double movement: architecture is internalized into domestic space and the private self is externalized onto objects through architectural form. Wharton does not call for interior decoration to mimic blindly architectural principles, nor does she espouse a picturesque organicism which treats architecture as the natural outgrowth of character and the pattern of life established inside the house. Instead she seeks to overturn the boundary between the interior and exterior to achieve a synthesis between them which modifies each realm.

Architecture remained an important metaphor for writing throughout Wharton's career. She originally thought of calling *The House of Mirth* "A Moment's Ornament," a title which would have identified the work with the main character, Lily Bart, who is continually referred to as an ornament, and who can only narcissistically create herself as an art object.[37] By choosing the title *The House of Mirth*, however, Wharton identified her own authorship with the architectural structure of the novel and differentiated her writing from Lily's self-ornamentation. Upon the publication of the novel, she wrote to her publisher: "Your seeing a certain amount of architecture in it rejoices me above everything."[38] For her, the achievement of architectural form in her fiction is related to her sense of attaining the status of professional author. She hoped that the architecture of the novel could bridge that split she found so debilitating in Eliot's late novels, between interior characterization and exterior structure. Twenty years later Wharton was to compare the choice of narrative perspective to the choice of a building site.[39] If professionalization defines the author as producer, "interior architecture" delineates the nature of the product. Having a professional identity means projecting the self onto the external form of the book, just as "interior architecture" implies the externalization of the self onto the structure of a room. Both imagine a strategy for abandoning the confines of domesticity and entering the public market with a sense of control.

Wharton's metaphor of "interior architecture" suggests a connection between writing and space often overlooked in discussions of women's literature. While spatiality has been an important coordinate in feminist criticism since at least *A Room of One's Own*, we often talk about language itself as a space from which women are excluded or absent, a space into which they inscribe themselves, or as a new space they must create. There is a tendency in some criticism, however, to treat spatiality in women's writing primarily in terms of enclosure and confinement. In their influential study of nineteenth-century women writers, *A Madwoman in the Attic*, Gilbert and Gubar see women writers "trapped in so many ways in the architecture—both the houses and the institutions—of patriarchy."[40] In their paradigm, women writers always start out entrapped in male texts and male genres, just as they are confined in the home. This confinement removes women from the source of their own authority and gives them only two alternatives. Gilbert and Gubar focus on a violent, enraged, and often self-destructive form of escape that can lead to the margins of language in silence and madness. The second alternative to entrapment, suggested by other critics, is a kind of literary separatism, either an acceptance of female biological space as the source of creative power, or the embrace of a prelinguistic void as a space exterior to language, which is male.[41] The first model situates women in a purely reactive role and attributes to male writers the total power to determine and circumscribe all discourse and literary genres, while the second imagines an essential and unchanging female space and language which can transcend or remain totally separate from social institutions and linguistic conventions.

A third approach found in discussions of American women novelists in the mid-nineteenth century stresses neither confinement nor separatism but the evangelical movement of women's fiction, a movement that strives to colonize and reform the male public sphere of the market with the more humane feminine values of the home.[42] In this view, the home becomes a source of female authority rather than its renunciation. This approach, however, still consigns women writers to a form of fiction rooted in and validating their own separate sphere of domestic and interior space.

Wharton's first book suggests that she was seeking a more dynamic model of authorship that was not based primarily on entrapment, escape, or the embrace of women's separate space. Wharton tries to reverse the direction of her American predecessors, who brought their wares and ideals into the public market only to entrench themselves more firmly in the domestic sphere. Her metaphor of "interior architecture" suggests the goal of appropriating a traditional male discourse of architecture to transform a traditional female discourse of interior space. "Interior architecture" turns domestic space inside out, to project a borderline area at the intersection of the private home and the streets of the public marketplace, which is neither governed nor subsumed by either realm. As an author, Wharton saw herself deploying her productive power to construct a novel as an architect would a house, not fighting her way out of monolithic male prisons which confine women to the interior.[43]

IV

If *The Decoration of Houses* takes Wharton as a writer out of her mother's drawing room into the marketplace, it still leaves her precariously balanced with one foot in each realm. Addressing a limited audience, those with the means to follow her opulent prescriptions, her manual presents an even tidier version of the drawing room, designed according to the timeless principles of classical architecture. In the stories and novellas written after *The Decoration of Houses*, Wharton plunges more intrepidly into a wider and more cluttered literary marketplace, to explore the perilous consequences of "interior architecture" as a metaphor for writing. If *Decoration* posits an ideal synthesis between the domestic interior and the public arena, Wharton's early fiction about writers explores the breakdown of these two realms as they dissolve into the market. On the one hand, Wharton fears that the self may be totally exposed through its externalization: the author who circulates her name on a title page may prove to be as vulnerable as the lady of leisure who displays herself as an art object. On the other hand, novel writing may easily turn into a sensationalist exposé of others. Wharton's mother may be correct, after all, that realism merely pulls aside the curtains to reveal an untidy drawing room.

Both these threats are embedded in the novella *The Touchstone* (1900), one of Wharton's few tales about a woman novelist.[44] The novella opens after the death of the writer, Mrs. Aubyn, with an advertisement placed in the *Spectator* by a professor seeking information for her biography. In her youth, Mrs. Aubyn had been close to a young man, Glennard, who rejected her as a lover after two years of friendship, when her growing fame began to make him feel inferior. Nonetheless, Mrs. Aubyn continued to write intimate letters to Glennard for the rest of her solitary life. The ad leads Glennard to sell her letters to a publisher in order to make enough money to marry a charming young lady and establish an ideal domestic retreat. The book of letters immediately becomes a scandalous success precisely for the reason that, as one reader says, "it's too much like listening through the keyhole" (p. 37).

Glennard justifies publishing the letters on the grounds that Mrs. Aubyn's fame made her most intimate letters "as impersonal as a piece of journalism" (p. 15). When he sees her name in the paper, he feels that it "had so long been public property that his eye passed it unseeingly, as the crowd in the street hurries without a glance by some familiar monument" (p. 4). The narrator explains that "in becoming a personage she so naturally ceased to be a person that Glennard could almost look back to his explorations of her spirit as on a visit to some famous shrine, immortalized, but in a sense desecrated by popular veneration" (p. 14). Glennard projects his own betrayal of Mrs. Aubyn's confidence onto her popular reception. Although the status of "personage" envelops the private person in the anonymity of public architecture, it is precisely the impersonality of Mrs. Aubyn's public identity that allows Glennard to justify exposing the private person revealed in her letters. Because she has a publicly known name, her letters do not remain in the private sphere and can be published like a novel to bring a price on the market. *The Touchstone* imagines the consequences of such a voracious system of exchange that refuses to stop at the product of the book alone but extends to the identity of the author as well. The story demolishes the premise it begins with, that two different orders of writing exist which can be kept separate: public novels and private letters. Both are reduced to the same exchange value on the market. In *The Touchstone*, written a year after the publication of her first book of fiction, Wharton explores the potential dangers of the literary market; by externalizing the self on a book jacket, the author may forfeit the self as private property and find her own life transformed into a commodity, an object as consumable as those novels devoured by her female relatives.[45]

Wharton's fears were not unfounded. She began her career at a time when the aggressive advertising of a growing publishing industry first promoted the "celebrity" and the "best-seller" as new, marketable items.[46] The figure of the celebrity epitomizes the contradictions that inform the professionalization of authorship. On the one hand, the writer achieved a new-found autonomy and authority determined and upheld by the recent copyright laws and the self-dictated standards of a professional community. On the other hand, the writer became more dependent on the demands of publishers and on the reception of the mass audience. While the author as celebrity gained a new public visibility, the author's private identity was made increasingly available for public consumption. Wharton explores these contradictions in "Copy," a satirical sketch about the meeting of two popular authors who were once lovers.[47] The two writers are engaged in a struggle to gain possession of their love letters written before their success, when "a signature wasn't an autograph." Each writer fears that the other will try to publish them and each is toying with the idea. Their most intimate dialogue is completely infused with the language of the publishing world:

> Mrs. Dale. . . . I died years ago. What you see before you is a figment of the reporter's brain—a monster manufactured out of newspaper paragraphs, with ink in its veins. A keen sense of copyright is *my* nearest approach to an emotion.
>
> Ventor (sighing). Ah well, yes—as you say, we're public property.
>
> Mrs. Dale. If one shared equally with the public! But the last shred of my identity is gone. (p. 278)

The status of celebrity both confers and denies identity; it protects the self's property rights to its productions, at the same time that it leaves the self prey to public consumption.[48]

"Copy" suggests an analogy between the author as celebrity and the lady of leisure. The public anonymity of the book cover allows an author to escape displaying herself in the privacy of the drawing room, but traps her in new forms of disembodied self-display. The author as celebrity subjects herself to the same combination of narcissistic self-exposure and self-effacement as the lady of leisure who produces herself as an ornamental object. In the writing of her apprenticeship, Wharton moves into the marketplace to escape the confines of the feminine domain, only to find that the market may instead be feminizing all writers through the process of commodification.

This process can be glimpsed in the parallel fates of Mrs. Aubyn and Lily Bart. Lily is described throughout *The House of Mirth* as an artist manqué, a woman lacking any creative outlet other than self-adornment.[49] She is also a merchant who cannot sell her wares—that is, her self—on the marriage market and who subsequently ends up "floating in a sea of disoccupation." In the pivotal *tableaux vivants* scene, Lily produces herself as an art object by imitating a Reynolds portrait. Instead of appearing fully veiled by art, by her total absorption into the figure in a painting, she paradoxically appears quite naked. While half the audience admires her transcendent beauty, others make lewd jokes about the lines of her body both draped and revealed by her gown. At the moment that she is most fully transformed into art, she is also most fully exposed. It is no accident that Trenor's attempted rape in the privacy of an empty drawing room follows this scene, erasing the line between public display of the self as art and the private vulnerability of the lady at home. In contrast to Lily, who projects herself into a painting as an object of art, Mrs. Aubyn becomes a producer of art and separates herself from her product; during her lifetime, her productivity provides a shield which allows her to resist becoming a commodity, as Lily cannot. Yet after Mrs. Aubyn's death, instead of achieving the traditional immortality accorded to the poet, she becomes as naked and vulnerable as Lily Bart in the Reynolds painting. The anonymity of the book cover ultimately provides Mrs. Aubyn with no better protection after her death than does Lily's flimsy gown, as the market turns her private identity into an object of exchange.[50]

Writing for a market not only leads to the risk of self-exposure, it equally threatens the exposure of others or the betrayal of intimacy. As the only living author in *The Touchstone,* Glennard turns his intimate knowledge of Mrs. Aubyn, obtained from her letters, into a commodity for mass consumption. He succeeds in maintaining his anonymity while publishing the letters and living off their sale, and he uses this transaction to fund his ideal domestic retreat. The maintenance of domesticity here depends not on the protection of intimacy but on its successful marketing. In *The House of Mirth* social intercourse depends similarly on the use of intimacy as a medium of exchange. Lily's withdrawal from this economy at key junctures in her life provokes her demise. Although she buys Bertha Dorset's letters to Selden, she refuses to trade them in turn for the restoration of her self-image in the public eye. If Lily is trapped in her self-creation as an art object, she is equally trapped by her reluctance to do the same to others. Her destruction has been attributed to her lack of a strong inner self, but what is of greater moment is that her clinging to the myth of an essential internal self that can be exempted from this system of exchange leads directly to her downfall. She refuses to accept her society's implicit dictum to expose or be exposed.

Many of Wharton's early works focus on the ways in which artists prey on their material and trade their intimate knowledge of others for their own success; her short fiction explores the fine line between disinterested realism and a more aggressive voyeurism. In one of her earliest novellas, *Bunner Sisters*, the narrative point of view in the opening paragraph is identified with that of the lady shoppers who frequent the store of two poor women: "In the days when New York's traffic moved at the pace of the drooping horse-car, when society applauded Christine Nilson at the Academy of Music and basked in the sunsets of the Hudson River School on the walls of the National Academy of Design, an inconspicuous shop with a single show-window was intimately and favorably known to the feminine population of the quarter bordering on Stuyvesant Square."[51] R. W. B. Lewis has suggested that Wharton represents herself in this tale as the mysterious lady shopper who appears in the store from time to time but has no function in the plot.[52] When the sisters, in dire need, consider going to her for help, she suddenly stops appearing in the store. As a figure for the writer, the lady intrudes into the lives of the sisters but remains aloof from their troubles. While *The Touchstone* represents reading as the act of eavesdropping at the keyhole, *Bunner Sisters* situates the reader peering through the shop window and watching the untidy lives behind it disintegrate. The story opens with the reader gleaning intimate knowledge through the window of the shop, and ends with the only surviving sister, Ann Eliza, walking through the city streets looking in windows for employment signs. As she moves from inside the shop to outside, the writer and the reader, in the role of shoppers, are implicated in the forces that dispossess the sister and expose her to the streets. By framing the story with shop windows, Wharton implicitly adapts and critiques the class tourism and voyeurism which is presented by her contemporary male naturalists as scientific objective investigation. She asks whether to write realistically means to shop for material in the lives of other people and to strip them of the lives they possess.[53]

Throughout her career, Wharton was sensitive to the charge that she practiced class tourism in the upper ranks of society, the charge that her fiction resembled the popular literature that exposed the glitter of high society to the ravenous public gaze. When *The House of Mirth* was first published, she was furious at Scribner's advertisement on the wrapper that said: "for the first time the veil has been lifted from New York society."[54] The ad was removed at her insistence, but the novel's appeal to a mass-produced voyeurism does help explain why it became a best-seller. This appeal is both embedded and denied in the narrative itself. The theatrical framing of the opening chapters of *The House of Mirth* can be read as lifting curtains on private scenes of intimacy and luxury from which the reader is excluded. During Lily's visit to Selden's apartment, for example, we share the inquiring glance of the washerwoman and Rosedale's smug and knowing smile. The novel is studded with references to society-page journalists telling the same story as the narrator. Newspaper reports even more strikingly frame Wharton's later novel, *The Custom of the Country:* the novel opens with a glimpse of high society through the clippings that Undine collects from *Town Talks*, and the novel ends with her son leafing through a scrapbook filled with newspaper pictures of his mother.[55] These references have a double-edged effect: on the one hand, they serve as a foil to differentiate the novels as works of art that transcend the mere curiosity of the marketplace. On the other hand, they suggest an uncomfortable likeness: a novel may use the society column as raw material, not to transform it into art, but to be consumed by the reader as though it beat the society pages at their own game by telling the *real* truth behind the gossip.

As late as *A Backward Glance*, Wharton was still defending herself against this implicit accusation of pandering to popular curiosity. Insisting on the autonomy of the imagination, she continually claims that she is not writing about real people: "it is discouraging to know that the books into the making of which so much of one's soul has entered will be snatched at by readers curious only to discover which of the heroes and heroines of the 'society column' are to be found in it" (p. 212). She then concedes that she has no control over her readers' responses: "If one has sought the publicity of print, and sold one's wares in the open market, one has sold to the purchasers the right to think what they choose about one's book" (p. 212). Yet Wharton remained uneasy about the power of readers to consume her work as they wished. In an oft-quoted passage from *A Backward Glance*, she explains that she wrote about a "frivolous society" in *The House of Mirth* in order to expose its destructiveness, its "power of debasing people and ideals," and its wastefulness (p. 207). The need for such justification may stem from her fear that a novelist indeed endorses society's wastefulness and even produces more waste when she preys on society's glamour and transforms it into a marketable commodity in the form of the novel. Despite her disavowal of this exploitation, she praises her friend Henry James for the activity she denies in her own writing, for "carrying with him all the loot his adventure could yield" when he abandoned fashionable society for his country home (p. 174). But although she lauds James for his looting, she cannot admit to the same source for her own material. The often obtrusive moralism in her narrating voice may in part be explained as a compensation for this predatory relationship, as an attempt to transcend the society column through the intervention of a higher moral goal. Although, unlike James, Wharton did produce best-sellers throughout her career, she never comfortably accepted the characteristic of fiction as a vicarious form of conspicuous consumption for a mass readership. Her apprenticeship thus led her out of the drawing room into the literary marketplace to face the difficult question of whether she had escaped turning herself into a sign of wealth and leisure only to produce novels that had the same cultural significance.[56]

Despite these ambiguities of the market, Wharton continued to find in the profession of authorship a viable alternative to the stifling constrictions dictated by her class and gender. At the culmination of her apprenticeship, when she wrote *The House of Mirth*, she again rejected the confines of her mother's drawing room in her depiction of Mrs. Peniston's glacially neat house. Lily Bart's aunt, writes Wharton, "had always been a looker-on at life, and her mind resembled one of those little mirrors which her Dutch ancestors were accustomed to affix to their upper windows so that from the depths of an impenetrable domesticity they might see what was happening in the street."[57] Mrs. Peniston embodies an authorial stance and tradition of realism against which Wharton differentiates her own writing. If Lily represents the woman objectified as art, Mrs. Peniston represents another conception of the author as the disembodied and self-contained subject who sees and represents the world around her only at the cost of removal from it. As the reference to Dutch ancestors suggests, Wharton also rejects genre painting as a heritage for her own art, a form which Eliot advocated as a model for realism. Wharton rejects this way of painting the world, which appears solid and stable only from a safe retreat within the home.

To define herself as professional, Wharton moved out of Mrs. Peniston's sphere of "impenetrable domesticity" first by writing of "interior architecture" as a way of overturning the false dichotomy that separates the interiorized female domestic space from the externalized male public sphere.[58] When Wharton entered the streets of the literary marketplace, she confronted the threat which Mrs. Peniston's posture avoids: the impossibility of seeing without being seen in turn, without risking either self-exposure or the exposure of others. If Mrs. Peniston peers at the changing society around her by retreating from participation, Wharton, in contrast, fully implicates her own identity and craft in the growing consumer society that she depicts. She imagines the self not as an enclosed or displayed ornament at home but as a public persona projected onto the architecture of the book. Throughout her apprenticeship Wharton explores the necessary link between making art and making a name for oneself in the streets of the literary marketplace. There we can imagine that she did not find a reflection of herself as an art object or an essential inner self, but that she looked in the window of a bookshop and found her own name on a book for sale.

4

CROWDED SPACES IN *The House of Mirth*

The House of Mirth opens in a crowded train station when Selden glimpses Lily Bart in the midst of the afternoon rush. In the "act of transition between one and another of the country-houses," the main character does not first appear ensconced in one of their interiors along with the other ladies of her class.[1] Instead she stands out as a "highly specialized" product against a throng of "sallow-faced girls in preposterous hats and flat-chested women struggling with paper bundles and palm-leaf fans" (p. 5). Although Lily remains "apart from the crowd," her relation to that crowd is enigmatic. On the one hand, it forms a background that outlines her brilliance: "her vivid head, relieved against the dull tints of the crowd, made her more conspicuous than in a ball-room" (p. 4). On the other hand, the passers-by comprise an audience of spectators, "who lingered to look; for Miss Bart was a figure to arrest even the suburban traveller rushing to his last train" (p. 4). As a privileged onlooker, Selden engages in "speculation" about Lily's relation to her setting, with a "confused sense that she must have cost a great deal to make, that a great many dull and ugly people must, in some mysterious way, have been sacrificed to produce her" (p. 5). By introducing the main character through Selden's confusion, the narrative introduces itself as a more accurate "speculation," a promise to clarify the mystery of Lily's production by computing her cost, by unfolding the relation between the veiled figure of the lady and the crowd that surrounds her.

The opening scene describes Lily Bart in precisely those idealistic terms which Howells dismissed as unrealistic: artificial, polished, painted, and covered with a "fine glaze," she appears behind a veil, like a mysterious heroine of a romantic novel. Howells's aesthetic of the common, in contrast, advocates representing the members of the crowd, who exhibit for Selden "the dinginess, the crudity of this average section of womanhood" (p. 5). The lady indeed represents all that is uncommon and superfluous, useless and rarefied, as far away from the financial world of the businessmen of her own class as from the working world of the lower-class women. Epitomizing the unreal qualities of modern life, the lady of leisure seems a most inappropriate subject matter according to the producer ethos underlying Howells's theory of realism, to which Wharton herself subscribed. Yet Wharton's opening scene can be read as a critique of Howellsian realism by posing the figure of Lily at center stage and then decentering her by revealing her social production. Just as Selden first views Lily against the crowd of average women rushing through the station, the reader approaches the coming scenes of upper-class luxury and intimacy against a crowded society in flux.

Realism in *The House of Mirth* explores the relation between two conflicting meanings of "society": as the exclusive realm of the elite, whose members are known or knowable to one another, and as the inclusive yet impersonal network of civic, political, and cultural institutions, in which the connections between members are binding yet elusive. Wharton poses this conflict at a time when both meanings were undergoing radical change, as the rapid growth of wealth destabilized the upper classes, and the increasing interdependence yet stratification of society as a whole made its inner workings and interconnections all but invisible. *The House of Mirth* represents high society as a predominantly female realm, whose relation to the hidden male arena of business and equally shadowy world of working women must be charted by the narrative, with Lily deployed as a scout. The novel maps a social terrain where these realms become increasingly interconnected not only through the relations of work and marriage but through the mediation of spectatorship. Wharton's realistic narrative as well becomes enmeshed in producing the spectacle of the unreal world it strives to unveil.

Although the narrative of *The House of Mirth* is tightly structured around Lily's progression from one enclosed interior to the next, the interstices of the novel are filled with crowds. Throngs of newcomers cram the entrance to the "charmed circle" of high society, while packs of onlookers lurk around its edges to peer inside. In contrast to Mrs.

Peniston's empty house, built upon inherited wealth and rigid decorum, the social set in which Lily circulates is presented as "a crowded selfish world of pleasure." At its center stands the guest-filled home of Judy Trenor, who "seemed to exist only as a hostess, not so much from any exaggerated instinct of hospitality as because she could not sustain life except in a crowd" (p. 41). Her own identity, like that of the other characters in the novel, depends upon the very crowd she dominates. Trenor's identity as hostess stems neither from kindness to strangers nor from the rituals among an established community, but from her power to control the crowd by regulating the influx of newcomers.

Haunting the outskirts of the Trenor's social world is a more amorphous and threatening crowd. What Lily sees at first as "the charmed circle about which all her desires revolved" (p. 50) later appears to her as a "great gilt cage" in which its members "were all huddled for the mob to gape at" (p. 56). Although the members of this "charmed circle" draw its boundaries through their power of exclusion, through "the force of negation which eliminated everything beyond their own range of perception" (p. 49) they paradoxically thrive on being recognized by those they negate. To legitimate their privilege, the upper class cannot afford to seclude itself in a private sphere, but depends upon displaying itself before the gaping mob. Such publicity must simultaneously appeal to the crowd by arousing its desire to belong and control that crowd by maintaining an inviolate boundary between actors and audience. High society in *The House of Mirth* is threatened less by the parvenus that enter it, as is commonly assumed, than by its need to turn the rest of society into an audience. If the demands of the urban poor threaten to disrupt the middle-class community in *A Hazard of New Fortunes*, the gaping mob in *The House of Mirth* threatens the power of the elite by entrapping them in its gaze, in their own dependence upon publicity.

One of Wharton's recurring narrative strategies is to give material substance to those threats which first appear in the text as figures of speech. The specter of the "gaping mob," for example, materializes during the first major social gathering of the novel, the wedding between Lily's cousin, Jack Stepney, and Miss Van Osburgh, another member of New York's older elite. The ritual of the wedding has the dual function of consolidating class unity and staging a gala spectacle for a mass audience. Although the ceremony takes place outside the crowded city, in "the village church near the paternal estate on the Hudson," it is performed against a background of voyeuristic crowds clamoring for a glimpse: "It was the 'simple country wedding' to which guests are conveyed in special trains, and from which the hordes of the uninvited have to be fended off by the intervention of the police" (p. 88). Not entirely excluded, the hordes gain a channeled entry in the form of the press, whose representatives "were threading their way, note-book in hand, through the labyrinth of wedding presents, and the agent of a cinematograph syndicate was setting up his apparatus at the church-door" (p. 89). In the role of mediator, the press, on the one hand, represents elite society by making it visible to the classes beneath them. On the other hand, the press represents these classes as mobs or hordes, and attempts both to arouse and contain their desire to enter a world they must serve as spectators.

Articulating the spectacular nature of this upper-class ritual, Lily imagines trading her place as "casual spectator" for the role of the "mystically veiled figure occupying the center of attention" (p. 89). Lily's contradictory self-image encapsulates that of her class, which to maintain its power as the center of attention must also remain mystically veiled. The combination of conspicuousness and elusiveness empowers the elite as the center of desire by simultaneously attracting the notice of the audience beneath them and keeping that audience at bay.

The upper-class woman plays a central role in this pageant. While the press displays the wedding presents to the gaping mob, those same presents stir the envy of the inner coterie. As spectator, Lily is especially struck by the bride's jewels, whose "precious tints [were] enhanced and deepened by the varied art of their setting." Lily identifies not only with the mystically veiled figure of the bride but with the fully exposed objects, the jewels: "More completely than any other expression of wealth, they symbolized the life she longed to lead, the life of fastidious aloofness and refinement in which every detail should have the finish of a jewel, and the whole form a harmonious setting to her own jewel-like rareness" (p. 91). Lily's desire for aloofness depends upon her attachment to the setting from which she wishes to be distinguished. Throughout the novel, Lily's identity is described in relation to a background against which she can outline herself, or a mirror in which she can be viewed. Yet each attempt to ignore that dependence contributes to her further decline.

The narrative of Lily's descent can be traced through her relation to the mirror, from the one in Selden's apartment in which he sees her as "a captured dryad subdued to the conventions of the drawing-room" (p. 12), to Mrs. Bry's admiration which "was a mirror in which Lily's self-complacency recovered its lost outline" (p. 114), to Gerty's mirror which reflects Lily's "disfigurement," to the "blank surface of the toilet-mirror" in her death room (p. 327). Lily's reliance on mirrors and settings for her identity has been viewed as either a weakness of moral character or an indication of her plight as a woman who exists passively as a beautiful object rather than acting in the world.[2] Yet this dependence also shows how the lady of leisure becomes emblematic of her class. Just as she can achieve an identity only from the gaze of those around her, the class she represents depends not only on the subservience but on the spectatorship of the crowds around it.

Wharton has long been seen to chronicle the rapid succession of New York's established elite by succesive waves of parvenus, who supplanted inherited wealth with industrial fortunes and traditional values with conspicuous consumption. *The House of Mirth*, however, shows that the dazzling ascendancy of new money did more than alter the demographic composition of New York's elite. The representation of this class and of its relation to other classes underwent fundamental transformations as "members of old and new money emerged into the public social life in a grand way."[3] The New York "old guard"—itself only as old as the merger of antebellum Knickerbockers with post–Civil War industrial fortunes—formulated rituals and rules of polite behavior designed to consolidate their class interests and regulate the admission of newcomers. Both their lack of stability and their attempt to achieve it was epitomized by the Astor Four Hundred Club, a grouping based on the notion that a select number of individuals could be designated as the upper crust of society. Their social gatherings took place in the formalized privacy of the dining room at home, or the equally circumscribed space of the elaborate formal ball.[4]

When the huge influx of wealth turned New York into the finance and trust center of the country in the late nineteenth century, the older families lost their authority to control the admission to an elite coterie. With fewer guarantees of social status, the wealthy focused more on competing for power with one another than on acknowledging their common interests. If the old guard had tried to cement its membership through exclusive rituals in a private setting, both new and old money now competed for status through extravagant public spectacles.[5] Rather than adhere to formal rules of etiquette to prove their worthiness to enter the upper echelon, the newer elites tried to outdo one another in innovative and often outlandish performances, staged as much for one another as for the masses beneath them. The change in upper-class leisure from private functions to public displays was reflected in the social geography of the city, with the building of palatial hotels and restaurants. These monuments served the double purpose of a meeting ground and competitive arena for the expanding elite, and an advertisement purveying their luxury and power to the masses. Social life was thus gradually moving out of the private dining hall and exclusive ball of the Astor Four Hundred Club to the public stage of the hotel and restaurant where anyone with wealth could come to see and be seen.[6]

In New York City, the struggle for economic power on Wall Street was manifest less in the political and civic arena (where it went on for example in Boston), than in the social realm of Fifth Avenue, a sphere dominated by women. Whereas Thorstein Veblen analyzed the conspicuous consumption that turned the lady of leisure into an ornamental display of her husband's power as an outdated vestige of barbaric customs, Wharton presented this role as pivotal in new modes of representing class power. Visitors to the United States in the 1890s and first decade of the twentieth century often commented on the female domination of a social scene vacated by men who were busy building economic empires. To Henry James and Paul Bourget, both friends of Wharton's, this division constituted "*the* feature of the social scene" of American life.[7] Wharton, however, takes this observation further to explore the hidden connections between these bifurcated realms. For the lady of leisure, domesticity was subordinated to publicity as the home became a stage setting for the gala social events orchestrated and acted out by women. The upper-class home functioned less as a private haven from the competition of the marketplace than as the public stage for that competition. Indeed the meaning of public and private underwent an interesting reversal. In *The House of Mirth* it is the dealings of the business world which seem private and unspeakable, while the cultural work of women dominates the public scene. The women of this group have a dual role: to display the wealth and social power of their husbands and to conceal the source of this power.

Thus Wharton does not simply chart the breakdown of the traditions of the old guard and the rootlessness of the new; rather she participates in changing forms of representing class power. The wedding scene in *The House of Mirth* stands at the crossroads of this transformation. On the one hand, the wedding takes place in the privacy of "the paternal estate" between members of the old guard with the traditional function of assuring their future through kinship. On the other hand, the wedding has a circus-like quality in that it is performed for a mass audience excluded from participation. The wedding, furthermore, challenges the traditional social and literary meaning of domesticity. Lily Bart longs to be the bride, not because this status promises to remove her to a secure domestic retreat, but because of the power it would afford her to star in the public eye. By having Lily miss her chance to play this role in the beginning of the novel, Wharton rejects marriage as the narrative teleology of the domestic novel, and implicitly calls attention to her own narrative as realistic.

The narration of Lily's fall away from the center of the older elite traces the rise not only of the nouveau riche but of new modes of upper-class leisure and self-representation. Whereas the Osborn wedding still maintains the sanction of a traditional ritual, the next major gathering in the novel, the Wellington Brys' *tableaux vivants*, has a purely theatrical function. The Brys stage this gala event to break into high society in a grand way, not by conforming to its preexisting rules but by redefining its terms of pleasure and leisure. The tableaux vivants enact imitations of famous old paintings, with fashionable ladies costumed as the main characters. Since the sixteenth century, oil paintings have had a double significance as property: they are not only owned as valuable possessions, they also represent in tangible and tactile detail those objects that the owner has the wealth to possess.[8] In addition to displaying the owner-spectator's power in the present, their solidity promises a permanent record of his image for the future. The Brys' tableaux vivants invert the way painting functions as a representation of social status by harnessing the cutural authority of the artistic tradition while transcribing it in a new context. Rather than buy paintings that represent the things they own, they spend money to imitate the art of the past. They hire a "distinguished portrait painter" not to paint a lasting portrait of themselves but to direct a show. If oil paintings are valued for their realism, for their tangible and lasting properties, the tableaux vivants advertise the ability of the Brys to copy the real thing and to perform it as something unreal and fleeting. They turn art into performance. These performances are not paeans to property and ownership, they flaunt the power of conspicuous consumption, the power to spend money for its own sake. Instead of buying unique and enduring works of art, the Brys spend money to deny the material reality of objects, and treat art merely as a means of producing "spectacular effects."[9]

The Brys' newly built mansion has the same effect as their evening entertainment. As opposed to a private setting for domesticity, the house is constructed for public display and is self-consciously built as a stage: "the air of improvisation was in fact so strikingly present; so recent, so rapidly evoked was the whole *mise-en-scène* that one had to touch the marble columns to learn they were not of cardboard, to seat one's self in one of the damask-and-gold armchairs to be sure it was not painted against the wall" (p. 133). In contrast to the older homes of Mrs. Peniston and Percy Gryce, which impose themselves on the spectator with their mausoleum-like solidity, the Brys' mansion flaunts its newness and improvised quality.

Although the performance of the tableaux vivants may appear as the antithesis of the activities of collecting and connoisseurship in the novel, it is the logical culmination of the collector's ethos. A member of the older elite, Percy Gryce, collects Americana for its "mere rarity," but his collection denies the historical content of the documents just as the tableaux vivants deny the historicity of the art of the past. While Gryce shuns the conspicuousness which the Brys court, his Americana collection has the exchange value for him less of money than of personal publicity: "Anxious as he was to avoid personal notice, he took, in the printed mention of his name, a pleasure so exquisite and excessive that it seemed a compensation for his shrinking from publicity" (p. 21). The collection, which he inherited from his father, serves as a mirror which allows him "to regard himself as figuring prominently in the public eye" (p. 21). Gryce's modest collection has the same purpose as the more voracious acquisition of Rosedale, who catches the "envious attention" of those who formerly shunned him by "buying the newly furnished house of one of the victims of the crash, who in the space of twelve short months, had made the same number of millions, built a house on Fifth Avenue, filled a picture gallery with old masters, entertained all New York in it, and been smuggled out of the country between a trained nurse and doctor while his creditors mounted guard over the old masters and his guests explained to each other that they had dined with him only because they wanted to see the pictures" (p. 122). Rather than accumulate art objects piece by piece, Rosedale acquires a whole collection at once; the value of the collection lies in the fact that he has taken over what someone else has lost, not in the objects themselves. Although Rosedale prides himself on being less aggressive and obvious than the Brys in his social ascent, his acquisition of real "old masters" has the same effect as the Brys' performance of the imitation, that of producing publicity for the social power of the owner.

Although the Brys present their tableaux vivants to an exclusive party of invited guests, "to attack society collectively," they stage their entertainment for a broader audience, for the larger crowd of the gaping mob. The next evening finds *Town Talk* full of innuendos about Lily's role in the performance, and her cousin, Mr. Ned Van Alstyne, claims to have read about her in "the dirty papers" (p. 158). *Town Talk* is an obvious parody of New York's *Town Topics*, a popular society magazine and scandal sheet. Although originally published for the inner circle of "gentle folk," the magazine began to appeal to a wider readership as its circulation passed fifty thousand in the 1890s.[10] The popular press has a function similar to that of the collection of high art; both reflect to the elite their own sense of importance in the eyes of others. If they invite their peers into their mansions to view enviously their art collections and entertainments, they depend upon the press to invite outsiders to participate vicariously in the same events.

As all social interaction in *The House of Mirth* becomes more staged and theatrical, the novel becomes more crowded with references to the media, to popular forms of representing the wealthy classes. The opening scene of book 2 parallels that of book 1, and demonstrates this progressive theatricalization of social intercourse. Book 2 opens in a public space that does not have the functionality of the train station but serves self-consciously as "sublime stage setting" (p. 183). Both scenes are framed by the observations of Selden, "who began to feel the renewed zest of spectatorship that is the solace of those who take an objective interest in life" (p. 184). Yet rather than stare at Lily, who seems caught unaware in Grand Central Station, Selden notices a "consciously conspicuous group of people" who

> advanced to the middle front and stood before Selden with the air of chief performers gathered together by the exigencies of the final effect. Their appearance confirmed the impression that the show had been staged regardless of expense, and emphasized its resemblance to one of those "costume-plays" in which the protagonists walk through the passions without displacing a drapery. The ladies stood in unrelated attitudes calculated to isolate their effects, and the men hung about them as irrelevantly as stage heroes whose tailors are named in the program. (p. 184)

In this scene, high society imitates the costume play, itself a theatrical form which imitated the manners of the wealthy. The copy and the original become indistinguishable, just as spectators and actors become inseparable when "it was Selden himself who unwittingly fused the group by arresting the attention of one of its members."

Selden is not the only spectator-participant in the scene; he is rivaled by the presence of "that horrid little Dabham who does 'Society Notes from the Riviera'" (p. 199). In the figure of Dabham, the gaping mob becomes ever more concrete. He gains entrance into closed circles that others merely glimpse from the outside. The next day, the same group chooses a restaurant which "was crowded with persons mainly gathered there for the purpose of spectatorship, and accurately posted as to the names and the faces of the celebrities they had come to see" (p. 216). It is Dabham's job both to keep the crowds posted and to provide those on the inside with the measure of their success. Lily Bart feels reinstated in her position in "high company" by "making her own ascendancy felt there so that she found herself figuring once more as the 'beautiful Miss Bart' in the interesting journal devoted to recording the least movements of her cosmopolitan companions" (p. 196). Securing her identity in such a setting, Lily manages to "throw into the extreme background of memory the prosaic and sordid difficulties from which she had escaped" (p. 196).

As the tone here indicates, the narrator disapproves of the theatricality of this setting which erases all traces of the past in the beam of the moment's publicity. She blatantly criticizes "the strident setting of the restaurant, in which their table seemed set apart in a special glare of publicity"; a setting in which the presence "of little Dabham of the 'Riviera Notes' emphasized the ideals of a world where conspicuousness passed for distinction and the society column had become the roll of fame" (p. 215). The intrusive narrative moralizing indicates particular discomfort with the presence of Dabham, whose "little eyes were like tentacles thrown out to catch the floating intimations with which, to Selden, the air at moments seemed thick" (p. 215). Dabham is a subject for scorn not simply because of his sordid voyeurism, but more importantly because of the similarity between his role and that of the author. Like the gossip columnist, the novelist takes us "behind the scenes" into the interior of *The House of Mirth* to reveal the nuances and intimations of an otherwise inaccessible elite circle. Expressing her own discomfort with capitalizing on such privileged knowledge, she concludes the description of the dinner's finale by suggesting that "the whole scene had touches of intimacy worth their weight in gold to the watchful pen of Mr. Dabham" (p. 216). How is this pen distinguished from that of the novelist using the same material?

To make this distinction, Wharton poses Selden as a model for the realist who has one foot in the gilded cage but still seems to keep the other outside by the power of detached, objective observation. He acts as a policeman monitoring Dabham, who "suddenly became the center of Selden's scrutiny." Yet precisely in this position as spectator of the spectator—watching over Dabham—Selden loses his objective status and participates in the same game of publicity and spectatorship that everyone else takes part in. His own complicity can be seen in his response to the crisis when Bertha Dorset publicly forbids Lily to return to the yacht. Rather than defend Lily in public, he "was mainly conscious of a longing to grip Dabham by the collar and fling him out into the street" (p. 217). Selden accepts Dabham's terms that what is staged for public exposure takes precedence over any other narrative of events. There is no distinction, just as no difference exists between the costume play and the drawing room. At key junctures in the novel, Selden is seduced by the immediacy of the spectacle, and cannot understand the countervailing evidence. Despite—or because of—his air of detachment, Selden participates fully in the social world in which conspicuousness turns effortlessly into notoriety, and Bertha Dorset can replay Lily's reinstatement as banishment.

When Lily returns to New York, she makes no attempt to prepare an alternative story to that initiated by Bertha and circulated by Dabham and his colleagues. In reply to Gerty's request for the truth, she explains, "it's a great deal easier to believe Bertha Dorset's story than mine, because she has a big house and an opera box and it's convenient to be on good terms with her" (p. 225). Throughout the novel, narration is impotent against the power of vision, not necessarily because sight is more accurate than stories, but because spectacles are staged by the wealthy and powerful. In Mrs. Peniston's outdated social world, she is horrified to learn that Lily has made herself "conspicuous," and she refuses to speak to Lily because it would be as "unwarrantable as a spectator's suddenly joining in a game" (p. 128). If Mrs. Peniston were to confront her, however, Lily would probably be incapable of telling her own story, "as she was of more service as a listener than as a narrator" (p. 108). Lily never tries to counter her conspicuousness with narrative, but instead with more conspicuousness in the right setting, until she reaches the point where she avoids being seen at all. Rosedale articulates this powerlessness of narrative when he proposes to marry Lily on the condition that she regain power over Bertha. Although Rosedale does not believe the stories about Lily, he claims that the truth or falsity of stories matters only in novels, "but I'm certain it don't matter in real life" (p. 256). He goes on to show that in real life what matters is the balance of power demonstrated solely by the visible. The impotence of narrative in *The House of Mirth* poses a peculiar dilemma for the realist, who sets herself up as the teller of truth rather than as the spectator or producer of scenes. Yet she thereby aligns herself with a position of social impotence not unlike that in which Lily finds herself.

Upon returning to New York, only to face her disinheritance, Lily enters the new social milieu of the Gormer family. After painstakingly mounting the social ladder according to the rules, they prefer to "strike out on their own: what they want is to have a good time and to have it their own way" (p. 233). Despite their initial success at social climbing, "they decided that the whole business bored them and that what they wanted was a crowd they could really feel at home with" (p. 232). Indeed, their notion of domesticity depends on effacing the difference between the crowd and the home, between spectators and performers. Instead of staging a major social event, as the Brys do, they "start a sort of continuous performance of their own, a kind of social Coney Island, where everybody is welcome who can make noise enough" (p. 233). In contrast to the Brys, they do not rely on the authority of tradition by imitating the old masters; instead they invoke the authority of novelty. They enact a new kind of upper-class leisure in which "ridiculing ritual substituted fun for formality. The search for sensation replaced the continuity of tradition which held the old guard together."[11] Instead of assembling an exclusive guest list of old names, the Gormers invite glamorous outsiders—actresses, artists, and celebrities, "everyone who's jolly and makes a row."

Among the Gormer set, Lily's former social disgrace only brands her "the heroine of a queer episode" as they accept her just like the others into the "easy promiscuity of their lives." In this group, Lily gains "the odd sense of having been caught up into the crowd as carelessly as a passenger is gathered in by the express train" (p. 233). Echoing the first scene, the change in Lily's status is marked by her membership in the crowd, rather than by her capacity to stand above it. The metaphor of being swept along is realized when she agrees to participate in the Gormers' motoring trip to Alaska. Despite the social distance she has traveled and the fact that "the Gormer *milieu* represented a social outskirt which Lily had always fastidiously avoided," it strikes her "now that she was in it, as only a flamboyant copy of her own world, a caricature approximating the real thing as the 'society play' approaches the manners of the drawing-room" (p. 234). Yet as Lily descends the social scale, she finds that the copy and the real thing become indistinguishable. The caricature of the Gormers easily turns into the real thing, when Bertha enlists Gormer in her campaign against Lily. "The real thing" thus is not the inimitable manners of the older elite but the "impregnable bank-account" which underlies the authority that sets standards against which imitators appear as caricatures.

As Lily descends the social scale, she visits regions which seem more and more unreal because of their distance from the center of her old world yet strangely interconnected with that world. After being snubbed by the Gormers, Lily becomes the "secretary for a western divorced ingenue," Mrs. Norma Hatch, who inhabits "the world of the fashionable New York hotel, a world over-heated, over-upholstered, and over-fitted with mechanical applicances for the gratification of fantastic requirements" (p. 274). Mrs. Hatch's hotel life exemplifies what James called "the sense of promiscuity which manages to be at the same time an inordinate untempered monotony."[12] Promiscuity refers not to sexual excess but to the older meaning of an indiscriminate and disorderly mixture of varied elements. The unreality of the hotel world is characterized by the lack of acknowledged distinctions and boundaries. Even more distant than the popular amusements of Coney Island, Norma Hatch's "habits were marked by an Oriental indolence and disorder peculiarly trying to her companion. Mrs. Hatch and her friends seemed to float together outside the bounds of time and space. No definite hours were kept; no fixed obligations existed" (p. 275). This lack of boundaries extends to people as well, as Mrs. Hatch makes no distinctions between her peers, her manicurists, her society friends, and her doctors. To Lily, the lack of distinction in time and social place makes the people seem to have "no more real existence than the poet's shades in limbo" (p. 274). The hotel seems to allow the gaping mob to enter in a controlled form, in the technological "blaze of electric light." Rather than appear in the elite column of the society pages, Mrs. Hatch makes her social debut in the photographs of the "Sunday Supplement." Like the hotel, the Sunday Supplement represents a closer step to the gaping mob. Begun in the 1890s with the boom in mass-circulation newspapers, these illustrated supplements represented a new form of celebrity. Mrs. Hatch aspired to be a member of the world she read about, as she "swam in a haze of indeterminate enthusiasms, of aspirations culled from the stage, the newspapers, the fashion-journals, and a gaudy world of sport still more completely beyond her companion's ken" (p. 277).

If Mrs. Hatch's world seems unreal to Lily, the most shocking aspect of it is the intersection with "her own circle," when she meets the sons of the oldest and most respectable New York families. Indeed the social life of upper-class young men in this period was bifurcated between allegiance to the proprieties of their own sphere and their freedom to frequent the new after-dinner clubs and hotels, "when released from the official social routine" (p. 276).[13] The appearance of these young men gave Lily "the odd sense of being behind the social tapestry, on the side where the threads were knotted and the loose ends hung" (p. 276). Throughout the novel, wealth means having the power to hide these loose ends, to render invisible the work on which one's existence depends. Lily herself has a horror of cleaning smells and of the sight of rumpled dresses the morning after a party because these sensations attest both to her dependence on those beneath her and her own proximity to a sphere of servitude. She finds one of the worst aspects of life in the boardinghouse to be the smell of cooking that seeps into her room, the absence of boundaries that keep out of sight her own means of subsistence. The luxury of the world which Lily leaves behind depends on keeping the "machinery" of its production "so carefully concealed that one scene flows into another without perceptible agency" (p. 301).

If the hotel of Norma Hatch yields Lily a glimpse of this agency behind the social tapestry, the next chapter finds her literally working there, the place "where threads were knotted and the loose ends hung." By taking a job at the milliner's, Lily finds herself creating the setting against which she had formerly displayed herself. She is driven to the job by her attempt to turn her only talent, that of producing herself as an ornament, into a marketable skill. Rather than play the role of model, the image of the consumer of these goods, she attempts to step over the line into that world of production which so horrifies her.

Lily's work at the milliner's returns to the opening question of her relation to the average working women of the crowd by thrusting her among them. These women have a double-edged relation to the society women above them: their labor produces the setting that creates the conspicuousness of upper-class leisure, and they become an audience that watches the same setting they produce. For Lily, the strangest aspect of working in the milliner's shop is hearing the names of her former peers, "seeing the fragmentary and distorted image of the world she had lived in reflected in the mirror of the working-girls' minds. She had never before suspected the mixture of insatiable curiosity and contemptuous freedom with which she and her kind were discussed in this underworld of toilers who lived on their vanity and self-indulgence" (p. 286). The working girls are members of the gaping mob, who provide not only the labor but the mirror in which upper-class ladies must reflect their own identity. This relation reverses the direction taken by Gerty Farish in her working-girl clubs. Reformers like Gerty assume a one-way mirror, in which they visit the lives of the poor in order to uplift them. The working girls are scrutinized by charitable ladies who expect in turn a passive gratitude and admiration, not a radical scrutiny in kind.

Thus in answer to the opening question of Lily's relation to the crowd, the price of making Lily is both the work of women who produce her and the cost of their spectatorship which sustains her. The narrative charts a social world in which class segmentation is highly spatialized, clearly marked in *The House of Mirth* by the spatial coordinates of Lily's descent, as she moves down the social scale through very different interiors, from her aunt's inherited mansion, to the country home of the Trenors, to the boardinghouse. These rigid boundaries, however, are penetrated through the relations of spectatorship and voyeurism. In *The House of Mirth* class stratification is not trascended by the common interests of domesticity, as it is for Howells. Instead both the bond between classes and their hierarchical difference depend on conspicuousness. At the end of the novel, the working girl, Nettie Struther, seems to represent a Howellsian solution of domesticity to Lily's wasted life, but Nellie's relation to Lily is mediated through spectatorship as well. She follows Lily's career in the newspaper and tells Lily that she talked over with her husband "what you were doing and read descriptions of the dresses you wore" (p. 314). If Lily first visits Nettie through the channel of the girls' club and the work of charity, Nettie follows Lily through the channel of the mass media. In addition, she names her baby after a character in a popular play, the French queen, "Marry Anto'-nette," who reminded her of Lily. Through her values of domesticity and productivity, Nettie may appear as an example of "real life" unavailable to Lily. Yet Nettie's life also becomes a parody of its own imitation of upper-class life, as she becomes a domesticated version of the gaping mob.

Throughout the novel, the gaping mob both defines and threatens the upper class, which depends on the mob's admiration and its exclusion. Lily similarly depends on the mirror of the gaping mob to maintain her identity. When she loses this mirror, she loses a self. At the end of the novel, Lily kills herself to avoid a mirrorless future in which time itself suddenly faces her as "a shrieking mob" (p. 322).

The gaping mob does more than play the role of a passive audience in *The House of Mirth*. Its threatening quality emerges in the first scene in the figure of the charwoman scrubbing the stairs and blocking the hall as Lily leaves Selden's apartment. Although Lily explains away her "persistent gaze" by imagining "the poor thing" to be "probably dazzled," she is visibly upset by the stare of the charwoman, who later turns her vision into a source of considerable power that shapes the trajectory of Lily's career. As a cleaning woman she has access to Selden's wastepaper basket, from which she retrieves Bertha's love letters. Mrs. Haffen resurfaces with the letters for sale almost as a confirmation of Lily's own fears of falling into a "future of servitude" at the same moment she resents the smells and sights of the women cleaning her aunt's house, "as though she thought a house ought to keep clean of itself" (p. 102). These retrieved letters, whose contents are never directly revealed, become a central medium for exchange throughout the novel. As writing, they form a kind of circuit which intertwines class and character in the novel—from Bertha to Selden to Mrs. Haffen to Lily, who purchases them fully aware of their exchange value, their power to reinstate her in her social circle.[14]

The exchange of letters thus offers an alternative narrative to the plot of decline which Lily follows. At any moment she can reverse her fortune by trading the letters, with their implicit threat of exposure, for Bertha's loyalty. Simon Rosedale governs this alternative plot: he sees Lily at the same time that Mrs. Haffen sees her, and he probably encourages Mrs. Haffen to sell the letters; and he continually urges Lily to sell them back to Bertha. As author of this plot, Rosedale plays the curious role of the demonic realist in opposition to Selden's romantic. Artistic qualities are attributed to Rosedale, who, like the realist, understands the hidden workings of society, the need to cloak and display his wealth with the "right woman to spend it." More important, he is the only one in the novel who knows as much about Lily as do the narrator and reader. Whereas Nettie posits knowledge as the cement of domestic love—"I knew he knew about me"—Rosedale, rather than Selden, is the one who knows about Lily: about her transaction with Trenor, and the truth of her relation with Bertha. He knows the story that Selden can only read with difficulty in her checkbook after her death. He knows that the truth value of stories matters less than conspicuousness: "the quickest way to queer yourself with the right people is to be seen with the wrong ones" (p. 257). Nowhere is Rosedale more the realist than in his proposal to Lily: he engages in "plain speaking" by expressing his desire to get into society which she finds "refreshing to step into the open daylight of an avowed expediency" (p. 259). Yet to act realistically in "open daylight," according to Rosedale, is to engage in a transaction which both the narrator and Lily find morally repugnant by virtue of reducing everything to "a region of concrete weights and measures" (p. 259).

By burning the letters, Lily treats them as unique content—the intimate knowledge of Selden's past—that cannot be reduced to weights and measures; she refuses to turn them into a medium of exchange and "trade on his name." Yet by breaking this circuit she must abandon her self as well. Wharton thereby divorces her own writing from Rosedale's plot, which treats writing as a medium for exchanging intimacy for power. Wharton saves Lily from Rosedale's plot by extracting her from the circuit of exchange; yet outside that circuit she can have no self and is left "unsphered in a void of social nonexistence." Wharton thereby refuses to treat writing as the retrieval of knowledge from the wastebasket of intimacy; but in burning those letters she replaces them with Lily, who ends her life "thrown out into the rubbish heap" (p. 308).

5

THEODORE DREISER'S PROMOTION OF AUTHORSHIP

In 1898 the first issue of *Success* magazine published an interview with the famous novelist William Dean Howells by a relatively unknown journalist, Theodore Dreiser.[1] Entitled "How He Climbed Fame's Ladder" and subtitled "William Dean Howells Tells the Story of His Long Struggle for Success, and His Ultimate Triumph," the interview bears a remarkable resemblance to the opening of *The Rise of Silas Lapham.* Dreiser steps into the shoes of Bartley Hubbard, the aggressive young representative of the new journalism, treated with such ambivalence in *A Modern Instance,* and Howells plays the role of a cagier Silas Lapham, able to manipulate the interview format to his own advantage. Although the stated purpose of Marden's magazine was to hold up prominent figures as models for their younger contemporaries, one of Dreiser's first questions to Howells belies this goal: "You began to carve out your place in life under conditions very different from those of to-day?" (p. 59). Bathed in a halo of nostalgia partly of Howells's own making and partly of Dreiser's "sincere reporter's rhetoric," Howells's apprenticeship appears strikingly remote from the young writer contending with the modern conditions of "to-day."

Two years later—the same year as the first publication of *Sister Carrie*—Dreiser published a better-known interview, entitled "The Real Howells," which critics often read as a more accurate account of Dreiser's appreciation of the novelist, untailored to fit the *Success* formula required by the magazine's editor, Orison Swett Marden.[2] It is here, they argue, that Dreiser projects an image of what Ellen Moers calls his "ideal reader."[3] In this literary history, Dreiser appears as the rightful heir to Howells's legacy of realism, which Howells himself could neither fulfill nor recognize in Dreiser. In the second interview, however, Dreiser's mixed tone of adulation and condescension enshrines Howells as a symbol of cultural authority and undercuts that image by consigning him as a venerated relic to a bygone era. If the first interview implicates institutional changes in the social production of writing that separate Howells's apprenticeship from Dreiser's, the second suggests equally important structural changes in the public persona of the author.

Dreiser's interviews with Howells serve here as an introduction to a reconsideration of Dreiser's apprenticeship in the 1890s and first decade of the twentieth century. The difference between the critical evaluations of these two interviews—between the formulaic and the real—reflects a common approach to Dreiser's early writing. Most critics acknowledge that Dreiser's apprenticeship was crucial in that it immersed him in a wide variety of mass cultural practices; he not only contributed regularly to the new, inexpensive magazines of the period—in which these interviews appeared—but before that he launched his career as an urban journalist and then worked as an editor and writer for a women's magazine of popular music and literature. Critics such as Robert Elias, Ellen Moers, and Yoshinobu Hakutani have successfully mined Dreiser's early work for the raw material of experience, reading, philosophy, and style which Dreiser later transformed into his serious works of realism.[4] Their implicit critical narrative, however, usually traces Dreiser's rise from conventional hack to iconoclastic realist, from the mass market to the production of serious art. In this view, if his commercial writing constrained Dreiser to formulaic conventions, then the writing of *Sister Carrie* culminated this apprenticeship by violating artistic and moral conventions, leading to the novel's rejection and Dreiser's consequent breakdown.

My purpose in this chapter is to renarrate the trajectory of Dreiser's apprenticeship, not to distill an incipient realism from his writing for the market, but to explore the way Dreiser's conception of the realist was shaped both within and against the institutions of mass culture; in the next chapter I will explore the reliance of his realistic forms on mass cultural conventions. Dreiser's apprenticeship, like Wharton's, involved not just learning how to write realistically, but learning how to promote himself as an author in the market and sell his product—his construction of reality. Like both Wharton and Howells, however, Dreiser tried at first to distance his authorship from the mass market he was writing for by adopting older images of the artist as genius, prophet, and orator. Ultimately his apprenticeship did not lead him away from the market to produce unconventional art, it led him to view the realistic author and his products as subjects of the mass market. Like Wharton, he achieved an unstable fusion of a marketable identity and a position outside that market, though less in her role of the professional than in the role of celebrity she found so threatening. This chapter examines Dreiser's construction of a social position for the realist—his own "carving of a place for himself" as represented in his newspaper articles, his editorship of the magazine, *Ev'ry Month,* his free-lance articles for *Success* magazine, and the posthumously published account of his neurasthenia in *An Amateur Laborer.* Each stage reveals a tension that Dreiser simultaneously resolves and deepens between the concept of writing as producing and as marketing. In this narrative, Dreiser's apprenticeship culminates not in the production of *Sister Carrie* in 1900 but in its successful reissue and promotion in 1907.

I

My narrative opens in the middle—with Dreiser's interview of Howells in 1898. Just as Howells had created Hubbard as a foil for his own stance as realist, Dreiser represented a Howells from whom he differentiated the shape of his own career and his conception of the work of writing. The first interview for *Success* magazine, written in question-answer format, focuses primarily on Howells's antebellum apprenticeship and then jumps to his current eminence. Howells's depiction of his training in his father's printing shop makes writing appear as a rural cottage industry, as the work of the country editor from which Hubbard flees. Given the choice by his father between school and the print shop, Howells stresses that "we could not be idle" (p. 60), that literature is not the province of leisure and privilege. His father's shop involved Howells in every aspect of the production process, from waiting for telegraphic news, to writing notices, to setting type, to delivering papers. He conducted his literary studies during free moments at home at a desk under the stairs. As Howells explains, there was little separation between labor at the print shop and the leisure to read, and equally little separation between home and work life: "It seemed, for a while, so very simple and easy to come home in the middle of the afternoon, when my task at the printing-office was done, and sit down to my books in my little study" (p. 60). In fact, his father was both his master at work and the teacher directing his reading. Howells uses an artisanal vocabulary to describe his first efforts at writing: "As soon as supper was over, I got out my manuscripts, and sawed, and filed, and hammered" (p. 61). When asked about his first published story, he explained that he "did not really write it, but composed it, rather, in type, at the case" (p. 62). Even the act of creation is represented as part of the craftsmanship of printing.

Most of Dreiser's questions focus on the nature of writing as labor in order to determine how hard work leads to success, and to mold Howells's narrative, as Hubbard does with Lapham, to the rags-to-riches formula. Yet Dreiser poses questions, evaded by Howells, which are clearly unsuited to the mode of literary production described by Howells. When Dreiser comments, for example, "then you began life in poverty," Howells responds, "but nobody was rich then" (p. 60). Asked whether he "chose the printing office" when given the two options by his father, Howells responds "not wholly." Dreiser continually tries to pin down Howells about his discipline and schedule for reading and writing, but Howells evades him by describing the erratic rhythms of work in the print shop. When asked, for example, "When did you have time to seriously apply yourself to literature?" Howells responds, "I think I did so before I really had the time" (p. 60). Dreiser then asks about "conveniences for literary researches," a term more applicable to the modern techniques of journalism than to Howells's answer that he imitated the writings of great authors, relying on tradition rather than research. Howells widens this disjuncture between old and new by recalling his rejection of a "city editorship" after "one night's round with the reporters at the police station." Instead, he returned to his father's print shop, where he spent his nights reading the poet Heine by candlelight with a German bookbinder (p. 61). By the time of this interview, however, as Howells knew well, an apprenticeship at a city newspaper had become commonplace for a younger generation of writers such as Dreiser, from whom Howells implicitly removes himself.

In response to Howells's romantic choice of rural candlelight over urban gaslight, Dreiser insists upon the question, "Did you find it labor?" to which Howells answers in typically equivocal fashion: "I fancy that reading is not merely a pastime, when it is apparently the merest pastime," (p. 61) but he later adds that the "endeavor that does one good—and lasting good—is the endeavor one makes with pleasure . . . pleasureable labor brings, on the whole, I think, the greatest reward" (p. 63). While Howells values reading as work and not idleness, he still tries to separate the pleasureable labor of literature from the industrial drudgery at a city desk or factory. Dreiser's next comment, however, interprets the term "reward" in a slightly different context: "You were probably fascinated by the supposed rewards of a literary career" (p. 63). Although Howells admits to his youthful fantasy of fame—and the entire interview attests to his achievement—he concludes with the claim that the goal of literature is service to the community, "a field for endeavor toward the happiness of the whole human family. There is no other success . . . the keenest joy, after all, and the toiler's truest and best reward" (p. 64). Thus Dreiser's interview with Howells reconstructs an idealized world no longer available to Dreiser's generation—nor indeed to Howells's—a world in which literature is integrated into other ways of life, whether the rhythm of the country newspaper or an ambassadorship in Venice, and in which writing is a pleasureable form of artisanal work, whose value lies in community service.

Howells's notion of a reading audience as community also appears as an outdated vestige of his rural roots. When, for example, Howells recounts the reception of his first story composed in type, he recalls discontinuing the serial upon overhearing an old farmer say "he did not think it amounted to much." According to Dreiser, Howells maintained a sense of addressing a knowable community even when he began to publish for a mass audience. In the second interview of 1900, "The Real Howells," Dreiser quotes a long passage from an article later incorporated into *Literary Friends and Acquaintances*, in which Howells expresses his delight in being recognized by two readers in a hotel in Montreal. He responds to them that "I was just looking for someone I knew. I hope you are someone who knows *me*" (p. 70). Howells recalls this meeting as the "precious first personal recognition of my authorship I had ever received from a stranger," and this acknowledgment in fact makes them no longer strangers; for many years Howells was to recognize one of these readers' names on the sign of a Wall Street law office. Although to Dreiser this anecdote exemplifies Howells's charming frankness, it must have struck him as evidence of a very different public world from the one for which he was writing. Howells's story assumes an intimacy with readers who share the same social world of mutual recognition, where strangers can be known from their publications or office signs. Dreiser's interview assumes a world in which important men do not represent themselves directly in their writing but must be made accessible to a curious public through the mass media. The interview both produces a sense of intimacy and elevates the person interviewed to a higher plane of fame. As a celebrity, Howells becomes known less through his works than through his image as a "personage," like Mrs. Aubyn in Wharton's *Touchstone*. Furthermore, by writing such interviews, the young journalist tries to break into this star system with the hope that the aura of the personality may rub off on him.

While Dreiser's first interview shows the conditions of Howells's work to be long unavailable to the aspiring young writer, his second interview, "The Real Howells," consigns Howells as a "personage" to an outdated world as well. Many critics have read this interview as a tribute to the man who should have been Dreiser's most appreciative reader, or as a request for patronage, but Dreiser's most recent biographer, Richard Lingeman, more accurately characterizes it: "as if he were prematurely writing Howells's obituary."[5] "The Real Howells" is written in essay form, and Howells does not speak back directly, as he does in the first interview. This second interview opens by dismissing Howells's writing through a backhanded compliment which claims that he "is greater than his volumes make him out to be" (p. 67). Dreiser commends Howells for his "sympathies" for the poor but notes his lack of experience of misery, praises him for his acute observations but notes that he "goes no further" and is "inclined to let the great analysis of things go by the boards" (p. 69).

Yet Dreiser purports to find these inadequacies compensated for by two related qualities, Howells's famous literary philanthropy and the warmth and sincerity of his character. Although Dreiser makes much of "this great literary philanthropist," such a designation relegates Howells to an earlier age of patronage. Whereas Dreiser indeed may have hoped through this glowing portrait to benefit from such philanthropy, he had elswhere satirized the image of Howells as a "look-out on the watch tower, straining for a glimpse of approaching genius" (p. 69). In an issue of *Ev'ry Month,* Dreiser wrote a caption under a picture of Abraham Cahan—the same example of a Howells discovery that he uses in this interview—which reads: "Mr. Howells has discovered a new 'great' novelist. . . . Critics do not, however, agree with Mr. Howells and it is now recalled that Mr. Howells once discovered a great Kentucky poet whose muse has not been heard of since. However, Mr. Cahan is fortunate in being discovered by so renowned a literary Columbus."[6] This caption suggests both the inadequacies and yet the market value of Howells's discoveries. While the interview reinforces Howells's stature as the "Dean of American letters," it undercuts his authority through the repeated use of markedly old-fashioned terms such as "dean," "nobleman," "character." It also suggests that while philanthropy may be as inappropriate to the market conditions of "today" as the rural print shop, Howells's philanthropy may be a prettified term for the modern patronage of the marketplace.

Dreiser concludes his second interview with the evaluation that "it does not matter whether Howells is the greatest novelist in the world or not, he is a great character." Dreiser uses the word "character" as

Howells does, for a figure "evidently so honest at heart that he is everywhere at home with himself, and will contribute that quiet, homelike atmosphere to everything and everybody around" (p. 67). Commenting on the anecdote about Montreal, Dreiser injects a doubt only to dismiss it:

> some may think that such open expression of sentiment and pleasure is like hanging one's heart upon one's sleeve for daws to peck at, but more will feel that it is but the creditable exuberance of a heart full of good feelings. He is thus frank in his books, his letters, his conversation. His family get no nearer in many things than those in the world outside who admire his charming qualities. He is the same constantly, a person whose thoughts issue untinged by any corroding wash of show or formality. (p. 70)

Although Howells becomes a representation of his own ideal of character, these qualities in Dreiser's hands sound quaint, unsuited to the changing society around him and to the publishing business, a world where "small things are no more." Dreiser notes that in contrast to Howells's honesty, "his field of endeavor is of that peculiar nature which permits of much and effective masquerading" (p. 70). In contrast to the foil of character he constructs in Howells, Dreiser himself enters a literary market more like the one Wharton confronted, in which the writer does not hang "one's heart upon one's" book jacket, but projects a personage as an objectified commodity. The literary market to Dreiser is a necessary masquerade in which the writer's character is indistinguishable from the changing mask of the book cover, a masquerade that took a myriad of forms in the apprenticeship of Theodore Dreiser.

II

It is well known that Dreiser followed the route of the urban journalist, a route rejected by Howells, and it is a commonplace that this apprenticeship initiated Dreiser into the underworld—so repellent to Howells—that provided Dreiser with raw material for his realistic novels.[7] Although Dreiser himself promoted this scenario in his autobiography, *Newspaper Days*, he also pointed to a stronger initial attraction to journalism. Whereas to middle-class writers such as Lincoln Steffens and David Graham Phillips, journalism may have confronted them with an uncushioned, brutal reality, for Dreiser, in contrast, the newspaper promised freedom from the streets he had been trodding daily as a collector for an easy-payment installment firm.[8] If Wharton sought in the work of writing an escape from the domestic idleness of the upper-class lady, Dreiser sought in writing an escape from work into the glamorous world of wealth and power. "Newspapers—somehow by their intimacy, seemed to be the swiftest approach to all of this of which I was dreaming," he wrote in retrospect and saw that he "confused inextricably, reporters with ambassadors and prominent men generally. Their lives were laid among great people, the rich, the famous, the powerful; and because of their position and facility of expression and mental force they were received everywhere as equals. Think of me, new, young, poor, being received in that way!"[9] The word "ambassador" suggests an interesting concept of representation that substitutes the figure of the writer for the words he writes, and raises the question of whom he represents to whom. Dreiser believed that the writer represents himself to the world he seeks to enter.

Dreiser's autobiography, not surprisingly, is structured around a narrative of disillusionment, from the promise of a glittering career in the Midwest to the disappointment of his short stint as a "legman" in New York, which left him sitting unemployed on a park bench, giving birth to the character of Hurstwood. But there is another, less obvious narrative in Dreiser's short career as a reporter. Although in retrospect Dreiser denounces the timid journalistic conventions and commercial interests which censored real news, in fact he adapted very well to these conventions and did become an ambassador of sorts. Most of his newspaper jobs cast him in promotional roles, which turned the reporter's writing into advertisements for the newspaper, and, when the advertisements were successful, promoted his own career in the market.

Dreiser's first newspaper position in 1891 was not as a reporter at all but as a temporary "clerk" for the *Chicago Herald*, distributing shoddy toys for the paper's Christmas campaign. In *Newspaper Days* Dreiser rails against such philanthropic crusades which cynically boosted circulation by exploiting young men, as needy as the recipients of the gifts. But this first promotional job was in many ways paradigmatic of the reporter's work on the newspaper. Dreiser obtained his first job as reporter on the *Chicago Globe* in exchange for peddling a novel written by one of the editors—"an immature imitation of *Tom Sawyer*"—by knocking on the doors of the girls who graduated from the editor's high school, a chore that replicated Dreiser's work as collector.

Dreiser's first series of feature articles for the same paper might be viewed as a more realistic muckraking that exposes urban vice: a crusade against fraudulent auction shops which, protected by the police, preyed on gullible country folk. Yet this campaign to close the shops also functioned as an advertisement by counterattacking the political enemies of the publisher, who used the articles "to call the attention of the public, via billboards, to what was going on in our columns" (p. 79). In addition, by contributing to the paper's prestige and growing circulation, Dreiser also boosted his own status as a reporter. He boasted of "personally serving warrants of arrest" and in almost every article mentioned his own participation, as in "Two of the squealers were yesterday taken to police headquarters by a Daily Globe reporter."[10] As the paper becomes the major actor in the drama it produces, even an attempt to bribe Dreiser becomes material for another story.

Although Dreiser charts his move from Chicago to St. Louis to Pittsburgh as growing evidence of his literary skills, his creativity developed not in opposition to the self-promotional techniques of the newspaper but in collusion with them. Dreiser's most successful story for the *St. Louis Republic* was a mock-heroic account of the preparations for an annual charity baseball game between two lodges, sponsored by the paper.[11] According to *Newspaper Days*, writing about such a nonevent both unleashed Dreiser's imagination for the first time and sparked the interest of people in the local community, who began to write congratulatory letters, thereby turning Dreiser into a "personage, especially in newspaper circles" (p. 231). Important citizens who liked to see their name in print invited him to their "mid-night smokers," and his editor encouraged him to write over ten more humorous articles about the preparations in order to boost attendance at the game. When Dreiser moved to St. Louis from Chicago in 1892, he feared that the dependence of the local papers on telegraphic news "did not promise much for a big feature, on which I might spread myself" (p. 97), but he did indeed "spread himself" by making up news, by turning a minor notice of a local event into a front-page drama. Dreiser's ability to write about an event before it occurred could prove to be a liability—as when he published a review, written in advance, of three plays that had been cancelled; his consequent humiliation led to his resignation from the *St. Louis Globe-Democrat*. Yet in his next job he turned this ability to write about nothing into a successful marketing device for himself and the paper. The popularity of his baseball series led to other promotional assignments such as his well-known trip to the World's Fair in Chicago, accompanying a group of female schoolteachers who had won a contest sponsored by the paper. Although in retrospect, Dreiser expressed embarrassment at riding in a carriage with a banner "advertising the nature of the expedition" (p. 245), his articles dutifully focused less on describing the fair than on the "*Republic*'s School Teachers" and their cute responses. Few paragraphs omit the name of the paper.[12]

Despite his later claim that his newspaper experience exposed him to a brutal urban reality censored by the narrowness of midwestern conventions, Dreiser played well to those conventions in his promotional role as reporter. He was delighted, for example, to participate in an advertising gimmick to verify the powers of a well-known medium, and even his more factual features about the construction of the public waterworks or the railroad depot read as forms of boosterism for the city of St. Louis.[13] When Dreiser arrived in Pittsburgh in 1894 he similarly adapted to the conventions he later decried as censorship. In *Newspaper Days* he tells of a city dampened by the aftermath of the Homestead strike, a city he never reported at the time, and he attributes the light tone of his articles to the powerful political censorship which demanded that he write about the "idle stuff which they could use in place of news" (p. 413). Yet his articles did more than fill space; they contributed to the paper's goal of downplaying the class violence that still structured city life. Many of his articles gently leveled class differences through universal "human interest" topics such as the rain which falls on the entire city, the feeling of "blue Monday" which hits workers and employers alike, the scraps of music that can be heard in doorways, and the literary aspirations of the "common man" represented nostalgically by "toll-gatherers and watchmen."[14] These features reinscribed the public arena of the city so recently marred by violent conflicts as a smaller and more intimate strife-free space. Although his stay in Pittsburgh is best known for his discovery of Balzac and realism, Dreiser characterized his first "dabbling in creative writing" not as realism but as the "mood or picture writing about the most trivial matters" he wrote for the censored *Dispatch* (p. 413). Throughout his apprenticeship, Dreiser's journalism reinforced what he later saw as stifling midwestern conventions, elaborating a cozy at-home tone, which mastered the violent qualities of urban life as a familiar community. Even his more lurid stories of crime and suffering in St. Louis, about a train wreck or a crazed man who killed his own children, borrowed from sentimental novels the comforting, familiar figure of the grieving mother.[15] Thus Dreiser's apprenticeship as a cub reporter might be reconceived not solely as an introduction to the American equivalent of the urban social upheaval he was reading about in Balzac. In addition, Dreiser was mastering journalistic conventions that constructed the real as a familiar locale or picturesque mélange for the promotion of the newspaper and its ambassador, the reporter.

During his early days as a reporter, Dreiser expressed discomfort with this promotional role, not by seeking to write of a more fundamental social reality than the one allowed by the papers, but by musing about the more traditional romantic figure of "the genius." His only known signed piece from this period, "The Return of Genius," tells the whimsical, Faustian tale of a young genius who longs for the success which will make him immediately wealthy and his name "assured for posterity."[16] The gods promise to fulfill all his desires on the condition that he "shalt not hear nor see [his] own glory" (p. 92). After living in a heavenly palace, where he receives reports of the world "written on sheets of pure gold" (p. 93), he restlessly longs to "see the world bow and smile, that I might feel its glances of admiration and hear its words of praise" (p. 93). The gods let him return, with the admonition that if he seeks such admiration, "then thy name dies with thee" (p. 94). This piece posits two alternative paths to making a name: the transcendent recognition that achieves immortality beyond and despite contemporary readership; and the need for an immediate performance to see one's own success in the eyes of an audience. Dreiser seems to choose the second avenue, the path of the contemporary market, when he mocks romantic notions of genius in several sketches for "Heard in the Corridors," a column conducted as an eavesdropping search for impromptu interviews with fictional celebrities in hotel lobbies. One piece parodies the figure of the budding poet who decides to "cap the climax and write an epic poem and then starve to death."[17] After losing his job as a collector, however, the poet decides to "ease up on literary work" and take a job as a traveling salesman "to have due assurance that I was going to eat regularly" (p. 131). This budding poet—given the name of one of Dreiser's former city editors and mentors—concludes: "I don't want to discourage any literary genius, but, by the way, I don't think real literary genius could be discouraged at all" (p. 131). Although the sketch debunks the romance of the starving artist who is discovered only posthumously, the ending maintains the transcendent notion of literary genius asserting itself despite material conditions. Dreiser similarly satirizes a fictional convention of poets as "the most ludicrous thing I ever ran across in my life," on the grounds that "true genius is a true and polished sphere, around which the world may gather to admire. But the other spheres cannot gather round. . . . Genius brooks no competition—acknowledges no peers."[18] If Dreiser opposed the competition of the market to the transcendence of genius, his writing in this period tried to fuse both spheres, in his desire both to "spread himself" on the unsigned pages of newsprint and to make an "undying name." The figure of "the genius" served the same ideological purpose that the professional did for Wharton—to imagine a way of entering the market while maintaining a distance from it. Dreiser did not reject the market in favor of a transcendent genius but redefined genius as the celebrity who could beat the market at its own game, who could compete so thoroughly as to defeat any competition.

If the figure of the genius posited a stance above a mass audience to whom he simultaneously appealed, the reporter faced another danger of sinking anonymously into that crowd. The star journalist may indeed enter those fashionable worlds inaccessible to his readers, as Dreiser suggested in a story about a society ball which starts with a description of the crowd lined up outside the hall: "All through the long evening hours the mass had gathered. Between the solid lines of anxious spectators they stepped, so gay of dress and heart, into the great resplendent hall and now they were to dance."[19] By implication the article differentiates the writer from the mass as he sweeps in with members of high society. Yet Dreiser often expressed the fear that his role as spectator aligned him less with the major performers than with the mass audience. A vivid symbol of this danger can be found in Dreiser's most successful "scoop" for the *St. Louis Herald.* After an explosion of an oil tank, "hundreds of sightseers" from neighboring villages drawn by "news of the burning wreck" became the victims of an even more horrific explosion, which charred many beyond recognition: "It was the sightseers from Alton, Ill., who suffered the loss of life and limb."[20] Dreiser's article about the wreck repetitively describes each burn victim's loss of an identifiable visage, descriptions that implicitly pose a question about his own role: how can the journalist, whom Dreiser often compares to a sightseer, avoid the same fate of being swallowed up by the event and losing his identity in the act of seeing? When his next article describes his retrieval of the names of the victims, it is as though he were also recuperating his own identity as an unmarred spectator.

One of Dreiser's only short stories about a reporter, "Nigger Jeff," also expresses this fear that the "hired spectator"—as the journalist is called in this story—may be submerged by the crowd.[21] A smug young urban reporter sent to witness an imminent lynching feels superior to the backwater townsmen in his sense of justice and dread of such unleashed violence. But the lynch mob is depicted less as bloodthirsty actors than primarily as a crowd of spectators, excited as is the reporter by the spectacle, and they parody the reporter's search for information in their "chorus of 'whos,' 'wheres' and 'whens'" (p. 81). The reporter is at first swept up by the fervor of the mob, and then set apart by his horror at the actual hanging, a response that evolves into the aesthetic distance of the artist who resolves at the end to "get it all in" (p. 111). According to

June Howard, this story treats the problematics of spectatorship that necessarily makes the writer socially ineffective and remote from the very events he observes and portrays.[22] Yet the writer's distance might be seen, instead, as a solution to an even more threatening problem: as "hired spectator," the journalist may become indistinguishable from his mass audience of sightseers or lynchers.

A more material threat drawing the reporter into the masses was the increasingly industrialized nature of newspaper work, which made Dreiser a laborer "out of sympathy with laborers" (*Newspaper Days*, p. 110). Where both Howells and Wharton valued writing as productive work, as opposed to the idleness of the aristocracy and the consumption of the masses, Dreiser made an effort throughout his career to distinguish writing from labor. What he valued in newspaper work was the leisure it afforded him to frequent hotel lobbies and gossip with important people (p. 140); or the status of the feature writer, at the top of the reporters' pyramid, that gave him the opportunity to write the "idle stuff" he associated with "creative writing." This need to dissociate writing from work stemmed both from his own class background and the changing conditions in the production of writing. Tramping the streets in search of news was not that different for Dreiser from collecting installment payments. More important, editors wielded the power both to dictate the content and to rewrite the form of the story. Indeed the attraction of the nonevent for Dreiser lay not only in imaginative freedom but in a relative degree of freedom from the editor's control. The limited attraction of journalism as labor was also evident in the fact that although Dreiser was seeking a name in the glamorous "Age of the Reporter," most of his articles were unsigned.

The lack of power and autonomy in journalism, as well as the small salary, led Dreiser away from St. Louis in 1894 in two directions, one nostalgic, the other more forward-looking. He was persuaded by a colleague to become a partner in purchasing a dying country newspaper in Weston, Ohio, out of nostalgia for a home he never had and desire for security and autonomy. Yet he found there only a decrepit press, like a ruin from Howells's youth, and a small town, which, treating the paper as a voice of narrow local interests, had no intention of supporting it through advertising. In contrast to Howells's Hubbard, Dreiser had no desire or opportunity to reorganize the paper around the "modern conception" and immediately left for a city job.

Although Dreiser later called this venture an "interlude between an old and a new life" (p. 370), it committed him briefly to a rural family life that he had never experienced before directly. His real "home"—that is, his broken-up family—ironically lay in New York City. His brother, Paul Dresser, a popular songwriter, had urged him to move to the city where "one might do, think, act more freely than anywhere else"; there Paul was persuaded that Dreiser would "be discovered" for his genius, and Dreiser was enticed with stories about star reporters such as Stanley and Kipling (p. 454). But after a short time in New York, Dreiser saw that he had moved from the inaccessible idyll of Howells's youth to one of the most industrialized institutions of writing. He finally found a position as a "legman," whose job was to collect the facts which another man would write up and who was paid not for his product but for his time. If Howells could describe his apprenticeship in artisanal terms which gave him hands-on control over all aspects of the writing process, Dreiser ended the first stage of his apprenticeship in an industry which did not even allow him to use his hands to write, where "such men as myself were mere machines or privates in an ill-paid army to be thrown into any breach" (p. 487). Dreiser's short-lived newspaper days enacted the contradictions that Howells rejected, between journalism as a glamorous profession which turns the reporter into one of the celebrities he writes about, and the industrialization of news production which turns the reporter into an unskilled laborer. Dreiser entered journalism to become an ambassador for himself, to make an "undying name," only to promote himself as a nameless ambassador for the newspaper, and he left the profession proletarianized, sitting on a park bench as a member of the nameless crowd.

III

If the New York newspapers reduced Dreiser to an industrial worker subject to a highly specialized division of labor, the next stage of his apprenticeship might appear as an adequate compensation, by giving him control over all aspects of the production of a new magazine, *Ev'ry Month*. His official capacity was "editor and arranger," as noted on the title page, but his small budget also made him the writer for the first issues, reviewer, advertising agent, and designer.[23] Editing, however, placed Dreiser in a contradictory, if familiar, role. His own control over the production was subordinate to the main purpose of the magazine: to promote the new music-publishing firm, Howley, Haviland and Company, of which Paul Dresser owned one-third. At the centerpiece of each issue lay the sheet music for the kinds of sentimental ballads written by Paul about lost loves, nostalgia for home, girls gone wrong in the city, and the good mother waiting at home. Although the songs may have been sentimental and nostalgic, their production grew out of the modernization of the "sheet music business [which] was undergoing a rapid transformation from cottage industry to mass-production operation."[24] Whereas popular songs had formerly endured for years through informal modes of transmission, the 1890s witnessed the phenomenon of the "hit," akin to the new best-sellers of the period. The hit was carefully orchestrated by a network of promotional techniques which Dreiser described in "Whence the Song," including the hiring of a host of "arrangers," paying singers on the vaudeville circuit to plug the song, as well as bribing organ-grinders on city streets.[25] Imitating the popular cheap monthlies of the 1890s, such as *Munsey's* and *Ladies' Home Journal*, Dreiser's magazine extended this promotional network from the arena of public entertainment into the parlor. At a time when the upright piano was becoming a standard fixture of the middle-class home, the magazine was cultivating a new, nonprofessional popular market for sheet music. If Dreiser himself served as a promotional link in the chain for his company, he employed others in the same way by doing regular features on popular artists which allowed him to fill his magazine with free illustrations, and by using advertising pamphlets from theaters and publishers, along with the photos of celebrities they distributed. The nature of the magazine can be seen in its cover design, which Joseph Katz compares revealingly to an array of shop windows whose contents Dreiser had to dress each month.[26]

Thus as editor, Dreiser played a similar, though less lucrative, role to that of his brother, the third partner of the firm. Dreiser later described Paul's contribution as a live advertisement, walking down Broadway, back-slapping, frequenting bars where he made friends and courted celebrities of the stage and sporting arena like himself. These activities had the effect of "attracting by his personality such virtuosi of the vaudeville and comedy stage as were likely to make the instrumental publications of his firm a success."[27] Paul contributed to the firm not so much a business sense, according to Theodore, as a personage, one who, by drawing vaudeville stars around him, simultaneously promoted his interest in the firm and an interest in himself as a minor celebrity.

Biographers have explored Dreiser's ambivalent relationship to his brother, caused in part by jealousy of Paul's success and Theodore's resentment at being dependent on him. But this ambivalence also was directed toward the nature of Dresser's art. Just as Dreiser turned Howells into a figure for genteel culture—at once authoritative and outdated, his brother became a figure for sentimental commercial culture, from which Dreiser was equally concerned to distinguish himself. Dreiser not only labeled his brother's songs sentimental and attributed their popularity to their "wide appeal to the heart," but he identified Paul by his warmth to his mother and by his own tender, motherly qualities. Although later in his life, Dreiser was to marvel at their affinities despite their great intellectual differences and Paul's thoroughly middle-class and sentimental values, at this stage of Dreiser's career he was attempting to disavow those affinities precisely because of the similarities in their conception of art. Even before *Ev'ry Month*, the trajectory of Theodore's career paralleled Paul's, who began his theatrical experience in a traveling medicine show just as Theodore started his newspaper work by distributing Christmas toys for a newspaper. Both started out as artists in promotional roles at different stages of the development of mass culture.

Evidence of Paul's threatening qualities can be found in Dreiser's first fictional use of Paul's name, in a sketch for "Heard in the Corridors," which starts with a "Paul Dresser" refusing the offer of a cigar from "a coterie of genials in the parlor" of a hotel. "Paul" then explains how as foreman in a powder mill he once made the mistake of smoking on the job while talking to a "steady promising young man" who worked under him. The young man's clothes caught fire and he burned to death, which led Paul to harbor a sense of criminal guilt: "The young man was so bright and promising that it seemed all the worse to have him die in that manner."[28] In this gratuitous choice of Paul Dresser as a character it is hard not to imagine the young man as Theodore. Why did Dreiser view Paul as a mortal threat to his own potential? What was the danger Dreiser saw in a brother whom he continually referred to as so tearfully good-hearted? This danger can be glimpsed in later anecdotes in "My Brother Paul" about Paul's generosity when, for example, he humiliates a beggar through a practical joke, at the same time that he gives him charity, or when he intercedes on behalf of an imprisoned young man from his hometown, who wrote to him after hearing one of his songs; Paul succeeds in having his death sentence commuted to a life sentence, a favor whose value Dreiser questions. Thus Dreiser seemed to see in Paul's sentimentality both cruelty to the recipients of his charity and an ultimate ineffectualness. In fact, Paul's appeal to the heart, which made his music so popular, appeared ultimately self-serving, advertising his own good heart. To Dreiser, Paul's culture of sentiment had a self-referential quality, similar to that of the new journalism, whose social campaigns worked to increase circulation.

Dreiser's two-year employment as editor of *Ev'ry Month* gave him both a form and a forum in which to explore his own relationship to the popular culture represented by his brother Paul. On the one hand, he identified his own writing with Paul's motherly aesthetic and implicitly with his female audience. On the other hand, he used the magazine to denounce the institutions of mass culture in which his magazine participated, and thereby elevated himself above his female consumers. Early in his editorship his alliance with Paul can be seen through his choice of pseudonyms. Since Dreiser wrote most of the articles, they had to appear under different names, but as in the name he used for his first signed article for the *Globe*—Carl Dreiser—most of his names were taken from his family; he used combinations of his brothers' names, such as Ed Al, and the initials of his fiancée for the sentimental pieces in the magazine. Thus the articles in *Ev'ry Month*, in contrast to the unsigned articles of the newspapers, gave Dreiser the opportunity to make a public name for himself on a masthead and to participate in the masquerade of mass culture (from which he excludes Howells). But Dreiser curiously masked himself in an amalgamation of family names, as though to root himself in a stable identity, as Paul did in the nostalgia for a lost home in his songs.

If Dreiser, like his brother, participated in the promotional machinery of the magazine, he also attempted to elevate himself above this machine in the regular column that introduced the magazine, "Reflections," which was signed "The Prophet." The very choice of this signature elevated him above the sentimental familial bonds implied in his other psuedonyms; by identifying himself with an older, oracular mode of address, he became a figure for the writer more akin to the genius, who both transcends the cheap print medium in which he is writing and speaks oracularly to the generalized future rather than in the intimate tones of the contemporary editor. Indeed one of his columns argued vehemently against the claims of the press that "oratory is dead," supplanted by the medium of print, a medium he earlier had called "trade, the facilities for buying and selling paper that has been written on."[29] The tone of "The Prophet" attempted to resurrect this figure of the orator within the masquerade of print.

Although the "Reflections" column has been mined by critics for Dreiser's developing theories of social Darwinism and art, it is equally rich in references to the institutions of mass culture, references that can be read as a process of self-definition within and against those practices. Throughout *Ev'ry Month*, Dreiser not only repeatedly attacked the newspaper world which rejected him but he also criticized the world of popular music and theater which he was hired to promote. Toward the end of his tenure at the magazine he wrote, for example, that "the vaudeville, like the new journalism, is but a passing show. Only the really high and good can endure," and he published Arthur Henry's satire of comic opera accompanied by a photograph of Paul in a scene from such an opera.[30] Yet "The Prophet," we shall see, did not merely rail against commercialized mass culture, he also established his own conception of popular art within that culture.

Two of his columns curiously treat both the evils of the press and the tendency of wealthy American women to ignore budding young geniuses. Commenting on "the recent marriages of a daughter of the House of Gould and a daughter of the House of Vanderbilt to noblemen of Europe," "The Prophet" chastises wealthy American matrons for not being "patrons" of American artists. "American girls" he complains, "are introduced and trained among snobs, are taught to pray with eyes turned Europeward, and are eventually wedded to the highest bidder, while the genius of our land wanders on neglected."[31] In the next section of the same column "The Prophet" comments wryly on how the *Times* "raised its languishing circulation of 15,000 to 95,000 simply by telling how girls worked in small, narrow, ill-lighted rooms" (p. 39). Such crusades about "man's inhumanity to man" merely work as sentimental fads to serve commercial ends. Six months later, "The Prophet" similarly rails against the new journalism "filled to overflowing with money changers of the most grasping and rapacious kind," and in the same column laments the fate of the young genius who "dreams of a brilliant future in these sharply contested days of business. . . . There is many a brilliant young nobody, who at twenty-six years old imagines that he is dying unrecognized because he has not attained fame, nor the love of some bright, dashing, beautiful and wealthy girl." This "great man in poverty" is usually "possessed of a wealth of knowledge . . . which will not circulate."[32] In both columns, Dreiser attacks two strange bedfellows, the organs of the mass media and wealthy, marriageable girls; the only common bond seems to be a conspiracy against the American genius.

This collusion between mass cultural institutions and upper-class snobbery can be seen in another column on the state of the American theater. Dreiser endorses the criticism of the decline of the theater into vaudeville, "something that is meaningless and showy. Nonsensical humor, paltry music, the most flippant of jesters—these are the desired and the financially befriended. There is no love for anything serious—that is, no great popular love. It is all variety—variety, variety, variety—until one wishes that the 'spice of life' phrase had never been thought of or promulgated."[33] Speaking in the lofty tone of one committed to the high art of serious drama, "The Prophet" then turns around to criticize the criticizers, the "respectable element" that "refuses to recognize the stage" because of the "rag-tag element that hangs onto it" (pp. 101–2). Indeed most of his venom is hurled at the "pharisaism" of the "so-called better element" who shut their eyes and ears to the "all but divine voices that are preaching a message no less important to the race than those emanating from the rostrum and the pulpit" (p. 102). Here he not only identifies his own prophetic preaching with serious drama but puts the blame for the disintegration of the stage less on vaudeville than on those "diamond begirded matrons" who crowd a metropolitan opera house "because it is fashionable" (p. 102). Like Wharton and Howells, Dreiser dissociates "serious art" both from the conspicuous consumption of a new aristocracy and from the working-class fare of "variety." Yet for Dreiser the middle ground between these two extremes is neither the realism of commonsense art and morality nor a professional identity, but a "genius": "great massive men, strong of intellect, high in ideals, who have worked and slaved for their art" (p. 101). In these columns, Dreiser reverts to his romantic notion of the artist as genius who transcends both the evanescent variety of popular culture and the conspicuous consumption of the wealthy. Indeed Dreiser's own signature and stance as "The Prophet" enact this ignored voice in the wilderness. (It is easy to imagine readers of the magazine skipping over the ponderous introductions to get to the music.)

Although Dreiser's "Prophet" seems to reinforce the critical distinction between the serious artist and the hack, he does not disdainfully condescend to his readership but seeks their engagement in his own definition of the popular; and his voice can be as intimate and chatty as it is aloof and ponderous. His ideal artist is not a genius whose epics would be discovered posthumously, or an orator who speaks to an empty house, for the genius, as he wrote earlier, "returns to men." One column deflates the common image of the artist's "retiring disposition" and argues instead that "an artist should be a man of general culture and so exert an influence in the avenues outside his own profession." The same column argues against the notion that special "knowledge" is required to appreciate great art; instead, the key to art appreciation is the "responsive heart"—"we are all connoisseurs if we are right-hearted."[34] Thus Dreiser's genius, like the orator and the prophet, must appeal to a popular audience, one he separates from both the audience manipulated by commercial journalism and the audience excluded from elite culture, but one which in fact incorporates elements of the sentimental culture of the heart to which Paul's songs appealed.

Dreiser combines elements of sentimentalism and consumerism to develop his own notion of realism. In the second issue of *Ev'ry Month,* he argues that "an instance in point of the assertion made in these columns once before, that those painters and sculptors who desire to gain enduring fame must paint and carve the scenes of today, is furnished by brilliant Broadway—and a furnishing store at that."[35] If he claims elsewhere that anyone can understand art because the artist himself is part of the workaday world, here he describes the common setting: Broadway. "In Broadway is everything: windows adorned with rare paintings and crowded with aged bric-à-brac; windows filled with rarest gems and gaudiest trifles, all displayed 'neath a hundred electric bulbs to attract attention" (p. 43). If Broadway brings together all commodities under the same leveling glare of electric lights, it also gathers all forms of "humanity . . . crowding itself here before a poster and there before a window." The "cosmopolitan, dallying crowd" appears to Dreiser not as a threatening mob, nor as automatons classified according to occupation as they are in Poe's "Man of the Crowd." Instead they come together as spectators and can be categorized according to the windows at which they stop to gaze.[36] "In Broadway, then, before many trifles, dawdle the mob, and from the size of the crowd and quality of the display one may infer that which is dearest to the popular heart" (p. 43). In delineating this popular heart, Dreiser too is seeking that middle ground between elite and mass art charted by Howells. Dreiser does not mourn the lack of an audience for the classics, as only "one lone onlooker" stops before "a painting of nine muses in classic garb." And the same sentence notes that "before a poster of the latest dancer in red and white some two or three pause momentarily" (p. 43). The variety show, like the classics, cannot command attention for too long. More admirers "linger" to "study" a modern form of art, Frederic Remington's painting of a western cowboy, and a statue of his in Tiffany's. Remington, also used as an example of a genius neglected by wealthy matrons, is here given due recognition by the crowd of onlookers. The duration of the time they spend—that they linger—as well as the fact that they "study the slightest details" indicates that his art appeals to intellect. But this is not the most popular attraction.

The largest crowd in this sketch surrounds the window of a haberdasher, in which, "quite the most glaring of any, with its hundred lights and neckties of yellow and red, was hung recently a copy of the painting by Delorme, entitled 'The Blacksmith'—a $50,000 production, though no placard said so" (p. 43). Dreiser describes the audience as much as the painting, and portrays a crowd of "an average mixture of men and women, workingmen and men of leisure, all deeply serious and gaining no little satisfaction from their observation of this work" (p. 44). The crowd is drawn into a sense of community through the experience of looking, which they share aloud through their comments. They are attracted by the realistic detail—"the thousand and one minute details which the artist had carefully worked in, filling every nook and cranny" (p. 44). Yet this realism is enhanced by the "pang of sentiment" produced by the "daub of green as of trees and flowers, through the rude window, where the white daylight contrasted so strangely with the smoky glare of the forge opposite" (p. 44). The painting similarly is an amalgam of old and new; though Dreiser calls it a modern subject, it depicts a lone rural artisan.

Dreiser's example of true popular art embodies a revealing contradiction between the content and the context in which it is displayed, a contradiction that can be seen in the window within the window. In the painting, nature outside the rude window contrasts conventionally with the darkness of work inside the shed; the work takes place in a natural setting which promises refreshment from physical labor at the forge. Dreiser finds a lesson in this scene: in the "free, serious, willing expression" on the face of the smith is the "evident moral of content in necessity" (p. 44). Yet the message of the painting is contradicted by the context in which it is displayed, as the content contrasts markedly with the city streets. The spectators are window-shoppers and the painting is a copy of a luxury item, which Dreiser makes clear by his own inside knowledge—"a $50,000 production, though no placard said so." Although the onlookers of different classes unite in their "observation of this work," most of course could not afford to own such a painting, nor as city dwellers could they reenter this lost rural world which arrests their gaze. The placement of the painting in the window of the haberdashery invites the onlookers to participate in the pleasure of looking as it obviously excludes them from ownership. Furthermore, the very act of looking at this painting in a Broadway window embodies an opposition to the producer ethos which the blacksmith himself represents: "content in necessity." According to another "Reflections" column, the urban equivalents of the blacksmith, those whose "days are all toil," are not contented with necessities but are "hounded by their desire to taste a few of life's pleasures and by those who wish to sell them the mockery of these exorbitantly."[37] Window-shopping fuels the "all-possessing desire to rush forward and join with the countless throng . . . to see the endless lights, the great shops and stores, the towering structures and palatial mansions."[38] Thus one of Dreiser's earliest statements about realism, "the scenes of today," reveals a contradiction at the heart of his own aesthetic and his conception of the role of the realist. Like "The Blacksmith," Dreiser appeals to an older system of meaning—to the prophet, orator, and genius; but by virtue of withdrawing from the commercial market and setting himself above it, he also seeks recognition from that mass audience that crowds around his work displayed in a shop window.

The magazine *Ev'ry Month,* like the painting "The Blacksmith," combines an appeal to nostalgia—for domesticity rather than work—with the practice of marketing products for the new woman (two of the magazine's most repeated advertisements are for pianos and bicycles). Regular columns at the end of each issue advise women who have new leisure time—"readers who may happen to be young married women with time on their hands, or girls living at home without any special duties"—how to create a "cozy corner," how to turn packing cases into furniture, how to decorate a "real home," how to make up an "honest bedroom" rather than use the folding beds of a makeshift boardinghouse.[39] This advice at the end of each issue implies that the "real home" is no more immediately accessible than the blacksmith at the forge, but that this home can be taught and reestablished in a new urban context under the tutelage of an anonymous advice column. Dreiser's concept of popular realism involves this duality as well. He envisions art forms—whether in painting, literature, or music—that have spontaneous and immediate access to the heart, and that circulate through preindustrial practices, like the tune whistled on street corners. But the success of modern art-forms also depends on a complex promotional machine—on booking agents, arrangers, organ-grinders, and the magazine which he himself edits. Or in the case of paintings and sculpture, the artworks must decorate shop windows as reproductions. "The Blacksmith" shares with Dreiser's editing and writing not a reverence for craftsmanship but a practice of promotion, a mode of calling popular attention to itself by serving as an advertisement on Broadway.

IV

The painting of "The Blacksmith" encased in the haberdasher's window is emblematic of the free-lance articles Dreiser was to write at the next stage of his career for O. S. Marden's *Success* magazine, whose stated aim was to inspire young men with examples of public figures who rose to prominence through "the application of industry and will-power."[40]

Just as the older work ethic of the craftsman is recontextualized as a new kind of advertisement on Broadway, the message of Dreiser's interviews with businessmen, scientists, and artists is the subordination of work to marketing. Like the sentimentality of "The Blacksmith," work in *Success* is imbued with a nostalgia that marks its impotence but that also gives it the authority to stamp a venture with value. Dreiser's interviews do not simply devalue work but revalue or reencode it as a form of salesmanship. Dreiser saw his own decision to free-lance as a form of marketing; "one day it occurred to him that he was wasting time 'fixing up other fellows' articles'," he told his first biographer, "Why not market his own? He could see that magazine readers were asking for lively stories about real people and things. They would take him nearer to his heart's desire—to write about life as he saw it."[41] For Dreiser to write about real life was also to learn how to sell that version of reality.

Most of Dreiser's interviews for *Success* open with the question of whether the keynote to success lies in innate ability or external opportunity, and most offer the solution of hard work to bridge any gap between those alternatives. The narrative that follows, however, usually counterbalances "industry" with another element, not the luck and patronage of the Horatio Alger myth, but the more calculated capacity to take advantage of opportunity through shrewd marketing. Philip Armour, for example, typically roots his success in his work on the family farm and country store, conditions no longer relevant to the need of outwitting modern competitors in the expanding packing industry. The stories that do illustrate his successful "work," in contrast, show his "mobilization of energy" to take advantage of the oncoming depressions in the financial market in 1864 and 1894.[42] While marketing may be an obvious asset for the businessman, Dreiser also shows that the scientist, Edison, develops his "inner gift" neither merely through hard work, nor through the accident of intuition, but through a diligent awareness "of the practical need of, and demand for, a machine, before expending time and energy on it." Edison keeps "strictly within the lines of commercially useful inventions" rather than "put on electrical wonders, valuable only as novelties to catch the popular fancy."[43] Thus in the case of both Armour and Edison their innate capacity for either business or science must be realized through work, which itself, however, remains incomplete without the capacity to market their products.

An interview with Andrew Carnegie makes clear that the worker must market himself as well as his product.[44] In a typical declaration of the importance of industry, Carnegie laments the difference between the younger generation of businessmen who have janitors to serve them and the older who swept the floors themselves. While he concludes that the aspiring young man should therefore occasionally pick up a broom, more important than such homely diligence is that the "rising man must do something exceptional, and beyond the range of his special department. He must attract attention" (p. 163). Carnegie suggests a difference between performing duties and performing "to show invincible determination to rise" (p. 163). The point here is not just to work harder to fulfill one's ambitions, but to call attention to oneself by advertising ambition as marketable in itself. The necessity for such self-promotion is suggested by an interview with Chauncey M. Depew, who notes that the main difference between contemporary conditions and those of his generation is that "we had to make the places and call ourselves to the tasks. Today a man fits himself and is called."[45] As historians of success have shown, the ideology of the self-made man who founds his own business had to be adjusted for the man whose place was behind the desk of a corporation. This new form of self-making requires, as Carnegie suggests, that one do something exceptional in order to be called to fit a corporate place. The repeated question in Dreiser's interviews about whether young people today have as many opportunities as their elders attests less to the helpfulness of the older generation than to skepticism about the relevance of their espousal of thrift and hard work; the question suggests anxiety about competition in the market over places for which a young man might "fit himself."

This anxiety extends in Dreiser's interview beyond the business and professional worlds to the world of art. Many of Dreiser's articles about artists, both in *Success* and other magazines, raise the question of whether hard work or clever marketing makes the artist, and some of Dreiser's most striking examples of the centrality of self-promotion can be seen in his interviews with artists and writers. Many of his articles start by displaying the "high market value" of the artist's work, whether indicated by the gifts of jewels surrounding the diva, Lillian Nordica, the high bidding by newspaper syndicates for the illustrator, Homer Davenport, or the list of prices commanded by Alfred Stieglitz's prints. Although Dreiser explains, for example, that "a great photograph is worth years of labor to make," he also emphasizes that Stieglitz "attracted attention by constantly securing an artistic photograph of something never before attempted."[46] Stieglitz's success resembles Carnegie's advice: call attention to your work by performing an unprecedented act. Dreiser in addition traces the abandonment of a traditional form of artistic preparation—such as Howells's imitation of the masters—for a quicker entry into the market. Nordica, for example, rejects the advice of her old singing teacher to study hard in private for many years and only then to enter the operatic world where she will be recognized immediately for her true talent. Instead she follows the advice of a younger teacher, who introduces her to the "right people," secures her a position traveling with a popular band, until she arrives at the point where she can discuss "terms" with the most prestigious opera companies.[47]

An underlying conflict recurs throughout Dreiser's articles on art between the relative value of making and marketing. This conflict can be seen in "He Became Famous in a Day," about the young sculptor Paul Weyland Bartlett.[48] The stated purpose of the article is to reveal the real story behind what the papers said, that Bartlett became famous in a day for his exhibition of hundreds of small bronze sculptures in the Paris Salon, and to show instead what the article's subhead declares: "Success Won by Toilsome Effort." In tracing the inception of this effort, Dreiser notes that Bartlett realized "his work might be good, but what of it? Paris is filled with artists of talent" (p. 244). The key was not to produce better work but to find a scheme for drawing attention to his work, which was apt, "along with hundreds of others . . . to rest unnoticed among the vast collection" (p. 243). For a solution, Bartlett does not risk his reputation on one large piece but enters over a hundred miniature bronzes (permitted in such a large number because of their size), which he made "after years of preparation, and months and months of particular and painstaking toil" (p. 244). This toil produced its rewards, as the case "containing his exquisite bronzes was the talk of the exhibition. Hundreds stopped to admire" (p. 244). As in the description of Stieglitz's photography, labor is important, though it is subordinated to the goal of making a splash, of promoting one's art. "Mr. Bartlett had done good work before this. Indeed he had considerable standing as a sculptor, but it had not crystallized into that thing called fame until this bright idea was carried out" (p. 244). Like "The Blacksmith" in the window, Paul Bartlett is a craftsman who casts his own bronzes and knows the value of hard work. In writing the article, Dreiser does reveal the hard work that contributed to overnight fame, but he also inverts a traditional causal relation to show that labor itself did not generate recognition, but that hard work was generated by the scheme of how to make a name in the Paris Salon.

If the question of what contributes to success involves how to draw attention to oneself, the practice of the interview is part of the answer. Dreiser's later reminiscence about his work for *Success* noted that great men love to talk about themselves;[49] he could have also noted that writers equally love to write about great men to share their spotlight. The interview is based on a kind of tautology: a person is interviewed because everyone knows he is a celebrity but the interview is part of the mechanism that creates that assumption. Many interviews start with a double-edged introduction, referring to common knowledge about the celebrity's prominence and to the exclusivity of this particular interview, thus calling attention to the reporter's special access to this figure. We read, for example, that "The name Choate carries the flavor of law," or that Anthony Hope is already known for "achieving distinction easily," or that Clarence Stedman has already been written about by many others, or that the sculptor, J. Q. A. Ward, has been placed "conspicuously and deservedly in the public favor." The interviewer countermands this reference to commonplace knowledge with an implied or explicit reference to his own special "scoop," as in Dreiser's claim to "unveil" the real Armour, who shuns publicity. Dreiser faithfully followed Marden's orders, which he later made fun of, to go beyond Samuel Smiles's "rehashed hearsay about these noble go-getters" and instead to employ the newly accepted technique of the interview to get the real facts: "to go personally to each of these and wheedle or extort from them the truth about their early struggles" (Pizer, p. 273). Interviews often start with a story of Dreiser's heroic efforts in tracking down the celebrity, or with a detailed description of his home or inner office. The journalist both invites the reader into a scene of intimate contact with the celebrity and makes the reader aware of the exclusivity of this scene and the remoteness of the personage, made available only through the special access of the journalist.

Both Dreiser and his biographers have suggested that he handled the theme of success ironically, slightly undermining the figures and myths which his articles were meant to glorify. But even Dreiser's occasional irony works to enhance the glamour of the celebrity. Several critics have pointed out, in one of his first assignments, Dreiser's ironic treatment of the lawyer Joseph Choate who, like many interviewed for *Success*, claims that he "never met a great man who was born rich."[50] Dreiser follows this with the comment, "This remark seemed rather striking in a way, because of the fact that Mr. Choate's parents were not poor in the accepted sense. The family is rather distinguished in the New England annals" (p. 122). While Dreiser may indeed undercut the ideology of hard work and character as the route to success, he participates in framing a new ideology of what Susman has called "personality," of treating Choate less as an example to follow than a celebrity to envy.[51] The interview starts by noting that, because the lawyer is too busy with important affairs during the day, he agrees to see the reporter at home. Choate then spouts the clichés of industriousness, abstinence, and frugality, with his back turned to Dreiser, who is busy describing something different: the grand atmosphere of the room and the tone of this imposing figure who enhances his authority by answering with his back turned to the audience. When Dreiser reworks this material in "The Real Choate" he is even more overtly critical of Choate's egotism, his lack of heart, and his shrewd and sarcastic manner. He attributes his ascendancy to "chance of location. . . . New York is half the battle—talent the other half. This city whose word of approval lends prestige to so many forms of effort throughout the land—how much has it given to this one of its many favorites?"[52] Yet despite its reproach, Dreiser's article itself participates in producing that "word of approval." By criticizing Choate's selfish pursuit of wealth, women, and fame, Dreiser makes him glamorous. Debunking a public figure because of that person's own self-promotion can serve as an even greater homage than the more traditional praise of self-sacrifice for the community. As in the interview with Howells, the overwhelming sense of many of Dreiser's articles is of the great distance between successful men like Choate and the conditions now for a younger generation. Many of the figures Dreiser interviews serve less as exemplars of hard work to emulate than as subjects created in the market to envy.

Thus if Dreiser subverts Marden's stated intentions for his magazine, it is not to undermine the cult of success but to redefine it in a direction in which Marden himself was moving. The masthead of *Success* read, "Work, Sagacity, Honesty, Truth, Courage and Energy." The last term may be linked less to a nineteenth-century producer ethos than to a later emphasis on self-help and New Thought, or Susman's culture of personality. "Energy," a word evoked often by Dreiser, is different from the other terms because, unlike work or truth which have an object, energy refers to a drive which is objectless, an attribute of self-projection which refers back to that self. Yet Dreiser also links energy to its etymology as a rhetorical term, the power to move and persuade men through speech. Dreiser often refers to oratory in his interviews, discussing Depew's oratorical training, noting that Armour "would have preferred to be a great orator rather than a great capitalist," and interviewing Frank Gunsaulas, the preacher who headed the Armour Institute, and who argues explicitly that his aim is to convince young men that their opportunities are not dwarfed by corporations.[53] Dreiser's interest in oratory and energy can be understood as another transposition of an older set of values and significations into a modern context.[54] Energy serves less the purpose of persuading and moving men to action than it does of standing above the crowd and calling attention to the self.

Dreiser's fullest portrait of an energetic young man can be found in "The Color of Today," an obituary for the young painter William Louis Sonntag, whom critics have seen as an early model for Dreiser's realism.[55] But the overwhelming impression of this essay is of Sonntag's frenetic energy, of someone constantly seeking to perform a new and astonishing act, regardless of the medium, whether simulating a miniature-train crash which can be photographed on a life-size scale, or running off to illustrate the Spanish-American War. Sonntag, however, also craved the equally conspicuous sanction of older forms of status, insisting on his baronial ancestry and his acceptance into a host of clubs. Dreiser's article stresses his intimacy with Sonntag, who is known to be important by virtue of his own contact with celebrities—Kipling visits his studio. Thus "The Color of Today" refers less to Sonntag's realistic work than to his work of promoting his exceptional yet eminently acceptable self-images.

V

The legendary first publication of *Sister Carrie* shows that Dreiser did not apply to his own career as a novelist the lesson of marketing which his *Success* articles taught.[56] By insisting that Doubleday publish his first novel against their will, he was able to commit them legally to the publication of the book but not to its promotion, which led to its poor showing in the market. A suggestive article by Christopher Wilson has revised the story of Doubleday's "suppression" of *Sister Carrie*. This was not a question of the unconventional Dreiser resisting moral censorship, but of his resistance to having his career managed by Doubleday, whose chief editor indeed expressed interest in publishing Dreiser's work but on their terms—which did not include issuing *Sister Carrie* as a first novel.[57] This management would have resulted in the kind of symbiotic promotional relationship in which Dreiser participated as a reporter for various newspapers and as editor of *Ev'ry Month*. Doubleday would have promoted him as a young author, who, like Frank Norris and Stephen Crane, would have served as an advertisement for a young publishing company. Yet by insisting on Doubleday's production of the novel on his own terms, Dreiser in effect withdrew both his career and his work from the market.

It is commonly assumed that Dreiser suffered a nervous breakdown following the disappointing reception of *Sister Carrie*. But as many critics have noted, *Sister Carrie* did receive good critical reviews, which led to its successful reissue in England two years later. In the unfinished manuscript *An Amateur Laborer*, written in 1904, Dreiser attributed his breakdown not to critical rejection but to finding himself "unable to write a line or to earn a living by my pen."[58] This loss led not only to a material crisis in his life but to an extreme loss of identity as well. Whereas the doctors diagnosed his neurasthenia as the result of some hidden shock, he diagnosed the shock as his sudden inability to "accomplish any saleable results," after supporting himself as a journalist for several years (p. 11). In contrast to the doctor's prescription of drugs and the diverting entertainment of the theater—neither of which his patient could afford—Dreiser himself prescribed manual labor. In the manuscript he describes his search for work as a matter of necessity: "I found myself bereft of the power of earning a living with my mind and was compelled to turn to my hands" (p. 4). This necessity, however, is also represented as a choice, as a form of therapy, the "change I needed, something to divert my mind from its old course, a new form of labor such as manual toil" (p. 5).

Why did Dreiser choose manual labor as the route to health, income, and the restoration of his former identity as a successful writer? While he posited manual work as the natural alternative for a neurasthenic writer with a block, his narrative also presented other alternatives, such as the financial support of his relatives; and it was his brother Paul who rescued him repeatedly, first by sending him to a sanatorium, then by supplementing his laborer's meager income, and finally by securing him a job writing again for the *Daily News*. It might seem that Dreiser turned to manual labor out of nostalgia for the maxims of hard work and honest labor that he reported in *Success*, that he hoped to find a bedrock of reality in work as the root of character, as Howells did in Silas Lapham. Or Dreiser may have been engaged in a search for revitalization—a strenuous encounter with real life, which Jackson Lears has shown as the path taken by upper-class neurasthenics in their flight from the weightlessness of modern life.[59] This description, however, suits Eugene Witla in *The Genius* more than Dreiser in *An Amateur Laborer*, where he neither romanticized the character-building qualities of work nor imagined the recuperation of a whole, primal self.

An answer might be sought in the title of the projected book: *An Amateur Laborer*. By posing as a laborer, and labeling himself amateur, Dreiser implies the oppositional term "professional author." The narrative enacts a search not for an identity as a common laborer—a role for which he has much scorn—or for a way of throwing off the veneer of commercial success, but for a way of securing his uncommon identity as a professional writer and assuring himself of *not* being a laborer at all; by virtue of his amateurish approach to labor, his inappropriateness to the jobs he tries, Dreiser secures an identity by negation. If manual labor functioned as therapy, it was not simply the wage that sustained him (for it barely did), or the mental ease it offered, but the assurance that he indeed was not identical to the workers among whom he labored. Later in his career Dreiser referred to his incomplete manuscript as *A Literary Apprenticeship*, which may sound inappropriate for a text that more accurately represents a break in this apprenticeship.[60] Yet, for Dreiser, working as an "amateur laborer" equaled a literary apprenticeship, not because it gave him materials of real life to write about but because it reaffirmed his identity as a professional writer by showing his failure as a worker.

This manuscript reveals a very different attitude toward the work of writing from that of Howells and Wharton. To conceive of writing as disciplined work legitimated literature for Howells against what he saw as the idleness of the leisured class and the mass consumption of the working class. Labor for Howells was both an expression of character and a form of identification with a community. For Wharton, writing as professional work allowed her to differentiate it from both the idleness of the lady and the commercialism of the popular sentimentalists. For Dreiser, however, to conceive of writing as work was neither ennobling nor liberating, and although Dreiser came to be seen as a champion of the working class, his conception of authorship meant distinguishing himself from wage laborers.

Around the time Dreiser decided to abandon his aborted attempts to write, he developed a peculiar symptom, the "idea or hallucination that angles or lines of everything—houses, streets, wall pictures, newspaper columns and the like, were not straight and for the life of me I could not get them to look straight" (p. 26). This sense of dislocation contrasts strikingly with his earlier description of returning to a New York whose "streets and avenues were as familiar to me as those of my native village. I was as familiar with the sights and the sounds which I had once so ardently craved to share as if they were personally arranged by me" (p. 4). While his ambition as a writer once transformed desire into the power to arrange the world around him, his loss of the capacity to write a marketable line destabilizes the boundaries of a once familiar physical environment—as well as its representations in the newspapers and pictures. Yet the solution Dreiser proposes, to seek physical labor in place of writing, has the effect of blurring more lines rather than straightening them. It upsets the boundary between writer and worker, between observer of the urban spectacle and participant in what he called, in *Ev'ry Month*, an invisible underworld. "And if I went to the shops for something to do," asks Dreiser, "those great black factories whose walls I had often surveyed with a melancholy and poetic interest over the wide reaches of the city, how would I be received?" (p. 14). Stepping through those walls does not heal the rift between the writer as spectator and the people he observes; on the contrary, it challenges a line most threatening to his identity as a writer. The narrative of *An Amateur Laborer* attempts to revive his poetic interest by rebuilding the very walls it seeks to penetrate.

Dreiser introduces his job search by contrasting it with a

> long account of the labor struggles of another writer who had dressed himself to look the part of a laborer and I had always wondered how he would have fared if he had gone in his own natural garb. Now I was determined or rather compelled to find out for myself and I had no heart for it. I realized instinctively that there was a far cry between doing anything in disguise and as an experiment and doing it as a grim necessity. (p. 18)

Although Dreiser posits an opposition between his "natural garb" and the disguise of a laborer donned as an experiment, his narrative breaks down the distinctions between these terms. After failing to find a job at a sugar refinery, he tries to find "a motorman's or conductor's position, a place I had long had in mind as I was sure it was something that I could do" (p. 18).[61] He had "vivid dreams" of obtaining this position by "forcing my way into the office of the president, who I conceived to be a man who could tell by my appearance that I was not exactly of the ordinary run of men" (p. 19).[62] Instead, he enters a room "filled with motormen and conductors who were there being measured for suits," all of whom "looked at me with curious eyes as I came in, for I was still comparatively well-dressed, and some of them stood aside in so deferential a way that I felt that I was sailing under false colors" (pp. 19–20). When he explains his purpose to a superintendent, who had mistaken Dreiser for a businessman, "he told me in brusque tones where to go. I felt like an imposter slinking out for it seemed to me I had in some indefinable way misrepresented myself to him. I had not turned out to be what he took me for" (p. 20). Yet what the superintendent takes as a misrepresentation, and Dreiser feels as an imposter, is precisely what he represents as his true "natural garb," his identity as above the "ordinary run of men."

Although Dreiser contrasts his natural "grim necessity" with the more luxurious disguise of an "experiment in misery," performed by a writer like Crane, a less obvious inversion of this genre is Dreiser's need to view himself as the one being observed by those workers who are usually the object of the realist's gaze. Disconcerting as it may be, however, this gaze is necessary to reveal his "natural garb" as a difference, or an absence. While looking for a job, Dreiser, like Carrie in Chicago, is obsessed with the fear of rejection and consumed with "what would people think of me?" Yet unlike Carrie, he translates his "cold fear of inability" into a desire for superiority. When he sees workers looking through a shop window, he imagines "they see me coming. They think I am someone who is above that kind of work. They will not believe that I need it and turn me away. And how will I look to them anyhow?" (p. 17). To maintain his "natural garb," he needs to imagine his inability to work as bestowing a kind of identity. While standing outside "all sorts of institutions," too paralyzed to enter, "I would contrast my appropriateness to that with my inappropriateness to this and then I would weaken and hurry away" (p. 17). Yet such weakening yields strength, because it proves that he is a "natural" writer—at a time when he cannot write—through his obvious inappropriateness to physical labor.

Dreiser pursues this job until the day he reaches a crowd surrounded by "other individual stragglers, who impressed me at once as people who like myself were anxious to register but were ashamed to go up. They were a little better dressed than those who were gathered about the door—not so strong-looking and not so coarse" (p. 21). Because Dreiser's identification with these figures is more threatening than his distance from the real laborers, he experiences a failure of nerve, the inability to "summon up sufficient courage to join that crowd" (p. 21). While he walks by, he reasserts his identity by imagining the others looking at him "as though they thought I was some critical business man or other citizen merely passing on my way to my office" (p. 21). He chooses to preserve this image rather than join the crowd, a choice that leads him to the most destitute stage of his existence.

At this nadir, living on bread and salt and stolen apples, Dreiser's physical deterioration makes it impossible for anyone to hire him: "People did not like my appearance. They seemed to take it for granted that I was physically unable to do anything and passed me by" (p. 27). By implication, however, he can still do something mentally and he attributes his survival to a split in the self which spawns "a sane, conservative oversoul" (p. 27) who observes his immediate physical exigencies while remaining untouched by them. This oversoul instills a faith in the future which is expressed through Dreiser's decision not to pawn his possessions—"I would be destroying my chances to do anything if I began to part with the things that made up my personal appearance" (p. 28). Indeed the greatest crisis in the narrative revolves precisely around this loss of personal appearance, when his hat blows away in the subway. "I do not know when in life before any situation ever distressed me quite so much" (p. 35), which leads Dreiser to conclude that "in all the waste and endlessness I was nothing" (p. 37). This loss of identity is manifest in his fifty-cent purchase of a laborer's woolen cap. Despite—or because of—the hat, which makes him wonder how he could go anywhere looking "like a freak," he bemoans his inability to find a job, for "every one seemed to see or to insist that I was cut out for something better and that their work was unsuited to me. I think if ever the literary life, and the curious ability to examine the characters and motives of people, seemed accursed to me it did then" (p. 39). Dreiser, however, turns this curse into a blessing, for even when "grim necessity" reduces him to donning a laborer's cap, this cap becomes a flimsy disguise through which the "natural garb" of the literary life shines ever more clearly.

An upswing in Dreiser's fortunes occurs only when he gives up looking for "work" and decides instead to market himself on the grounds that earning your bread is "silly. In nature no such rule held as earning anything singlehanded. Each one was favored or discriminated against before he began. I was favored. I was given to write and no one had ever taught me. It came to me. Another was given to shine as a beauty, or a wit or a financier" (pp. 44–45). But this does not lead him to conclude that individuals are naturally placed in a social scale: "And then I thought of another side of the question. How many there were to care for. How full every nook and cranny of nature is with a great mass struggling to live" (p. 45). Rather than infer a bitter social Darwinian struggle over scarcity, he claims that "everything was in demand. It was only a question of getting hold of the means of grasping something with a strong hand and keeping it" (p. 45). Yet to keep something means paradoxically to sell it, to have "something which the world would buy—beauty, wit, strength, muscle—anything which nature provides and yet does not provide generally, and there would be no question of poverty" (p. 45). Thus Dreiser's solution to his dilemma is not to work hard but to find a commodity to sell: "The most saleable I thought would be either beauty or wit, but of course I had neither and no means of procuring anything else" (p. 45).

But Dreiser does have something to sell; if not his writing, then his identity as a writer (which he has worked so hard to preserve by not working). So he "put a few letters from publishers and people of note in my pocket, solely to identify and verify my claims to a slight distinction" (p. 44). He then applies for a job at the New York Central Railroad Company to the general passenger agent, "a man who made himself known to literary pople by reason of his interest in literary matters. . . . He liked writers and boasted of his acquaintance with some of them" (p. 46). Dreiser decides this time not to say "work," but instead to "put on the air of a superior being" and tell the man that he was looking for manual labor to recuperate his health (p. 46). He markets his neurasthenia as a sign of his writer's identity, and the agent in response procures a job for "Mr. Theodore Dreiser, 'a writer and author'," for his health (p. 47). Although Dreiser concludes from this experience that "the mystery of 'attitude' and personality was greater to me than ever," there should have been no mystery. Dreiser sells himself as a minor celebrity whose aura the agent purchases to enhance his own value.

When Dreiser finally finds work by seeking it as therapy, he runs into his brother, Paul, who insists on sending him to an expensive sanatorium, on the grounds that railroad work is no less a form of charity than Paul's generosity. If Dreiser saw work as a form of therapy, the ex-heavyweight champion who ran the sanatorium, Muldoon, turned therapy into a kind of work. Wharton, as a woman, was treated for her neurasthenia by the rest cure, but Dreiser's treatment involved rigorous exercise. Yet both methods worked similarly, by infantilizing the patient. Dreiser describes Muldoon as something between a mother and the foreman of a chain gang—ordering his patients to wash between their toes, forcing them to drink their buttermilk, and badgering them into playing games. In their daily exercise of tossing around a heavy medicine ball, Muldoon yells, "if you can't do the work, get out" (p. 79). The logic of Muldoon's therapy is directed toward wealthy executives and businessmen who seek rest and therapy in being ordered around instead of in commanding others. Dreiser finds himself as out of place among the wealthy businessmen as among common workers, a difference which he again turns into both a lament and a badge of distinction: "no skill in any manual trade, and no training in any professional one" (p. 93). His treatment remains necessarily incomplete, as he finds after several weeks that "authorship was a long way off," and his "eyesight still manifested that tendency to see things at a wrong angle" (p. 92). When he leaves the sanitorium, the stableman, assuming Dreiser is a wealthy businessman, charges him an exorbitant fee, and he again feels like a "faker in disguise," though not as a laborer but as "some beggar masquerading as a man of wealth" (p. 95). Yet this is a masquerade that reasserts his natural garb.

When Dreiser leaves the sanatorium he renews his determination to work on the railroad, which he envisions first as a romantic escape to nature "picking away through a long summer's day earning my bread by the sweat of my brow" (p. 94). His return to the city, though, rekindles his old desires through the view of the "fine spectacle to the eye . . . a Tantalus bunch of pleasures before the eye, but forever beyond reach" (p. 96). Although earlier in his career writing had promised the opportunity of attaining such magnificence, turning craving into participating, he now decides that it would be better for him to "abandon desire and [to] retreat. Be satisfied with the humble life. It was the only way" (p. 96). He decides to withdraw from the market and in effect to enter the painting of "The Blacksmith," a world in which manual labor becomes both a romantic escape from the city and the abandonment of desire. But work on the railroad provides a haven neither from the city nor from desire; instead it offers confinement which separates him from the natural landscape he views around him and only increases his desire to escape—"Outside was the world. Outside was life. Outside was something that was not toil" (p. 105).

Although the manuscript of *An Amateur Laborer* breaks off in the middle of Dreiser's short stint on the railroad, and the next stage of his career is somewhat obscure to biographers, it seems clear that the "recreative career of labor" (p. 113) did not cure Dreiser by enabling him to abandon desire and to withdraw from the market. In fact his road back to health lay in reentering the market as assistant editor of the *Daily News*, where he could "spread himself" again on the features pages. Through the sentimental patronage of his brother Paul, who used his connections to find this job, Dreiser recuperated his health—which he defined as the ability to make money with his pen—by competing successfully in the writing market which had destroyed him. Next, the former legman appalled by the industrialization of publishing joined one of the most industrialized institutions, the "fiction factory" of Street and Smith as editor of dime novels. He then moved up the industrial hierarchy to become editor of *Smith's* magazine, *Broadway* magazine, and finally to the lucrative and powerful position of editor of *The Delineator*. In returning to the familiar role of editing a women's magazine, he no longer tried to distance himself through the lofty but insecure tone of "The Prophet." Instead he assumed a more intimate yet authoritative voice in columns entitled "Concerning Us All: Talks with the Editor," or "Just You and the Editor"; this engagement allowed him greater control over his staff and readers and success in the market.[63]

Dreiser's position at *The Delineator,* which, once again, was in the business of promotion, for Butterick's fashions, has been viewed as a compromise, or a detour from his trajectory as a realist—not what one would expect from an author who wrote in 1903: "The extent of all reality is the realm of the author's pen, and a true picture of life . . . is both moral and artistic whether it offends conventions or not."[64] Yet Dreiser's assumption of this position in 1907 coincided with his republication of *Sister Carrie;* these two inseparable acts represent the culmination of Dreiser's apprenticeship by transforming him from an amateur laborer avoiding the market to a professional writer mastering the market. Only with the successful promotion of both the magazine and the novel did Dreiser start his prolific production of realistic novels. To reissue *Sister Carrie,* Dreiser chose the new, aggressive firm of B. W. Dodge and Company, and to guarantee some control over this publication he bought stock in the firm and became its director (duplicating his brother Paul's relation to his music-publishing company). For *Sister Carrie*'s second American debut, Dreiser barely revised the manuscript; instead he worked closely with Dodge on a lavish advertising campaign, which included a long promotional brochure with reviews of the first edition and a story of its "suppression" on the first page.[65] Dreiser thus turned a past failure in the market into promotional material. To understand self-promotion as central to Dreiser's conception of authorship is not to undercut his stature as realist, or to see his claims to tell the truth about reality censored by marketability. If realism "offends conventions," as Dreiser argues, this opposition is deeply enmeshed in those same conventions that Dreiser employed to promote his authorship in the market.

6

THE SENTIMENTAL REVOLT OF *Sister Carrie*

Chapter 5 suggested the inadequacy of opposing Dreiser's hack work written for the mass market to his realistic art written to defy marketable conventions. At each stage of his apprenticeship, Dreiser found the promotion of authorship in the market to be integral to the production of both the realist and his work. This chapter focuses on Dreiser's first novel, *Sister Carrie,* to address the problem of sentimentalism, which has been seen to entrap his prose in popular conventions that block his full achievement of realism.

Sentimentality in *Sister Carrie* does not simply lurk as a vestige of a residual convention, it is recontextualized and given new life in Dreiser's aesthetics of consumption. To understand the relation between sentimentalism, realism, and a consumer ethos, it is necessary to reconsider the role of consumption in the novel, both as a compensation for social powerlessness and as an expression of a utopian desire for change, for that which is unrealized. The interpenetration of realism and sentimentality is figured in the novel's second half through the newspaper and the popular theater, institutions of mass culture which shaped Dreiser's writing.

I

It is well known that *Sister Carrie* opens on two discordant narrative registers: the documentary description of a young girl's journey to the city, and the sentimental commentary on the moral ramifications of her venture. The first, most notable in the opening paragraph, details "her total outfit," consisting of "a small trunk, a cheap imitation alligator-skin satchel, a small lunch in a paper box, and a yellow leather snap purse."[1] The second casts her in a melodrama or sentimental novel, where "either she falls into saving hands and becomes better, or rapidly assumes the cosmopolitan standard of virtue and becomes worse" (p. 1). This narrative disjuncture follows a long tradition of the realistic novel in which the romantic illusions of the characters are dashed by their contact with the commercial reality of urban life. Stylistically, in this tradition, the dispassionate journalistic descriptions dismantle the black-and-white moralism of the sentimental commentary.

The problem with this reading, however, is that Dreiser's narrative proceeds not to debunk Carrie's dreams but to fulfill all her romantic and material aspirations of the first chapter, in which she is "venturing to reconnoitre the mysterious city and dreaming wild dreams of some vague, far-off supremacy, which should make it prey and subject—the proper penitent, grovelling at a woman's slipper" (p. 2). It is striking that this highly sentimental passage dubs Carrie "a half-equipped little knight," and in her first small success on Broadway she is promoted to lead the chorus line in the role of a "little gaslight soldier," complete with "epaulets and a belt of silver, with a short sword dangling at one side" (p. 290). The theater, the traditional symbol of illusion, becomes the vehicle for realizing Carrie's "wild dreams," and reencodes her romantic fantasies in a modern context when the city, in effect, does grovel before her photograph on a Broadway billboard. Even Carrie's disillusionment only fuels rather than diminishes the force of her fantasies, which are expressed in the sentimental language that concludes the novel: "Oh blind strivings of the human heart!"—language which has caused much discontent among critics.

One of the most vexing problems for Dreiser criticism has remained how to reconcile his power as a realist—power that has been located in his challenge to moral and literary conventions—with his reliance on sentimental codes. Although sentimentalism has its own complex literary history, critics equate it in its broadest sense with Dreiser's notoriously bad writing: his cumbersome prose style, his high-flown moralizing, his investment in the tawdry dream-worlds of his characters, his melodramatic chapter titles, and his flowery endings; in other words, everything that seems the antithesis of a realism that directly portrays social conditions in lucid and unencumbered prose. Leslie Fiedler even relegated *Sister Carrie* to the tradition of popular sentimental women's fiction.[2] In addition, Dreiser's sentimentalism is associated with elements of commercial popular culture figured in *Sister Carrie* not only through Carrie's reading but through her spectacular theatrical career, first as an amateur in Daly's famous melodrama, then as a chorus girl on Broadway, and finally as a star in the Sunday supplements. These anti-realistic elements have been problematic to critics because, as I have suggested in the introduction in this book, Dreiser has served as the test case for the viability of American realism—not only for detractors such as Trilling, but for supporters such as Alfred Kazin, who wrote: "It is because we have all identified Dreiser's work with reality that, for more than half a century now, he has been for us not a writer like other writers, but a whole chapter of American life."[3]

The problem of Dreiser's sentimentalism has been met by four major critical solutions. The most common solution privileges his lucid portrayal of social conditions—represented best by Hurstwood's decline—and downplays the maudlin flights of Dreiser's prose—represented by the plot of seduction and Carrie's longings and cheap success.[4] Another solution is offered by the new Pennsylvania edition of *Sister Carrie*, which restores Dreiser's original manuscript to what it was before his friend Arthur Henry revised it for the market: "Dreiser was composing a serious work of art," claim the editors, who retrieve it from Henry's "trying to revise it into saleable fiction."[5] Not surprisingly, the restoration of the "serious work of art" deletes the embarrassing chapter titles, which have been likened to Paul Dresser's popular ballads, and substitutes Hurstwood's suicide for the sentimental ending of Carrie in her rocking chair. A more compelling solution has been offered by Sandy Petrey, who argues that the straightforward narrative style of Dreiser's "social realism exposes sentimental posturing as absurd," as a hollow, outdated tradition no longer capable of attributing meaning to modern urban experience.[6] Other critics have shown similarly how Dreiser's plots and characters parody sentimental conventions to "controvert all the basic messages of popular fiction."[7]

These three different critical approaches recuperate Dreiser's realism by subordinating or deleting his sentimental qualities and differentiating his writing from the popular forms he employs. Another approach inverts his hierarchy. In *Sister Carrie*'s Popular Economy," Walter Michaels, echoing Fiedler but disagreeing with his evaluation, claims that Dreiser is indeed a sentimentalist, or at least, in contrast to Howells, embraces the sentimental ethos of capitalism which values excess over restraint.[8] Philip Fisher, while not directly addressing the issue of sentimentality, makes similar claims for Dreiser's writing as a form of popular art, which rather than controvert or parody popular ideology makes its readers at home in a new world of consumer goods.[9]

Earlier critics equate Dreiser at his most realistic with his critical "depiction of conditions" of work and unemployment, while those critics who privilege Dreiser's popular and sentimental side see his writing emerging from and embracing the consumer aesthetic of the late nineteenth century. This chapter argues that the critical opposition associating sentimentalism with consumption and desire, and realism with work and deprivation, is already generated by the narrative strategies of *Sister Carrie*, as a way of imagining and managing the contradictions of a burgeoning consumer society.

Although Dreiser starts by undermining the traditional locus of sentimental value in the virtue of the heroine and the middle-class home as a haven from the market, he does not thereby erase sentimental conventions; rather he reconstitutes marriage and domesticity as subjects of the market.[10] When Carrie steps off the train in Chicago to be greeted by her sister, the narrative dashes the conventions of the sentimental novel in which the middle-class home provides a shelter from the public marketplace. As Carrie embraces her sister, she loses the "affectional atmosphere" felt with the stranger on the train, Drouet, and finds "cold reality taking her by the hand" (p. 8). The Hansons' working-class flat not only offers no haven from the market but lies on a continuum with the workplace. In addition to inviting Carrie to live with them only to help them pay the rent, the Hansons distrust spending money for pleasure or for anything not related to "a conservative round of toil" (p. 10). Saving the little money they earn for a far-off plan to buy property, they spend money the way they work, hooked to a routine of delayed gratification. When Carrie leaves the Hansons, the narrative abandons the interrelated framework of domesticity and the work ethic which holds, in the Hansons' view, that "Carrie would be rewarded for coming and toiling in the city" (p. 11). As Dreiser was to articulate in *An Amateur Laborer*, Carrie soon discovers the absurdity of the notion of "earning your bread," and the greater importance of having "something which the world would buy."[11] To escape the dead end of the Hansons' home and the "round of toil" at the factory, Carrie finds she has only her self to sell in exchange for Drouet's "two soft, green, handsome ten-dollar bills" (p. 47).

Although Hurstwood is a member of a different social class, his home serves as an extension of his work rather than as an alternative source of value. Just as his job requires that he act as an advertisement for the resort he manages, his family's conspicuous consumption serves as a banner for his own success and affluence. The hollowness of Hurstwood's home life is summarized by the chapter title "Convention's own

Tinderbox" (p. 62). Where Carrie seeks an escape from the claustrophobia of working-class life by standing on the street outside the Hansons' apartment and then entering the world of the salesman, Drouet, Hurstwood escapes from the frigid atmosphere of his middle-class home to the warmth of hobnobbing with celebrities at his resort.

Domesticity in *Sister Carrie,* however, is never abandoned; rather it is reencoded as a marketable value. Like the readers counseled in *Ev'ry Month,* Carrie, at each stage of her life, recreates the conditions of domesticity in her makeshift homes and her play-act marriages. Dreiser describes the interiors she decorates for Drouet in Chicago and Hurstwood in New York in more detail than he does the sensuality between the lovers. Even these two men seem to value Carrie less for a risqué liaison than for a cozy domesticity. Drouet proudly invites guests to his home, and when Hurstwood flees to New York, he is especially gratified by his homey interior created with furniture bought on the installment plan. Hurstwood's final disintegration is marked not only by Carrie's abandonment but by his being forced to sell back the furniture. If sentimental domesticity is exposed as a convention in families at the beginning of the novel, it is reconstructed later in improvised settings, as though the couples were playing house. The reencoding of sentimental conventions in *Sister Carrie* can be seen further in the omnipresent rocking chair in the novel. Jane Tompkins has pointed to the rocking chair in the Quaker kitchen in *Uncle Tom's Cabin* as the seat of what she calls "sentimental power."[12] In *Sister Carrie,* the rocking chair mediates not only between motion and stasis in a mechanized society, or between private and public space, as Philip Fisher has shown, but between sentimentalism and realism, as the chair magically resurfaces, not in the kitchen, but in each rented room, from the Hansons' apartment to the Waldorf Astoria.[13] The rocking chair is the place where characters do not just observe the world outside their windows, but where they dream their sentimental fantasies of escape.

Just as domesticity is relocated in *Sister Carrie* from the stable home to rented spaces, sentimental language is divested of its traditional familial ties and reinvested in market-engendered values and consumer goods. Carrie's initial attraction to Hurstwood, for example, is described through a sentimental commentary on the inadequacy of words to "but dimly represent the great surging feelings and desires" that pass unspoken between two people (p. 88). When Hurstwood does speak, however, Carrie hears behind his words not feelings but, "instead of his words, the voices of things which he represented" (p. 88). This passage inverts sentimental signification, in which objects speak for the human heart. Dreiser attributes to the voice of "inanimate objects" more emotive power than he does to the words of any character. When Drouet, for example, takes Carrie to a restaurant for the first time, rescuing her from another job search, "as he cut his meat, his rings almost spoke. His new suit creaked." It is this voice, rather than his own incessant chattering, that "contributed the warmth of his spirit to her body" (p. 45).

If things speak louder than both people and words, what language do they speak? They speak in the melodramatic cadence of seduction to a country girl bound for the city in search of work. During her train ride to Chicago, Carrie's dreams leave no room for the main purpose of her journey—a job; instead they revolve around the things she wants to buy. Whispering in her ear like the serpent in Eden, Drouet voices her desires and recasts the melodramatic role of seducer in the appropriate form of the traveling salesman. He describes the city as a vast department store for which his own appearance affects Carrie as an advertisement: "the purse, the shiny tan shoes, the smart suit, and the *air* with which he did things, built up for her a dim world of fortune, of which he was the centre" (p. 6). Like Hurstwood, Drouet is an "ambassador" for the things he represents.

Sentimental power in an earlier tradition lies in the home as retreat from the market; in this novel, sentimental power is reinvested in a market of consumer goods which serve as a retreat from both the home and the workplace. Carrie significantly enters the city at dusk, "that mystic period between the glare and gloom of the world when life is changing from one sphere or condition to another," two spheres governed by the opposing conditions of work and leisure (p. 7). As the narrative switches perspective from Carrie's first glimpse of the city to the people leaving work, her desires are joined to the general excitement of the "lifting of the burden of toil." The "soul of the toiler" speaks to itself in slightly archaic sentimental tones: "I shall soon be free. I shall be in the ways and the hosts of the merry. The streets, the lamps, the lighted chamber set for dining, are for me. The theatre, the halls, the parties, the way of rest and the paths of song—these are mine in the night" (p. 7). This desire, however, is labeled "the old illusion of hope," an illusion dashed for Carrie by her sister, whose "cold reality" is defined by the "grimness of shift and toil" (p. 8). Although Carrie moves to Chicago to work, her desires—marked by the language of sentiment—are invested in the escape from work. The opening of the novel divides Chicago into two cities not by space or even class, but by time—a liberated evening sphere of desire conceived of in terms of consumption, and the daytime confining sphere of work, in which cold reality is equated with the thwarting of desire. Most of the significant changes—or escapes—in the novel occur at night: Carrie's move with Drouet, her flight with Hurstwood, and her meeting with Ames. In contrast to Hanson's work, which begins at dawn, appealing jobs take place at night and seem like amusement rather than work, as in Hurstwood's resort or Carrie's theaters.

The allure of the city at night inverts a familiar trope of "the mystery of the city," in which the threatening shadows of the city refer to lower-class haunts.[14] To Carrie on her first day, walking through the city as an applicant for a job, the "great streets" appear as "wall-lined mysteries" that exclude her from a world not of a dangerous underclass but of opulent objects of desire. Her first tour of the city in search of a job overwhelms her with a sense of her own powerlessness, "a sense of helplessness amid so much evidence of power and force which she did not understand" (p. 12). While new firms advertise their prosperity through large plate-glass windows, these windows are curiously opaque, as the labor that produces their wealth takes place in the back of the building, invisible from the streets. Carrie's small-town upbringing teaches her to read meaning on the surface of things. She interprets the windows as she would "the meaning of a little stone-cutter's yard at Columbia City, carving little pieces of marble for individual use," but she cannot fathom "yards of some huge stone corporation" (p. 12). Thus when Carrie finds her job, she assumes the identity conferred by this "goodly institution," with its "windows . . . of huge plate glass" (p. 21). Only when she goes to work does she see through the windows to the hidden factory.

Carrie does not remain passive before such overwhelming evidence of her own powerlessness. Like the Marches in *Hazard*, she actively creates significance out of the city's impenetrable facades. She scales down the vast city to a manageable, unthreatening size by translating its intimidating social structures into the sentimental language of consumption, transforming the city into a showcase for tangible commodities which speak to her. Unable to imagine people engaged in a social process of production, she does not question "what they dealt in, how they labored, to what end it all came," but instead imagines "far-off individuals of importance . . . counting money, dressing magnificently and riding in carriages" (p. 13). This desire for commodities and immediate pleasure provides Carrie with her strongest impulse to act, her "guiding characteristic" (p. 15); she is willing to argue with her taciturn brother-in-law to spend money on the theater, although in the same chapter she barely has the courage to enter a firm to apply for a job. Thus when she enters a department store for the first time, "she realised in a dim way how much the city held—wealth, fashion, ease—every adornment for women, and she longed for dress and beauty with a whole heart" (p. 17). The commodities in the department store speak the language of sentiment to the "whole heart" because they project in a "dim way" what is to Carrie an unrealized but desirable world that lies outside her current sphere of work.

The consumption of commodities in *Sister Carrie* functions in the novel to compensate for social powerlessness. Although Carrie and Hurstwood occupy opposite ends of the social scale, both are driven by their lack of social power. Despite Hurstwood's managerial position, he has no financial control over the business, and is not even permitted to handle the money in the cash register. His job is to act as though he were not working, to appear as the generous host rather than as the paid employee. He is described through the oxymorons of an "active manner" and "solid, substantial air," which create an image of solidity composed of the objects with which he adorns himself: "his fine clothes, his clean linen, his jewels, and above all, his own sense of his importance" (p. 33). Acting the role of host "lounging about," he transforms the conditions of powerlessness into a display of power through his studied pose of leisure. Yet clothes do not make the man, not because Dreiser opposes an interior self to an externalized masquerade, but because of the contrast between the display of status and the possession of social power. Hurstwood's precarious position as manager and husband is curiously similar to Lily's in *The House of Mirth*. At home Hurstwood is almost as powerless as Carrie at the Hansons'. His family surrounds him with an air of affluence and authority that ultimately lends prestige to his resort, but the discrepancy between his family's conspicuous consumption and its lack of social power undermines his authority at home. His wife and children long to enter the high society—families of bankers and industrialists—that they imitate. Thus Hurstwood's ambiguous social position spawns desires in his family which he cannot fulfill, and his impotence leads them to ignore him as head of the family. Although as a "man of authority" it "irritated him excessively to find himself surrounded more and more by a world upon which he had no hold, and of which he had a lessening understanding" (p. 153), he never really had the control over his family he thinks he has lost (he had signed over all his property to his wife), just as he has no financial control over his work. Hurstwood's passion for Carrie can be understood less as a romantic rebellion against convention than as compensation for his lack of authority at home. One of her chief attractions for Hurstwood is her submissiveness: "nothing bold in her manner. Life had not taught her domination—superciliousness of grace, which is the lordly power of some women" (p. 107). When he first feels his control slipping at home, he consoles himself with the thought that "things might go as they would at his house, but he had Carrie outside of it" (p. 106). His treatment of Carrie as a commodity lies not only in spending money on her but more importantly in projecting into her the image of recovered authority he loses at home and at work.

The consumption of commodities in *Sister Carrie* not only compensates for the lack of power at work and at home but also expresses and channels a utopian desire for change, for the "good" which consumer goods promise.[15] Carrie's desire for change can be seen in her response to her first day at the shoe factory. She expresses her dissatisfaction most acutely walking home on the city streets which make her feel "ashamed in the face of better dressed girls who went by. She felt as though she should be better served, and her heart revolted" (p. 31). "Revolt" is linked to the voice of sentiment—the heart—and Carrie's sentimental rebellion turns not against factory work but against a discrepancy between the well-dressed girls and herself, a gap that could be filled by consumer goods. Later in the novel, when Carrie moves to New York, she has a similar reaction to her first stroll down fashionable Broadway:

> The whole street bore the flavor of riches and show, and Carrie felt that she was not of it. . . . It cut her to the quick, and she resolved that she would not come here again until she looked better. At the same time she longed to feel the delight of parading here as an equal. Ah, then she would be happy! (p. 227)

Carrie translates the desire for change—for equality with other people—as she translates revolt, into the sentimental language of acquisition. This translation effaces any difference between dressing and parading as an equal and actually being one. Hurstwood similarly enacts his desire to become a celebrity by socializing with celebrities at his resort, where he in fact is hired to serve the people he treats as equals. When this position is threatened by his wife's ultimatum for a divorce, he worries obsessively not about responding but about receiving Carrie's response to his love letters. Carrie serves the same function for Hurstwood that clothes do for her; she promises magically to change him without his having to act.

The novel is interspersed with glimpses of alternative activities to the frenetic acquisitiveness of the main characters. Streetcar workers on strike, for example, attempt to gain power collectively by changing the conditions of their work. Later, as a strikebreaker, Hurstwood can no more join the strikers, when asked, than Carrie can follow Ames's advice to become a serious actress. "If I were you," says Ames, "I'd change" (p. 357). Both Carrie and Hurstwood share with Ames and the strikers the desire for change, yet rather than actively effect that change, they seek to possess the object, or person, that promises magically to transform them. Carrie's conversation with Ames does not prod her to action. Instead it only makes her more acutely conscious of her lack of the "better thing" which Ames represents, and it increases both her "inactivity and longing" (p. 357). Wanting to be different takes the form of longing to have more, as identity is defined by the power to spend money. Thus, as Hurstwood loses this power, he becomes more and more anonymous. Although desire in *Sister Carrie* propels constant motion, it also becomes a substitute for actively changing either the social order or the individuals within it. This form of desire contributes to the paradoxical sense of stasis in the text at the times of greatest motion; Carrie is constantly on the move up the social scale—from one city, one man, one job to the next—yet she always seems to end up in the same place, as the final scene suggests: rocking, and dreaming, and longing for more. In *Sister Carrie* the desire for social change is channeled into the desire for novelty, the desire to construct a social reality in which change most often yields more of the same.

It has often been noted that desire, by definition, in *Sister Carrie* is never satisfied, that longing continually outstrips its objects, which lose their value as soon as they are possessed.[16] The characters always seem to be in pursuit of something that commodities promise but never quite deliver, because they seek in things around them an image of themselves. Unlike the Marches, who look for a familiar and stable self-image in an apartment, and Lily Bart, who seeks the outlines of a self in the eyes of others, the characters in *Sister Carrie* continually pursue an image of themselves as they might be—not as they are. Carrie is enamored of the theater for the same reason she desires clothes, because she believes that by dressing or by playing a part she can actually be transformed into the glamorous creature of her fantasies. Like Drouet, she hopes that the atmosphere of the fashionable resorts and theaters can rub off on the identity of those who frequent them.[17] Carrie desires things not for their own qualities or for pleasures they afford, but for the new self-image they seem to offer. Therefore, "seeing a thing, she would immediately set to inquiring how she would look, properly related to it" (p. 75). And Hurstwood's desire for her resembles Carrie's relationship to things, as he pursues in her an image of himself as he would like to be:

youthful, powerful, and independent. Unable to fulfill this image by acting on the choices before him, he projects these attributes onto his ability to possess Carrie.

Dreiser's characters, however, look for themselves in things and in other people only to find what they are not. When Carrie observes the well-dressed clerks in the department store, she sees herself in their eyes "only to recognize in [them] a keen analysis of her own position—her individual shortcomings of dress and that *shadow* of manner which she thought must hang about her and make clear to all who and what she was. A flame of envy lighted in her heart" (p. 17). Carrie defines "who and what she was" by what she is not—by the fact that she is not as well dressed as the clerks. Carrie's only friend in the novel, Mrs. Vance, similarly serves as a yardstick for Carrie, who sees in Mrs. Vance all that she lacks: "the air of the petted and well-groomed woman. . . . She looked as though she was dearly loved and her every wish gratified" (p. 225). When they meet again, after Mrs. Vance has read of Carrie's stardom in the newspapers, Carrie looks down on, rather than up at, Mrs. Vance. It occurs to Carrie "that she was as good as this woman now—perhaps better. Something in the other's solicitude and interest made her feel as if she were the one to condescend" (p. 332). No two people in *Sister Carrie* meet as equals; one either condescends or is condescended to, is enviable or envies.

In a major study linking Dreiser's art to a culture of consumption, Philip Fisher suggests that commodities are projections of a collective psyche and that, in Dreiser's novels, the self is completely externalized in the surrounding city, which itself can be seen as a collection of commodities. "Far from being in any simple way estranged in the city," Fisher writes, "man is for the first time surrounded by himself. . . . Within the city anything outside the body is there only because it was projected there by will and need."[18] Consequently, identity is conferred on the self by the things around one. He therefore sees Carrie and Clyde Griffiths, the main character of *An American Tragedy*, as "blank center[s] engulfed by worlds" constituted by things, places, and the atmosphere they radiate.[19] Fisher, however, overlooks the contradiction exposed by Dreiser's novels in the structure of commodities: that they create common needs within a social hierarchy. Clyde may enter Gilbert's "world" by wearing the right clothes, but he has no foothold there because as a factory manager he cannot reproduce his cousin's position in the social hierarchy. Like Carrie, Clyde is trapped by this discrepancy between the desires evoked by commodities and the limits to his ability to fulfill those needs through his social position. Thus, the city does not only project human "will and needs" as Fisher suggests; it also projects the unequal social relations of power and domination. Fisher furthermore claims that "nowhere in Dreiser's novel is there the slightest trace of society, as that word is understood in nineteenth-century novels. Instead there are worlds," and "worlds are neither economic, nor public, nor are they permanent centers of activity. Worlds are not generated by the webs of work because in Dreiser work itself is only one kind of atmosphere."[20] Echoing the romance thesis of American fiction, Fisher implicitly links the absence of society in Dreiser's novels to the lack of social classes structured by productive relations—"the webs of work." Yet in both *Sister Carrie* and *An American Tragedy,* the "worlds" projected by desire are generated by and continually come in conflict with a "society" constructed on relations of power located in the workplace. Work in Dreiser's novels is not reduced to atmosphere, but is the site of those power relations which fuel the desire for change that commodities promise but never fully realize.

It is this gap between desire and social power that reopens the space for sentimentality. Walter Michaels identifies Dreiser's sentimentalism with the excess of the capitalist economy, but the sentimental voice of commodities can also be seen to address the contradictions of a capitalist economy which locates desire solely in the realm of consumption generated by the power structure of production.[21] By marking the longing of the characters as sentimental, Dreiser shows how capitalism in the late nineteenth century gives rise to desires for "goods" that it cannot fulfill, and translates desire into the realm of the unreal.

II

In the second half of *Sister Carrie,* Carrie's ascent on the stage has long struck critics as unconvincing and unreal, while Hurstwood's decline has been singled out as the apogee of Dreiser's realism. The language describing Hurstwood's deprivation has similarly been viewed as Dreiser's more realistic plain style, while Carrie's aspirations seem draped in the sentimental language of melodrama. The narrative itself suggests opposing sites of the real and the unreal by juxtaposing Hurstwood's newspaper reading with Carrie's acting career. It is as though Hurstwood becomes a character in the newspaper sketches of misery he reads, just as Carrie becomes a star performer featured in the Sunday supplements. Rather than choose one narrative stance as more realistic than the other, we might see them constructing competing versions of the real as do the theater and the newspaper. The point is not to claim that the chorus line is as real—if not more so—than the breadline in a society of spectacle, but to pose the question of why one comes to seem more real than the other.

In a compelling analysis of Dreiser's style, Sandy Petrey has shown how sentimentality is undermined by its inability to account for the juxtaposed straightforward narration.[22] If sentimental commentary, however, seems incommensurate with the narration of facts, we still ought not to privilege Dreiser's documentary style as adequate in itself and somehow closer to reality, as Petrey does. Indeed, as June Howard suggests, the plain-speaking documentary strategy can be as ideologically loaded as sentimental moralizing.[23] Details in *Sister Carrie* often appear autonomous and unrelated either to the immediate scene or to the narrative structure.[24] In a typical example of Dreiser's realistic style, for instance, the narrator interrupts his account of Hurstwood's flight from Chicago to inform us that "he stopped at a famous drugstore," which "contained one of the first telephone booths ever erected" (p. 194). The inclusion of this detail signals historical specificity. Yet it also has a more disruptive effect: it marks the disjuncture between background and foreground by pointing to its own irrelevance, to the lack of connection between the action of the narrative and the details of the setting. The fixation on details in *Sister Carrie* can be seen to parallel the infatuations of the characters with things. According to Richard Poirier, "the floods of language by which [Dreiser] embraces things outside himself are a verbal equivalent to the visual obsessions of his characters."[25] Each detail can be embraced as a fact only to be found as curiously empty and meaningless as sentimental gestures, just as the characters pursue commodities which lose their value and mystique as soon as they are possessed. Descriptive details in *Sister Carrie* evoke a contradictory sense of concreteness and insubstantiality.

The power and the limits of Dreiser's documentary style are explored through the newspaper in the second half of the novel. Hurstwood reads the paper as Petrey would wish, as the literal rendition of the bare facts of urban experience. After Hurstwood, however, escapes to Montreal with the stolen money, he looks for himself in the newspaper, only to find that the facts of his case are divorced from his own narrative of events. He is disappointed to find that "the newspapers noted but one thing, his taking the money. How and wherefore were but indifferently dealt with. All the complications which led up to it were unknown. He was accused without being understood" (p. 210). Although the newspaper extracts Hurstwood's crime from its context, reading the newspaper in New York reembeds him in a new social context. As he grows immobile and anonymous in New York, he depends more and more on the newspapers for his contact with the city around him. The papers give him access to people on all levels of the social scale. He carefully reads about the activities of high society, to which he once longed to ascend, and about the 80,000 people thrown out of jobs, into whose ranks he fears to sink. In the newspapers he also takes note of the city as a whole—its development, corruption, and the storms that beset it. After Carrie leaves him, Hurstwood depends upon the notices of her plays for any sense of personal connection in the city. The newspapers thus reposition him socially in the city, and Hurstwood increasingly substitutes reading for any direct experience. During a winter storm he stops going out to look for a job and stays at home to read about the storm and the hardships it causes. The newspapers thus become more than a repository for information; they form an escape for him from the very realities they report. Hurstwood soon finds that "his difficulties vanished in the items he so well loved to read" (p. 256), in the "Lethean waters . . . these floods of telegraphed intelligence" (p. 252). Hurstwood reads in the rocking chair, the place where Carrie indulges in her sentimental fantasies which serve the same function for her that the newspaper does for him.

If the newspapers construct a new reality for Hurstwood, his mistake lies in reading literally, in trying to enter that reality by participating in the streetcar strike. Although Hurstwood usually substitutes reading for actively seeking a position in New York, it is the newspaper which leads him out into the city in his last-ditch effort to find work. After following the account of a Brooklyn streetcar strike for a few days, he comes across a want ad for workers to take the place of the strikers. Once on the job as a strikebreaker, his overwhelming impression, however, is that "the real thing was slightly worse than the thoughts of it had been" (p. 308). When his car is attacked by a group of strikers, "it was an astonishing experience for him. He had read of these things, but the reality seemed something altogether new" (p. 310). Hurstwood then flees from the job during another violent confrontation, unable to tolerate the antagonism from the strikers and the cold, miserable working conditions. When he gets home to his comfortable rocking chair, however, he reads about the strike "with absorbing interest." What was an intolerable experience in person becomes transformed into an absorbing spectacle in the headlines: "Rioting Breaks Out in All Parts of the City" (p. 313).

Hurstwood's participation in the strike appears to exemplify the incompatibility of what Walter Benjamin has called "information" and "experience."[26] The purpose of the newspaper, according to Benjamin, is not "to have the reader assimilate the information it supplies as part of his own experience"; its effect, on the contrary, is to "isolate what happens from the realm in which it could affect the experience of the reader."[27] Hurstwood's mistake lies in trying to convert that information into experience. Yet Hurstwood's case also suggests a different kind of opposition than that delineated by Benjamin; an opposition not between atomized information and the plenitude of experience but between two different versions of reality. Newspapers, as Michael Schudson has shown, employ both storytelling and information, not only decontextualizing isolated bits of information but recontextualizing them in a storyline.[28] When Hurstwood ventures into the strike, he encounters not the coherence of experience but the incoherence of social conflict, which the newspaper represents and contains. While reading about the strike, he can sympathize with both sides, just as he can read about different social classes. The newspaper in this respect evokes a sense of community, of shared experience filtered through information, at the same time that it upholds the reader's sense of himself as outside observer. Hurstwood's experience of the strike dispels both senses—of community and neutrality; when he ventures out of his apartment as a scab, he is not prepared for the intensity of the social conflict, and is forced to take sides. He must either be seen and attacked as a scab, join the strikers, or leave. There is no neutral position. Reading the newspaper allows him to take all three positions simultaneously.

Dreiser implicitly defines his own realism against the newspaper that Hurstwood reads and the bewilderment that Hurstwood experiences. When Dreiser comments on a policeman's ambivalence toward the strike, he notes that "of its true social significance, [Hurstwood] never once dreamed. His was not the mind for that" (p. 300). By implied contrast, the realist represents the "true social significance," which readers have often found in the chapter on the strike. Yet a comparison of this scene to the one in *Hazard* will show that Dreiser's realism, like that of the newspaper, also works to contain conflict, precisely through his documentary stance, through the elaboration of what Howells might have called "useless information." March and Hurstwood each confront a strike that shatters their previous conceptions and eliminates their comfortable distance from such events. In *Hazard,* however, the strike crashes through the closed world of the characters in the foreground, and is viewed in terms of its effects on that settlement. The strike itself remains shadowy; it serves as a catalyst for the changes in the lives of the characters and in the narrative of the novel. In *Sister Carrie,* Hurstwood leaves the world of his life with Carrie and enters an entirely separate realm in which the strike takes place. While in *Sister Carrie* we do view the strike from the inside, its depiction, like the individual details in the text, has little effect on the narrative trajectory or the lives of the characters. Carrie knows little about it and Hurstwood continues on the same downhill direction as before. While the representation of the conflict is more vivid and detailed than in *Hazard*, it is also more contained and less threatening—as though roped off in a separate sphere. The detachment of this scene is indicated in several ways. While in *Hazard* the strike occurs in the heart of Manhattan where the characters live, in *Sister Carrie* Hurstwood must travel to Brooklyn and back; this is the only scene in the second part of the novel set outside of Manhattan. In addition, the strike scene is marked off by its chapter heading. Entitled only "Strike," it is one of the few chapters without both a sentimental and a metrical heading; it therefore seems more straightforward and realistic but also more removed from any interpretive context. Thus, in *Hazard* the strike is assimilated into the lives of the characters and into the narrative at the cost of its visibility; in *Sister Carrie* the strike is rendered quite visible at the cost of any narrative context.

The conventional opposition that associates realism with the newspaper and illusion with the theater is both invoked and undermined by *Sister Carrie*. While Hurstwood reads of the tens of thousands of unemployed and becomes one of them, Carrie finds in the "Oriental" splendor of the theater a "wondrous reality." While the literal reading of the newspaper misleads Hurstwood about the nature of urban reality, the theater realizes Carrie's fantasies of success and makes them literal. If Carrie's career, like Hurstwood's newspaper reading, provides an escape from the "cold bitter reality" of city life, it is an escape with a particular form. Every stage of Carrie's theatrical career reproduces the conditions of powerlessness that she encountered in her work in Chicago and that Hurstwood encounters unemployed in New York. The fairy-tale quality of Carrie's stardom transforms work into play and anonymity into identity. If, in the first part, Carrie's desire to consume expresses a utopian longing for change, her theatrical career puts this change into effect by turning her into a commodity.

Carrie's search for a job in the New York theater reproduces her job hunt in Chicago. As she begins her search she finds out that she is no different from a common laborer, that

> in the opera chorus, as in other fields, employment is difficult to secure. Girls who can stand in line and look pretty are as numerous as labourers who can swing a pick. She found there was no discrimination between one and the other of

applicants, save as regards a conventional standard of prettiness and form. Their own opinion or knowledge of their ability went for nothing. (p. 276)

Thus, she is in the same powerless position as she was as a job applicant in Chicago. But while she was ashamed in Chicago to be looked at and labeled as a job-seeker, in New York her looks have become the only commodity she has to sell, and she is not ashamed when a manager stares at her, judging "women as another would horseflesh" (p. 278). Once she finds a job as a chorus girl, the rehearsal on the chorus line resembles work on the assembly line of the shoe factory. She is subject to the same tedious drilling and to the tyranny of the manager, "who had a great contempt for any assumption of dignity or innocence on the part of these young women" (p. 280).

When she obtains her first position, Carrie makes no distinction between herself working as an actress and the customers who pay to see the play. The theater has the power not only to recast her dreams as a reality but her reality as a dream. The Oriental appearance of the theater lobby evokes her sentimental response:

> Blessed be its wondrous reality. How hard she would try to be worthy of it. It was above the common mass, above idleness, above want, above insignificance. People came to it in finery and carriages to see. It was ever a center of light and mirth. And she was of it. Oh, if she could only remain, how happy would be her days! (p. 280)

Her response here resembles her initial reaction to the facade of the shoe firm. There the sight of the large windows at first conceals her own position in the power structure. Here she similarly makes no distinction between the conditions of her role as worker and the luxurious atmosphere of the playhouse which is designed for the audience's consumption. Yet the fairy-tale quality of the stage allows her to reimagine work as a form of leisure and consumption.

Even disillusionment with work can be turned in the theater into a marketable commodity. Disappointed with her marginal role as a silent Quaker, Carrie unconsciously stands on stage pouting. Although her frown expresses her feelings of insignificance, within the theater it magically endows her with significance. The director finds her expression funny and tells her to frown even more; she then becomes "the chief feature of the play." Her passive expression of discontent is transformed into a springboard to success. She falls into this success as passively as Hurstwood falls into stealing the money. She does not even have to act, but succeeds through exposing her most common expression of longing and unhappiness. Her career as an actress turns passivity into the fantasy of being discovered.

Just as her discontent can be turned into a marketable commodity that can be sold and resold on the stage, so can her sexuality. At the factory she was embarrassed by the sexual taunts bantered among the workers. Yet in the theater the same lewdness contributes to her success:

> The portly gentlemen in the front rows began to feel that she was a delicious little morsel. It was the kind of frown they would have loved to force away with kisses. All the gentlemen yearned toward her. She was capital. (p. 326)

On stage Carrie truly is "capital," for her looks and her sexuality become a valuable commodity. The leering boy on the elevator in the shoe factory is replaced by these portly gentlemen. Although the life of the actress may represent the ultimate form of commodification, for Carrie it represents the utopian element of this commodification in which she offers a version of herself for the consumption of an audience without being touched or consumed by them.

Carrie's position as a star allows for another kind of reconciliation, one between the market and the home. The greatest measure of her success in the novel occurs when her name and image are employed as an advertisement. She is asked to live at a new residential hotel for a nominal fee because her "name is worth something" (p. 329). As soon as she does make a name for herself it too becomes a commodity, which she trades for "such a place as she had often dreamed of occupying" (p. 331). Carrie exchanges her name for the realization of her fantasies, the reconstitution of domesticity in a rented space.

The compensatory and transformative nature of the theater can be seen in Carrie's first encounter with the amateur production at Drouet's lodge:

> the nameless paraphernalia of disguise, have a remarkable atmosphere of their own. Since her arrival in the city many things had influenced her, but always in a far-removed manner. This new atmosphere was more friendly. It was wholly unlike the great brilliant mansions which waved her coldly away, permitting her only awe and distant wonder. This took her by the hand kindly, as one who says, "My dear, come in." It opened for her as if for its own. (p. 128)

The very anonymity of the theater turns it into a welcoming home and counteracts her sense of powerlessness. In her first acting experience at the lodge, Carrie finds that she must feel utterly alone in order to act well. She must ignore the presence of the other actors and the audience, especially during the love scene. Carrie appears just as alone during her love affairs offstage.[29] Yet this loneliness on stage powerfully affects the audience as intimacy. Her lines "came to the audience and the lover as a personal thing" (p. 139). And Drouet and Hurstwood each experience an ardor for Carrie which neither ever expresses face-to-face and which is described in the language of melodrama. Yet that personal connection which the men feel with Carrie seems possible only in the midst of a crowded theater. The loneliness of the individual in a city crowd is transformed in the theater into an ephemeral intimacy between the actress and the audience. The performance forges a momentary community of projected desire out of the isolated members of the audience, who share a common sense of personal intimacy with the actress. If in the theater Carrie can turn isolation in the city into intimacy, she similarly transforms anonymity into identity. The narrative juxtaposes her progress in the theatrical world with Hurstwood's descent into anonymity. After she leaves him, he becomes a part of the faceless and nameless impoverished masses, and dies unknown to anyone, an unidentified corpse transported out to a potters' field. Carrie turns this same anonymity and passivity into the valuable commodity that allows her success as an actress, "that passivity of soul which is always the mirror of the active world" (p. 117).

Critics have often wondered about the discrepancy between the narrowness and cheapness of Carrie's tawdry career on Broadway and the artistic idealism Dreiser attributes to her. The narrator criticizes Hurstwood for believing that Carrie

> would get on the stage in some cheap way and forsake him. Strangely, he had not conceived well of her mental ability. That was because he did not understand the nature of emotional greatness. (p. 271)

Yet Hurstwood is correct—Carrie does get on the stage because of her pretty face and she does forsake him. What then is this "emotional greatness" that makes Carrie an artist? It is not her ascent from popular art to more serious drama, the position advocated by Ames and accepted by many critics. Rather her art as an actress lies in reproducing the urban conditions of everyday life as play. If the theater provides an escape, it is not to some transcendent realm outside the city, as the final pastoral image suggests. Rather, the theater allows Carrie to translate the threats of city life into a form of art that can be instantly consumed by an audience, without consuming her. She is the artist Dreiser learns to be in *An Amateur Laborer*—one who not only produces great works but sells herself in a repetitive gesture that constructs that self. Acting for Carrie is in many ways an escape into the world she enjoyed as a spectator, a world

> showing suffering under ideal conditions. Who would not grieve upon a gilded chair? Who would not suffer amid perfumed tapestries, cushioned furniture, and liveried servants? Grief under such circumstances becomes an enticing thing. Carrie longed to be of it. She wanted to take her sufferings, whatever they were, in such a world, or failing that, at least to simulate them under such charming conditions upon the stage. (p. 228)

Carrie is indeed a sentimental escape artist, whose acting, like the sentimentality of Dreiser's writing, gestures toward the desire for social change that infuses his realism.

The new Pennsylvania edition of *Sister Carrie,* which concludes with Hurstwood's suicide, confirms and resolves what critics have long suspected, that the novel's previous ending, with Carrie dreaming in her rocking chair, was inadequate. The problem of Dreiser's conclusion raises a larger question: why do realistic novels in general have such trouble ending? Or why do we as critics have such trouble accepting their endings? We tend to find the conclusion of American realistic novels singularly unsatisfying, on the grounds that they retreat into nostalgia and sentimental or genteel rhetoric which undermine their realistic premises. In other words, why do realistic novels seem to end so unrealistically? (This is a vexing question for other well-known works of American realism not discussed in this study, especially *The Adventures of Huckleberry Finn* and *The Red Badge of Courage.*)

In the recent editing history of *Sister Carrie,* we have been lucky as critics to find, according to the Pennsylvania editors, that Dreiser's original intention corresponded with our own desire for a more realistic conclusion. Our dream has come true of rewriting the ending, substituting Hurstwood's suicide and his final words, "What's the use?" for Carrie's fantasies expressed in Dreiser's gushy, archaic prose. It is appropriate that the novel long considered the apogee of American realism should enact the critical wish-fulfillment that informs our reading of other novels as well. We wish we could have the divorce in *A Modern Instance* without the final withdrawal into polite conversation. We wish we could have the violent urban strike of *A Hazard of New Fortunes,* without the subsequent retreat into nostalgia for a small-town utopia. We wish we could have Lily's suicide in a boardinghouse in *The House of Mirth* without the sentimentalized working-class domesticity and the aristocratic fantasy of an ancestral estate. In each case we expect the realistic ending to be the one that banishes these alternatives.

Our critical desire seems to be for a more hard-boiled, dirty reality in an open-ended narrative that is not prettified or contained by conventional romance forms; but in fact, this desire works to sanitize and flatten realism by either ignoring or taking one side of the dialectic that informs realistic narratives. We have seen realism in the novels of this study as a debate with competing definitions of reality, either from a past discourse or an even more threatening emergent one. Howells's realism evolves from a debate with the conventions of outdated romance and the discourse of the contemporary mass media. Wharton's realism differentiates itself from the sentimentalism of popular domestic fiction as well as from the voyeuristic intrusions of a literary mass market. In both cases the "opponents" that realism posits for itself are incorporated into the realist's enterprise. This incorporation can be seen most fully in Dreiser, whose realism engages the commercial promotion of authorship and the sentimentalism of consumer culture. The dissonance at the end of realistic novels exposes the way in which the terms of the realistic debate have become polarized rather than resolved.

Realistic novels have trouble ending because they pose problems they cannot solve, problems that stem from their attempt to imagine and contain social change. In fact, the very premises that make the problems visible and available to representation make their resolution impossible in the narratives. The final disjunctures at the ends of the novels raise questions about our own expectations of realism: how does a certain order of experience come to be identified as real and another as unreal? Why does the representation of suicide and defeat appear realistic and the counterpoint that voices the desire for change sound unrealistic? These are some of the questions which the conclusions force upon us. The "unrealistic" endings of realistic novels embody the desire to posit an alternative reality which cannot be fully contained in the novels' construction of the real, and they challenge our notion that the real is that which cannot be changed. As the endings lay bare the unresolved debates with competing versions of reality, we are better able to see the social construction of realism.

NOTES

INTRODUCTION

1. Henry James, *Nathaniel Hawthorne* (1879), reprinted in *Literary Criticism: Essays on Literature, American Writers, English Writers*, ed. Leon Edel and Mark Wilson (New York: Library of America, 1984), p. 351.

2. Ibid., p. 320.

3. Richard Chase, *The American Novel and Its Tradition* (New York: Doubleday, 1957). Versions of the romance thesis, which holds that American writers characteristically escape from society and history, have informed a variety of studies, from D. H. Lawrence, *Studies in Classic American Literature* (New York: Penguin, 1923), to Richard Poirier, *A World Elsewhere* (New York: Oxford, 1966). Another statement can be found in R. W. B. Lewis, *The American Adam* (Chicago: University of Chicago Press, 1955).

4. No area of American literature is more contested today than that of the canon. But testimony to the power of the romance thesis is the fact that feminist criticism of American literature has focused predominantly on the sentimental novelists of the mid-nineteenth century as the countertradition of American fiction. See, for example, Ann Douglas, *The Feminization of American Culture* (New York: Avon, 1977); Nina Baym, *Woman's Fiction: A Guide to Novels by and about Women in America, 1820–1870* (Ithaca, N.Y.: Cornell University Press, 1978); Jane Tompkins, *Sensational Designs: The Cultural Work of American Fiction, 1790–1860* (New York: Oxford University Press, 1985). Although excellent studies have been done of individual women writers in the late nineteenth century, few full-length synthetic studies comparable to those of the earlier period have focused on the generation of American women writers—contemporary with the male American realists—as a group or coherent "tradition" or movement.

5. Another sign of the power of the romance can be seen in the fact that the

most powerful critiques of the ahistorical nature of American criticism still focus on the same sacred American texts that constitute Chase's "tradition." See Myra Jehlen, "New World Epics: The Middle-Class Novel in America," *Salmagundi* 36 (Winter 1977): 49–68; and Carolyn Porter, *Seeing and Being: The Plight of the Participant Observer in Emerson, James, Adams, and Faulkner* (Middletown, Conn.: Wesleyan University Press: 1981).

6. Lionel Trilling, "Manners, Morals, and the Novel," in *The Liberal Imagination* (New York: Viking Press, 1950), pp. 206–7.

7. Chase, *The American Novel,* p. 158.

8. Trilling, "Reality in America," in *The Liberal Imagination,* p. 13. It is important to note that Trilling conflates critics with very different political and aesthetic theories. Parrington considered "critical realism" as the culmination of an American progressive tradition with roots in the eighteenth century; by portraying objective conditions, critical realism "questioned the excellence of the industrial system." Vernon Louis Parrington, *The Beginnings of Critical Realism,* vol. 3 of *Main Currents in American Thought* (New York: Harcourt Brace, 1930), p. 238. For Marxists in the thirties, such as Granville Hicks and Bernard Smith, the goal of realism was to expose underlying forces of the capitalist system. Matthiessen, in contrast, placed Dreiser's "picture of conditions" squarely in an American democratic tradition by comparing him to Whitman, in *Theodore Dreiser* (New York: William Sloane, 1951), pp. 59–60. Yet even these critics tend to treat realism as a goal never fully achieved in American fiction. While to explore these theories of realism in detail would require another study, my argument is based on the claim that Trilling and Chase in effect won the argument and shaped the consequent study of American realism.

9. Trilling, "Reality," p. 11.

10. Trilling, "Manners, Morals, and the Novel," p. 221.

11. Ibid., p. 222. On Trilling's conception of "moral realism," and his attack on liberalism as thinly veiled Stalinism, see Mark Krupnick, *Lionel Trilling and the Fate of Cultural Criticism* (Evanston, Ill.: Northwestern University Press, 1986), pp. 57–75. Krupnick, however, naively accepts Trilling's characterizations of Parrington, liberalism, and popular-front politics as accurate historical description.

12. Larzer Ziff, *The American 1890s: Life and Times of a Lost Generation* (Lincoln: University of Nebraska Press, 1966); Alfred Kazin, *On Native Grounds: An Interpretation of Modern American Prose Literature* (1942; rpt., New York: Anchor Books, 1956).

13. Although many studies combine both literary history and formalist criticism, those primarily formalist include Charles C. Walcutt, *American Literary Naturalism: A Divided Stream* (Minneapolis: University of Minnesota Press, 1956); Donald Pizer, *Realism and Naturalism in Nineteenth-Century American Literature* (Carbondale: Southern Illinois University Press, 1966); Harold Kolb, *The Illusion of Life: American Realism as Literary Form* (Charlottesville: University Press of Virginia, 1969). The New Critical discovery of Dreiser might be

marked by Robert Penn Warren's essay on *An American Tragedy* in the *Yale Review* 52 (October 1962): 1–15.

14. Warner Berthoff, *The Ferment of Realism: American Literature, 1884–1919* (New York: Macmillan, 1965); Jay Martin, *Harvests of Change: American Literature, 1865–1914* (Englewood Cliffs, N.J.: Prentice-Hall, 1967); see also Kazin, *Native Grounds*, and Ziff, *1890s*.

15. Eric Sundquist, *American Realism: New Essays* (Baltimore: The Johns Hopkins University Press, 1982).

16. Richard Brodhead, "Hawthorne Among the Realists: The Case of Howells," in Sundquist, *American Realism*, pp. 25–41. In his book *The School of Hawthorne* (New York: Oxford University Press, 1986), chap. 5, Brodhead revises his argument to situate Howells's realism in a social context, but he still concludes that realism is subverted by Howells's moral preoccupations with fiction as a source of cultural value.

17. Joan Lidoff, "Another Sleeping Beauty: Narcissism in *The House of Mirth*," in Sundquist, *American Realism*, pp. 238–58.

18. See also essays in Sundquist, *American Realism*, by Laurence Holland and Evan Carton, who argue that Mark Twain's novels, long noted for their fresh use of the vernacular, self-consciously expose a fictionality that informs their linguistic and moral structure; and Donald Pease, who claims that *The Red Badge of Courage*, once viewed as the major realistic portrayal of the Civil War, undermines the very possibilty of representation.

19. Sundquist, *American Realism*, p. 9.

20. Ibid., p. 23.

21. Ibid., p. 7.

22. Howard Horwitz, "'To Find the Value of X': *The Pit* as a Renunciation of Romance," in ibid., pp. 215–37; Walter Benn Michaels, "Dreiser's *Financier*: The Man of Business as a Man of Letters," in ibid., pp. 278–96 (reprinted in Walter Benn Michaels, *The Gold Standard and the Logic of Naturalism* [Berkeley: University of California Press, 1987]).

23. Mark Seltzer, "*The Princess Casamassima:* Realism and the Fantasy of Surveillance," in Sundquist, *American Realism*, pp. 95–119.

24. June Howard, *Form and History in American Literary Naturalism* (Chapel Hill: University of North Carolina Press, 1985), p. ix.

25. Philip Fisher, "Appearing and Disappearing in Public: Social Space in Late Nineteenth-Century Literature and Culture," in Sacvan Bercovitch, ed., *Reconstructing American Literary History* (Cambridge, Mass.: Harvard University Press, 1986), p. 177.

26. Rachel Bowlby, *Just Looking: Consumer Culture in Dreiser, Gissing, and Zola* (New York: Methuen, 1985).

27. Mark Seltzer, *Henry James and the Art of Power* (Ithaca, N.Y.: Cornell University Press, 1984).

28. Alan Trachtenberg and June Howard are exceptions to this tendency to conflate capitalism with a culture of consumption and to ignore the underlying

anxieties about social change. In *The Incorporation of America: Culture and Society in the Gilded Age* (New York: Hill and Wang, 1982) chap. 6, Trachtenberg views realism, especially on the part of Howells, as an expression of those democratic tendencies which ultimately support a middle-class effort to impose homogeneous genteel standards. Howard focuses on naturalism as a genre rather than on realism.

29. Philip Fisher, *Hard Facts: Setting and Form in the American Novel* (New York: Oxford University Press, 1985), chap. 3.

30. Walter Benn Michaels, "*Sister Carrie*'s Popular Economy," *Critical Inquiry* 7 (1980): 373–90 (reprinted in Michaels, *The Gold Standard*).

31. T. J. Jackson Lears, "From Salvation to Self-Realization: Advertising and the Therapeutic Roots of the Consumer Culture, 1880–1920," in Richard Wight Fox and T. J. Jackson Lears, eds., *The Culture of Consumption: Critical Essays in American History, 1880–1980* (New York: Pantheon, 1983), p. 6.

32. Henry James, *The American Scene* (Bloomington: Indiana University Press, 1968), p. 76.

33. Ibid., p. 82.

34. Ibid., p. 83.

35. Fredric Jameson, *The Political Unconscious* (Ithaca, N.Y.: Cornell University Press, 1981), p. 193.

36. Though my use of the concept "social construction" is indebted in the broadest sense to Peter L. Berger and Thomas Luckmann, *The Social Construction of Reality: A Treatise in the Sociology of Knowledge* (New York: Doubleday, 1966), I am not directly applying their theory to American realism. While Berger and Luckmann see the construction of reality maintaining stability against the threat of competing definitions of the real (*Social Construction*, pp. 147–49), I aim to relate realism to the struggle for social power (which is not central to their argument) and see the construction of reality as an unstable process that confronts and incorporates competing definitions of the real in the form of each novel.

This is not intended as a thorough consideration of the theory of Berger and Luckmann; instead I am drawing on their basic insight in order to intervene in the literary critical debate that treats realistic representation either as a reflection of an external social world that literature cannot act upon, or as an artistic convention or linguistic fiction which can only undermine its own claims to referentiality. To conceive of a more dialectical relationship between literature and society, I approach realism as social construction in a double sense: realistic novels construct the social reality they present as "the way things are"; yet this process does not take place in a linguistic vacuum because realism as a theory and a practice is itself constructed and reconstructed by society, as it was at the end of the nineteenth century and in each subsequent generation of novelists and literary critics.

Some scholars have called for the direct application of Berger's and Luckmann's theory to the methodology of American studies. See R. Gordon Kelly,

"The Social Construction of Reality: Implications for Future Directions in American Studies," *Prospects* 8 (1983): 49–58; Kay Mussell, *"The Social Construction of Reality* and American Studies: Notes toward Consensus," *Prospects* 9 (1984): 1–16.

37. James, *American Scene*, p. 86.

38. Howard, *Form and History*, chap. 4, analyzes the portrayal of working-class characters as brutes in naturalistic representations as a form of class control.

39. Alfred Habegger, *Gender, Fantasy, and Realism in American Literature* (New York: Columbia University Press, 1982).

CHAPTER ONE

1. Edwin Cady, *The Realist at War: The Mature Years, 1885–1920, of William Dean Howells* (Syracuse: Syracuse University Press, 1958), p. 38.

2. Analysis of realism as a debate within the novel form also may help explain and overcome the divided critical response that Howells has received since his lifetime. For all those who have lauded him as a crusader on behalf of reality in fiction, as many, if not more, have condemned him for his genteel avoidance of American reality in his adherence to "the smiling aspects of American life." Both positions tend to judge him in terms of mimetic fidelity to social reality. To understand realism as a debate with other cultural practices shifts the focus away from questions of accuracy to suggest that realism works on two fronts: it breaks down encrusted conventions while it erects new ones to protect its construction of the real against competing versions. For the divided critical response to Howells, see Edwin Cady and David Frazier, eds., *The War of the Critics over William Dean Howells* (New York: Row, Peterson, 1962). More recently Alfred Habegger has reinterpreted Howells's warring side as an attack on the popular sentimental tradition of women's novels. See Habegger's *Gender, Fantasy, and Realism in American Literature* (New York: Columbia University Press, 1982).

3. William Dean Howells, "Editor's Study," *Harper's Monthly* 75 (September 1887): 639.

4. Howells, "Editor's Study," *Harper's Monthly* (April 1887): 825.

5. Howells, "Editor's Study," *Harper's Monthly* 75 (September 1887): 638.

6. Alan Trachtenberg, *The Incorporation of America: Culture and Society in the Gilded Age* (New York: Hill and Wang, 1982), p. 198.

7. Howells, "Editor's Study," *Harper's Monthly* 74 (April 1887): 824. On the boom in the publication of novels, see John Tebbel, *A History of Book Publishing in the United States*, volume 2: *The Expansion of an Industry, 1865–1919* (New York: R. R. Bowker, 1975), pp. 170–74.

8. On the differences between these two types of editors and their institutional context, see Christopher Wilson, *The Labor of Words: Literary Professionalism in the Progressive Era* (Athens, Ga.: University of Georgia Press, 1985), chap. 1. Although my sense of Howells as a transitional figure is indebted to Wilson's discussion, he locates Howells primarily in the genteel tradition.

9. On these modern techniques, see Christopher Wilson, "The Rhetoric of

Consumption: Mass-Market Magazines and the Demise of the Gentle Reader, 1880–1920," in Richard Wight Fox and T. J. Jackson Lears, eds., *The Culture of Consumption: Critical Essays in American History, 1880–1980* (New York: Pantheon, 1983), pp. 39–64.

10. Howells, "Editor's Study," *Harper's Monthly* 72 (January 1886): 321.

11. Ibid.

12. My account of Howells's realism in the 1880s is based on his criticism and on his fictional meditations on the social representation of authorship and its interpenetration with the mass media. More scholarly work remains to be done on Howells's actual role as editor: whom he published and reviewed and whom he rejected and ignored, how he interacted with those writers, how his editorship intersected with stands and policies adopted by the magazines he worked for, how the economics and the institution of publishing affected him. Most of the studies of Howells's vocation treat his relation to the Brahmin culture of Boston—represented by specific figures and by the *Atlantic*—rather than to the actual work of editing. See Lionel Trilling, "William Dean Howells and the Roots of Modern Taste," *Partisan Review* 18 (1951): 516–36; Edwin Cady, *The Road to Realism: The Early Years, 1837–1885, of William Dean Howells* (Syracuse: Syracuse University Press, 1956), pp. 127–98; Kenneth Lynn, *William Dean Howells: An American Life* (New York: Harcourt, Brace Jovanovich, 1971), pp. 152–89; Lewis P. Simpson, "The Treason of William Dean Howells," in *The Man of Letters in New England and the South: Essays on the History of the Literary Vocation in America* (Baton Rouge: Louisiana State University Press, 1973), pp. 85–128; Michael Davitt Bell, "The Sin of Art and the Problem of American Realism," *Prospects* 9 (1984): 115–42.

13. Howells, "Editor's Study," *Harper's Monthly* 74 (April 1887): 824.

14. T. J. Jackson Lears, *No Place of Grace: Antimodernism and the Transformation of American Culture, 1880–1920* (New York: Pantheon, 1981), chap. 1.

15. Quoted in John W. Crowley, *The Black Heart's Truth: The Early Career of W. D. Howells* (Chapel Hill: University of North Carolina Press, 1985), p. 124.

16. Henry James, "William Dean Howells," *Harper's Weekly*, June 19, 1886; reprinted in *Literary Criticism: Essays on Literature, American Writers, English Writers*, ed. Leon Edel and Mark Wilson (New York: Library of America, 1984), p. 502.

17. Howells, "Editor's Study," *Harper's Monthly* 75 (September 1887): 639.

18. Ibid., p. 639.

19. Ibid., p. 639.

20. Howells, "Editor's Study," *Harper's Monthly* 77 (September 1888): 315, 317.

21. Erich Auerbach, *Mimesis* (Princeton, N.J.: Princeton University Press, 1953), p. 491.

22. Howells, "Editor's Study," *Harper's Monthly* 75 (September 1887): 339.

23. Howells, "Editor's Study," *Harper's Monthly* 74 (May 1887): 987.

24. See, for example, his review of James's novels in "Henry James, Jr.," *Century Magazine* 25 (November 1882): 25–29.

25. Howells, "Editor's Study," *Harper's Monthly* 75 (September 1887): 638.

26. Warren I. Susman, "'Personality' and the Making of Twentieth-Century Culture," in *Culture as History: The Transformation of American Society in the Twentieth Century* (New York: Pantheon, 1984), pp. 271–85.

27. Howells implicitly links the story both to contemporary mass culture and to an outdated oral tradition: "In one manner or other the stories were all told long ago; and now we want merely to know what the novelist thinks about persons and situations" (Howells, "Henry James, Jr.": 29). By identifying character-painting with the novel and "novelty" (as opposed to "long ago"), Howells links character less with the producer's ethos than with the culture of personality based in a consumer's ethos. This problem will be treated below in the discussion of Bartley Hubbard.

28. The summary in this paragraph is based on Frank Luther Mott, *American Journalism: A History, 1690–1960* (New York: Macmillan, 1962), chaps. 25–30; Michael Schudson, *Discovering the News: A Social History of American Newspapers* (New York: Basic Books, 1978), chaps. 2–3; Richard Ohmann, "Where Did Mass Culture Come From? The Case of Magazines," *Berkshire Review* 16 (1981): 85–101.

29. See for example, Schudson, *Discovering The News*, pp. 71–76; Ziff, *1890s*, chap. 7.

30. William Dean Howells, *Years of My Youth* (New York: Harper, 1916), p. 141.

31. William M. Gibson, "Introduction" to *A Modern Instance* (1882; rpt., Boston: Houghton Mifflin, 1957) pp. v–xviii; Cady, *The Road to Realism*, pp. 206–11; Habegger, *Gender, Fantasy, and Realism*, pp. 86–102.

32. In a footnote to *The School of Hawthorne* Richard Brodhead suggests that the "coming of the new mass media—and especially of the mass media as successors to older institutions of public consciousness-formation—might be said to be a secret theme of *A Modern Instance*" (Oxford: Oxford University Press, 1986), p. 234. This chapter argues that this development is a central theme, which has only been overlooked because it has so thoroughly shaped the mass culture that we take for granted.

33. William Dean Howells, *A Modern Instance* (1882; rpt., Boston: Houghton Mifflin, 1957), p. 22. Subsequent references will be cited parenthetically in the text.

34. See for example, Gibson, "Introduction," vi.; Lynn, *William Dean Howells*, pp. 256–58; Henry Nash Smith, *Democracy and the Novel: Popular Resistance to Classic American Writers* (New York: Oxford University Press, 1978), p. 91.

35. Gibson, "Introduction," p. vii.

36. Schudson, *Discovering the News*, p. 93.

37. Ibid.

38. Hubbard introduces *The Rise of Silas Lapham* (1885) and is referred to in *A World of Chance* (1893).

39. In *The Rise of Silas Lapham*, the Boston patrician, Bromfield Corey,

characterizes Lapham, in his strict devotion to business and lack of culture, as not "grammatical" (New York: Norton, 1982), p. 56. Further references cited parenthetically in the text.

40. Susman, "'Personality'," 279–84.

41. Ibid., 277.

42. On the weakness of the novel as it shifts focus in chapter 31, see Cady, *The Realist at War*, p. 210; Kermit Vanderbilt, *The Achievement of William Dean Howells* (Princeton: Princeton University Press, 1968), pp. 80–83; Smith, *Democracy and the Novel*, pp. 93–103; Brodhead, *The School of Hawthorne*, pp. 99–103.

43. Mott, *American Journalism*, p. 444; Schudson, *Discovering the News*, p. 66.

44. William Dean Howells, "The Man of Letters as a Man of Business," *Scribner's Magazine* 14 (October 1893): 430.

CHAPTER TWO

1. Reverend Josiah Strong, *Our Country: Its Possible Future and Its Present Crisis* (New York: The American Home Missionary Society, 1885), p. 129. Subsequent references will be cited parenthetically in the text.

2. For a well-known eighteenth-century example see Thomas Jefferson, *Notes on the State of Virginia*, ed. William Peden (Chapel Hill: University of North Carolina Press, 1955), p. 165. On the response to the strikes of 1877, see Paul Boyer, *Urban Masses and Moral Order in America, 1820–1920* (Cambridge: Harvard University Press, 1978), pp. 125–26.

3. Boyer, *Urban Masses*, pp. 126–28; Henry David, *The History of the Haymarket Affair* (New York: Farrar and Rinehart, 1936).

4. Dreiser quoted in Boyer, *Urban Masses*, p. 128. Richard Sennett, "Middle-Class Families and Urban Violence: The Experience of a Chicago Community in the Nineteenth Century," in *Nineteenth-Century Cities: Essays in the New Urban History*, ed. Stephan Thernstrom and Richard Sennett (New Haven: Yale University Press, 1969), pp. 391–97.

5. Jacob Riis, *How the Other Half Lives: Studies Among the Tenements of New York* (1890; rpt., New York: Hill and Wang, 1957). Subsequent references will be cited parenthetically in the text.

6. See Boyer, *Urban Masses*, pp. 155–58.

7. Howells, "Editor's Study," *Harper's Monthly* 72 (May 1886): 973.

8. In a retrospective preface to *Hazard*, Howells singled out these two events as the major autobiographical inspiration for his novel; William Dean Howells, "Biographical," *A Hazard of New Fortunes*, ed. David Nordloh et al. (Bloomington: Indiana University Press, 1976), p. 4. On the impact of Haymarket on Howells's thinking, see Edwin Cady, *The Realist at War: The Mature Years of William Dean Howells, 1885–1920* (Syracuse: Syracuse University Press, 1958), pp. 67–68; Howard A. Wilson, "W. D. Howells' Unpublished Letters about the Haymarket Affair," *Journal of the Illinois State Historical Society* 56 (1963): 5–19.

9. Riis, *The Other Half*, p. 87.

10. Howells, "Biographical," p. 3.

11. Raymond Williams, *The Country and The City* (London: Paladin, 1973), pp. 202–20. Williams uses this term for the alleged face-to-face social relations depicted in literature about country life. He shows that the "knowable community" depends on an implicit process of selection and exclusion; not only on what is known but on "what is desired and needs to be known." Howells in *Hazard* strives to achieve this knowability for an urban community and founds it on a similar principle of implicit exclusion.

12. Among those who criticize Howells for not presenting an accurate portrayal of New York City and its lower-class life are Larzer Ziff, *The American 1890s: Life and Times of a Lost Generation* (Lincoln: University of Nebraska Press, 1966), pp. 38–39; David Weimer, *The City as Metaphor* (New York: Random House, 1966), pp. 53–55; Blanche Gelfant, *The American City Novel* (Norman: University of Oklahoma Press, 1954), p. 44. This criticism can be understood in part as the heritage from the 1920s rejection of Howells's writing as middle-class, prudish, squeamish, and effeminate. For this attack, led by H. L. Mencken and Sinclair Lewis, and the ensuing controversy in the 30s, see Edwin Cady and David Frazier, *The War of the Critics over William Dean Howells* (New York: Row, Peterson, 1962), pp. 113–78.

13. On the figure of the walker in the city, see Williams, *The Country and the City*, pp. 280–96; Walter Benjamin, "On Some Motifs in Baudelaire," in *Illuminations*, ed. Hannah Arendt (New York: Schocken, 1969) pp. 166–76.

14. For a typical criticism of this "lapse of technique," see Everett Carter, *Howells and the Age of Realism* (Philadelphia: J. B. Lippincott, 1950), p. 204. Howells himself felt the need to justify this scene twenty years later by assuring readers of its "fidelity and accuracy in the article of New York housing as it was in the last decade of the last century." He must not have been satisfied, however, with this empirical reasoning because he added the following apology: "In my zeal for truth I did not distinguish between reality and actuality in this or other matters" (Howells, "Biographical," p. 5).

15. Quoted in Cady, *The Realist at War*, p. 120.

16. William Dean Howells, *A Hazard of New Fortunes* (1890; rpt., Bloomington: Indiana University Press, 1976), p. 58. Subsequent references will be cited in the text.

17. Gwendolyn Wright, *Building the American Dream: A Social History of Housing* (New York: Pantheon, 1981), p. 135.

18. This approach is taken for granted by most readers whether they praise Howells for his accuracy or criticize him for his lack of realism. For two examples of the former see Cady, *The Realist at War*, pp. 100–102; Lionel Trilling, "William Dean Howells and the Roots of Modern Taste," *Partisan Review* 18 (1951): 528.

19. Walter Benn Michaels, "*Sister Carrie*'s Popular Economy," *Critical Inquiry* 7 (1980): 378. In contrast to Dreiser's unstable "economy of excess," Michaels poses Howells's realism as an aesthetic and ethos based on the princi-

ple of containment. This view oversimplifies Howells by taking his pronouncements about realism to represent his practice. Even in *The Rise of Silas Lapham,* which Michaels discusses, there is the countermovement in realism to undermine containment.

20. Cady, *The Realist at War,* p. 102.

21. The amphibious quality of Lindau's language is further suggested by the fact that Howells represents Lindau's German conversations with March in standard English. In addition, Lindau's German represents another interesting crossing of boundaries at the banquet, when Lindau attacks Dryfoos on political grounds in German, assuming incorrectly that Dryfoos will not understand him. It is the fact that Dryfoos does overhear him that sets off the conflict.

22. Most critics have interpreted March's defense of Lindau as a turning point in his moral development from an amused, passive spectator to someone who embraces moral complexity; see Cady, *The Realist at War,* p. 112; Carter, *Howells,* p. 202. For a more ironic view see Kenneth Lynn, *William Dean Howells: An American Life* (New York: Harcourt Brace, Jovanovich, 1970), pp. 300–302. It is generally accepted that Howells modeled March's defense of Lindau on his own defense of the Haymarket anarchists in 1887. This connection is usually drawn to laud both Howells's and March's moral courage. While Howells's isolated public support of the anarchists was truly a courageous act, in creating Basil March's dilemma Howells surely did more than applaud his own heroism. One might conjecture instead that in the portrayal of March's powerlessness, Howells was expressing his own frustration about political powerlessness, his disillusionment with the justice system, and his pessimism about the potential for reform. The protests of Howells and many others did not, after all, succeed in preventing the Haymarket hangings ten days later. His cynicism about peaceful reform has not been given enough attention because of the lingering stereotype of Howells as a complacent believer in "the smiling aspects of life." The more critical side of Howells's political thought is suggested in his letters, especially the one he wrote to the newspapers but never sent on the day after the hangings; Cady, *The Realist at War,* pp. 73–77.

23. A similar distinction between the public, or the community, on one side, and labor and capital on the other, can be found in the newspaper accounts of the actual strike on which Howells based his story:

> The community likes to have labor well paid and well treated and is always willing to see it make any legitimate effort to improve its conditions. But this community, at least, will not contemplate with patience the spectacle of organized labor committing acts and exhibiting a spirit a thousand fold more heartless and hateful than the worst offenses of its employers. (Editorial, *New York Herald Tribune,* 30 January 1889, p. 6)

In *Hazard,* Howells both participates in and critiques this broader realignment of forces in the political discourse of the late nineteenth century.

24. Cady, *The Realist at War,* p. 102.

25. The lack of closure at the end of *Hazard* has disturbed most critics, whether they find it symptomatic of the novel's overall weakness, whether they take this inconclusiveness as its central point, or whether they try to impose a unifying moral theme on the ending; see, for example, Warner Berthoff, *The Ferment of Realism: American Literature, 1884–1919* (New York: Macmillan, 1965), p. 56; Carter, *Howells,* pp. 215ff; Cady, *The Realist at War,* pp. 107ff. I find in the ending both a desire for closure and a denial of it.

26. Vernon Louis Parrington, *The Beginnings of Critical Realism in America: 1860–1920* (1930; rpt., New York, 1968), p. 242.

CHAPTER THREE

1. Alfred Kazin, *On Native Grounds* (New York: Doubleday, 1956), p. 61. On Wharton's antimodernism, see also Irving Howe's introduction, "The Achievement of Edith Wharton," in *Edith Wharton: A Collection of Critical Essays,* ed. Irving Howe (Englewood Cliffs, N.J.: Prentice-Hall, 1962), pp. 1–17, and essays in this anthology by Alfred Kazin, Diana Trilling, and Q. D. Leavis.

2. On Wharton's feminist critique, see Cynthia Griffin Wolff, *A Feast of Words: The Triumph of Edith Wharton* (New York: Oxford University Press, 1977), pp. 109–33; Judith Fetterley, "'The Temptation to Be a Beautiful Object': Double Standard and Double Bind in *The House of Mirth,*" *Studies in American Fiction* 2 (Autumn 1977): 199–211; Elizabeth Ammons, *Edith Wharton's Argument with America* (Athens, Ga.: University of Georgia Press, 1980).

3. Elaine Showalter, "The Death of the Lady (Novelist): Wharton's *House of Mirth,*" *Representations* 9 (Winter 1985): 147. For a new approach to Wharton which combines traditional and feminist views, see Wai-chee Dimock, "Debasing Exchange: Edith Wharton's *The House of Mirth,*" *PMLA* 100 (October 1985): 783–92. While Dimock shows that the language and the ethos of the market pervade all social interaction in the novel and not just the treatment of women, she endorses the traditional view of Wharton as an aristocrat.

4. Edith Wharton, *A Backward Glance* (New York: D. Appleton-Century, 1934), p. 209. Subsequent references will be cited parenthetically in the text.

5. R. W. B. Lewis, *Edith Wharton: A Biography* (New York: Harper & Row, 1975); Wolff, *A Feast of Words.*

6. On the institutional transition from genteel to professional authorship, see Christopher Wilson, *The Labor of Words: Literary Professionalism in the Progressive Era* (Athens, Ga.: University of Georgia Press, 1985), chap. 1.

7. Wharton, *A Backward Glance,* pp. 22–25, 56–57. On the shadowy nature of business for the members of her class, see also Edith Wharton, *The House of Mirth* (1905; rpt., New York: Berkley Books, 1981), pp. 30, 86, 122.

8. Frederic Cople Jaher, *The Urban Establishment* (Urbana: University of Illinois Press, 1982), pp. 246–79.

9. Charlotte Perkins Gilman, *Women and Economics,* ed. Carl Degler (New York: Harper & Row, 1966), pp. 330–31. On the relationship between feminini-

ty, idleness, and sickness, see Barbara Ehrenreich and Deirdre English, *For Her Own Good: 150 Years of the Experts' Advice to Women* (New York: Anchor Books, 1979), pp. 101–40.

10. On Gilman's treatment, see her *The Living of Charlotte Perkins Gilman: An Autobiography* (1935; rpt., New York: Harper Colophon Books, 1975), pp. 90–121. For a fictional rendition of the debilitating effects of the rest cure, see her "The Yellow Wallpaper" (Old Westbury, New York: The Feminist Press, 1973). On Wharton's rest cure, which was believed to have a more salutary effect than Gilman's, see Lewis, *Edith Wharton*, pp. 82–84; Wolff, *A Feast of Words*, pp. 85–86.

11. Lewis, *Edith Wharton*, pp. 353–54.

12. Thorstein Veblen, *The Theory of the Leisure Class* (1899; rpt., New York: Penguin, 1981), pp. 68–101.

13. Ibid., pp. 179–180.

14. On the recurring theme in women's writing of creating the self as an art object, see Susan Gubar, " 'The Blank Page' and the Issues of Female Creativity," in *Writing and Sexual Difference*, ed. Elizabeth Abel (Chicago: University of Chicago Press, 1982), pp. 73–94.

15. On the popular female novelistic tradition in the mid-nineteenth century, see Ann Douglas, *The Feminization of American Culture* (New York: Avon, 1977); Nina Baym, *Woman's Fiction: A Guide to Novels by and about Women in America, 1820–1870* (Ithaca, N.Y.: Cornell University Press, 1978); Jane P. Tompkins, "Sentimental Power: *Uncle Tom's Cabin* and the Politics of Literary History," *Glyph* 8 (1981): 79–99, reprinted in Jane Tompkins, *Sensational Designs: The Cultural Work of American Fiction, 1790–1860* (New York: Oxford University Press, 1985); Mary Kelley, *Private Woman, Public Stage: Literary Domesticity in Nineteenth-Century America* (New York: Oxford University Press, 1984); Gillian Brown, "Getting in the Kitchen with Dinah: Domestic Politics in *Uncle Tom's Cabin*," *American Quarterly* 36 (Fall 1984): 503–23.

16. Quoted in Baym, *Woman's Fiction*, p. 32.

17. Ibid., p. 33.

18. Sedgwick, quoted in Kelley, *Private Woman*, p. 30; Stowe, quoted in Douglas, *Feminization of American Culture*, p. 129.

19. Kelley, *Private Woman*, p. 249.

20. On the identification of the novel as a genre associated with women readers and writers, see Henry Nash Smith, "The Scribbling Women and the Cosmic Success Story," *Critical Inquiry* 1 (September 1974): 47–70; Alfred Habegger, *Gender, Fantasy, and Realism in American Literature* (New York: Columbia University Press, 1982), pp. 3–6.

21. Kelley, *Private Woman*, p. 26.

22. *The Woman's Book* (New York: Scribner's, 1894), p. 362.

23. In *Novels, Readers, Reviewers: Responses to Fiction in Antebellum America* (Ithaca: Cornell University Press, 1984), Nina Baym has recently shown that the Puritan suspicion of fiction is less pervasive in antebellum America than

is commonly held. She argues, however, that critics and reviewers were often uneasy with fiction's genuinely popular appeal.

24. Elizabeth Abel, Introduction, *Writing and Sexual Difference*, ed. Elizabeth Abel (Chicago: University of Chicago Press, 1982), p. 2.

25. Alfred Habegger, *Gender, Fantasy, and Realism*, p. ix.

26. Edith Wharton, "The Pelican," in *The Collected Short Stories of Edith Wharton*, ed. R. W. B. Lewis (New York: Scribner's, 1968), 1: 88–103. All short stories discussed are cited from this volume; references will be included parenthetically in the text.

27. Quoted in Wolff, *A Feast of Words*, p. 45.

28. This is the thesis of Douglas, *The Feminization of American Culture*, which focuses on an earlier period of the mid-ninetenth century.

29. Wharton, "George Eliot," *The Bookman* (May 1902): 247–51. Subsequent references will be included parenthetically in the text.

30. On the use of science as the major source of authority for the professions, see Thomas L. Haskell, *The Emergence of Professional Social Science: The American Social Science Association and the Nineteenth-Century Crisis of Authority* (Urbana: University of Illinois Press, 1977); Burton J. Bledstein, *The Culture of Professionalism: The Middle Class and the Development of Higher Education in America* (New York: Norton, 1978), pp. 88–94, 326–30.

31. On women as the objects and clients of the medical profession, see Caroll Smith-Rosenberg and Charles Rosenberg, "The Female Animal: Medical and Biological Views of Women," in Charles Rosenberg, *No Other Gods: On Science and American Social Thought* (Baltimore: John Hopkins University Press), pp. 54–70.

32. Rosalind Rosenberg, *Beyond Separate Spheres: Intellectual Roots of Modern Feminism* (New Haven: Yale University Press, 1982), pp. 1–27.

33. For a different interpretation of Wharton's relation to Eliot, which emphasizes Eliot's legacy of female disinheritance, see Sandra M. Gilbert, "Life's Empty Pack: Notes Toward a Literary Daughteronomy," *Critical Inquiry* 11 (March 1985): 355–84.

34. Wharton coauthored this book with Ogden Codman, Jr., *The Decoration of Houses* (1897; rpt., New York: Norton, 1978). Further references will be cited parenthetically in the text.

35. Wharton, *A Backward Glance*, p. 106.

36. Edmund Wilson, "Justice to Edith Wharton," in *Edith Wharton: A Collection of Critical Essays*, ed. Irving Howe, p. 23.

37. Lewis, *Edith Wharton*, p. 109. Both Wolff and Susan Gubar call attention to this earlier title as evidence of Wharton's dilemma about representing herself as artist; they see Lily as the heroine/victim of a thwarted *Künstlerroman*. They both overlook the fact that Wharton did change the title, thus identifying authorship and narration with "The House," the architectural structure, instead of with the victim entrapped within that house. It seems important not to identify the woman character as the only figure of authorship in the novel,

nor to insist too closely on the autobiographical identification of Lily and Wharton. In general we tend too readily to collapse a discussion of women's writing into a discussion of women characters. See Gubar's "The Blank Page," pp. 73–93.

38. Roger Burlingame, *Of Making Many Books* (New York: Scribner's, 1946), p. 33.

39. Wharton, *The Writing of Fiction* (New York: Scribner's, 1925), p. 46.

40. Sandra Gilbert and Susan Gubar, *The Madwoman in the Attic: The Woman Writer and the Nineteenth-Century Literary Imagination* (New Haven: Yale University Press, 1979), p. 85.

41. On discussions of women's writing based on biological models see ibid., pp. 93–104; and Elaine Showalter, "Feminist Criticism in the Wilderness," in Abel, *Writing and Sexual Difference*, pp. 17–20. On women's space and language as a prelinguistic void, see, for example, Claudine Hermann, "Women in Space and Time," in *New French Feminisms: An Anthology*, ed. Elaine Marks and Isabelle Courtivron (New York: Schocken, 1981), pp. 168–73. For a cultural-historical approach to Wharton and space, see Judith Fryer, *Felicitous Space: The Imaginative Structures of Edith Wharton and Willa Cather* (Chapel Hill: University of North Carolina Press, 1986).

42. On the evangelical politics of sentimental fiction, see Tompkins, "Sentimental Power." For a critique see Brown, "Getting in the Kitchen." My view is closer to that of Brown and Douglas (*Feminization of American Culture*), who argue that the reforming power of women's influence espoused by these novels reinforces the dominant political economy.

43. In " 'The Blank Page' and the Issues of Female Creativity," Susan Gubar takes at face value the following comment of Percy Lubbock about Wharton: "she was herself a novel of his [James's], no doubt in his earliest manner" (p. 81). Gubar uses this to support her own thesis that women writers must deal with the anxiety of finding themselves defined as the creation of male artists. According to Wharton's recent biographers, however, Wharton herself never seemed to experience this anxiety of being trapped in James's definition of her; she had largely formulated a sense of herself as artist before she and James became friends. This trap seems to have been set by critics, often building on Lubbock's *Portrait of Edith Wharton* (New York: Appleton Century, 1947), a biography which has since been proven to be erroneous and malicious (Lewis, *Edith Wharton*, p. 515). In response to Gubar's argument, we also have to remember that Wharton's concept of interior architecture and her use of architectural metaphors for fiction writing did precede James's famous description of the house of fiction in his preface to *The Portrait of a Lady*. So who, here, is trapped in whose house or text? Anxiety can go both ways.

44. Wharton, *The Touchstone* (1900), in *Madame de Treymes and Others: Four Novelettes by Edith Wharton* (New York: Scribner's, 1970). Subsequent references are cited parenthetically in the text.

45. Although Vernon Lee was the direct model for Mrs. Aubyn, according to R. W. B. Lewis, it is likely that Wharton also had George Eliot in mind, since she was to write in her review about the damaging effects of Eliot's status as a

"literary celebrity" on her writing and her life. See Lewis, *Edith Wharton*, p. 96; Wharton, "George Eliot," p. 251.

46. On the best-seller, a term coined by *The Bookman* in 1895, see James D. Hart, *The Popular Book: A History of America's Literary Taste* (1950; rpt., Westport, Conn.: Greenwood Press, 1976), pp. 184–85. On the author as celebrity, see Wilson, *Labor of Words*, pp. 17–33.

47. Wharton, "Copy," in *The Collected Short Stories* (note 26 above), pp. 275–286.

48. On the way in which the 1891 international copyright law transformed literary work into property, see Wilson, *Labor of Words*, pp. 72–74.

49. For Lily's artistic sensibilities, see *The House of Mirth*, pp. 10, 35, 132.

50. Lily Bart's own death scene, in fact, echoes the *tableaux vivants*, as it begins with her viewing the gown she wore that night and ends with Selden's adoration, as did the *tableaux vivants*.

51. Edith Wharton, *Bunner Sisters*, in *Madame de Treymes and Others* (New York: Scribner's, 1970), p. 225. *Bunner Sisters* was written in 1892 but not published until 1916.

52. Lewis, *Edith Wharton*, p. 67.

53. *Bunner Sisters* is one of Wharton's few stories written in a naturalistic mode, and one of the few to be rejected by Scribner's as too depressing and too long. Can Wharton's quotation of Johnson in relation to Eliot also be applied here, that naturalistic representation is "indelicate in a female"?

54. Lewis, *Edith Wharton*, p. 151.

55. Edith Wharton, *The Custom of the Country* (1913; rpt., New York: Berkley Books, 1981).

56. In her diaries of 1905 and 1906, Wharton proudly recorded the number of copies sold of *The House of Mirth* each month and noted that the novel continued to be a best-seller across the country (Lewis, *Edith Wharton*, p. 151). Her fear of being read as a mass-marketed "society novelist" was probably fueled by her success in that market and her own acute business sense.

57. *The House of Mirth*, p. 37.

58. Wharton continued to explore the double tension between professionalism and domesticity, and realism and sentimentalism throughout her career, a topic which requires more investigation from critics. An especially striking instance is *The Fruit of the Tree* (New York: Scribner's, 1907), the first novel Wharton published after *The House of Mirth*. The novel pits a professional nurse against a wife and mother, who appears as a figure from a sentimental novel. The nurse in an act of euthanasia kills the other woman and eventually marries her husband. The novel raises fascinating questions about the relation between professionalism and domesticity (which is lethal and parasitic at once), as ways of defining both womanhood and artistic production. This focus may, in addition, provide a link among what critics have seen as the inadequately connected plots and themes of the novel: the love story, the moral issue of euthanasia, and the problem of industrial work and reform which is posed by the factory town in which the novel takes place.

CHAPTER FOUR

1. Edith Wharton, *The House of Mirth* (1905; rpt., New York: Berkley Books, 1981), p. 3. Subsequent references will be cited parenthetically in the text.

2. See for example, Judith Fetterley, "'The Temptation to Be a Beautiful Object': Double Standard and Double Bind in *The House of Mirth*," *Studies in American Fiction* 2 (Autumn 1977): 199–211, and Cynthia Griffin Wolff, *A Feast of Words: The Triumph of Edith Wharton* (New York: Oxford University Press, 1977), pp. 109–33. For a psychoanalytic interpretation of Lily's narcissism, see Joan Lidoff, "Another Sleeping Beauty: Narcissism in *The House of Mirth*," in Eric Sundquist, ed., *American Realism: New Essays* (Baltimore: The Johns Hopkins University Press, 1982), pp. 238–58.

3. Lewis Erenburg, *Steppin' Out: New York City's Restaurants and Cabarets and the Decline of Victorianism* (Westport, Conn.: Greenwood Press, 1981), p. 37.

4. This paragraph is based on ibid., chaps. 1 and 2, and Frederic Cople Jaher, *The Urban Establishment* (Urbana: University of Illinois Press, 1982), pp. 246–79.

5. Erenburg, *Steppin' Out*, pp. 34–40.

6. Ibid., pp. 37–40; Frederic Cople Jaher, "Style and Status: High Society in Late Nineteenth-Century New York," in *The Rich, The Well-Born, and the Powerful: Elites and Upper Classes in History,* ed. Jaher (Urbana: University of Illinois Press, 1973), pp. 259–84.

7. Henry James, *The American Scene* (Bloomington: Indiana University Press, 1968), p. 65; Paul Bourget, *Outre-Mer* (New York: Scribner's, 1895), chap. 4.

8. John Berger et al., *Ways of Seeing* (London: Viking Press, 1973), pp. 83–112.

9. On the relation between the spectacle and the intangible qualities of commodity culture, see Jean-Christophe Agnew, "The Consuming Vision of Henry James," in *The Culture of Consumption,* ed. Fox and Lears, pp. 65–100.

10. Frank Luther Mott, *A History of American Magazines, Volume 4: 1885–1905* (Cambridge, Mass.: Harvard University Press, 1957), pp. 751–55.

11. Jaher, "High Society," p. 274.

12. James, *The American Scene,* p. 104.

13. Erenburg, *Steppin' Out,* pp. 51–56.

14. On the centrality of exchange in *The House of Mirth,* see Wai-chee Dimock, "Debasing Exchange: Edith Wharton's *The House of Mirth,*" *PMLA* 100 (October 1985), pp. 783–92. While Dimock demonstrates the pervasiveness of the language of exchange throughout the novel, she does not extend this analysis to writing as an act and medium of exchange.

CHAPTER FIVE

1. Theodore Dreiser, "How He Climbed Fame's Ladder," *Success* (April 1898): 5–6; reprinted in Ulrich Halfmann, ed., *Interviews With William Dean*

Howells (Arlington, Texas: University of Texas Press, 1973), pp. 59–64. Subsequent references will be cited parenthetically in the text.

2. Theodore Dreiser, "The Real Howells," *Ainslee's* (March 1900): 137–42; Halfmann, *Interviews*, pp. 67–71.

3. Ellen Moers, *Two Dreisers* (New York: Viking, 1969) p. 55.

4. Robert Elias, *Theodore Dreiser: Apostle of Nature* (New York: Knopf, 1949), chaps. 1–5; Moers, *Two Dreisers*, pt. 1, "Apprenticeship in the 1890s"; Yoshinobu Hakutani, *Young Dreiser: A Critical Study* (Rutherford, N.J.: Fairleigh Dickinson University Press, 1980). See also the biography of Dreiser by Richard Lingeman, *Theodore Dreiser: At the Gates of the City, 1871–1907* (New York: Putnam, 1986).

5. Lingeman, *Dreiser*, p. 236.

6. Unsigned caption, *Ev'ry Month* (September 1896), p. 22. Moers quotes this as evidence of Dreiser's appreciation of Howells and misses the obvious irony (*Two Dreisers*, p. 44).

7. For a recent discussion of Dreiser's journalism, see Shelley Fisher Fishkin, *From Fact to Fiction: Journalism and Imaginative Writing in America* (Baltimore: The Johns Hopkins University Press, 1985), chap. 4. She argues that Dreiser's "greatest strengths and weaknesses as a writer may be traced to his work in journalism in the 1890s. He would return as a novelist to subjects, styles and strategies he had first explored as a journalist. His awareness of the limitations of journalism, however, would imbue that return with a special sensitivity to the liberating possibilities of fiction" (p. 88). Fishkin charts a familiar trajectory from the constraints of hack work to the freedom of art.

8. On the careers of Steffens and Phillips, see Christopher Wilson, *The Labor of Words: Literary Professionalism in the Progressive Era* (Athens, Ga.: University of Georgia Press, 1985), chaps. 6, 7, and on institutional changes in journalism see his excellent chapter on "The Rise of the Reporter." For further background on newspapers in this period, see Larzer Ziff, *The American 1890s: Life and Times of a Lost Generation* (Lincoln: University of Nebraska Press, 1966), chap. 7; Michael Schudson, *Discovering the News: A Social History of American Newspapers* (New York: Basic Books, 1978), chaps. 2 and 3.

9. Theodore Dreiser, *Newspaper Days* (New York: Horace Liveright, 1931), p. 4. Originally published in 1922 under the title *A Book About Myself*. Subsequent references will be cited parenthetically in the text.

10. Theodore Dreiser, "Fakes," *Chicago Daily Globe*, Tuesday, 18 October 1892, p. 1; reprinted in Blair Ferguson Bigelow, "The Collected Newspaper Articles, 1892–1894, of Theodore Dreiser" (Ph.D. diss. Brandeis University, 1973), p. 47. For all fourteen articles, see Bigelow, pp. 9–89.

11. Bigelow, "Articles," pp. 258–458.

12. The titles indicate the focus of the articles: "Teachers at the Fair," "The Republic Teachers Will See Everything," "The Teachers' Fourth Day"; Bigelow, "Articles," pp. 467–501.

13. See "Blindfolded He Drove," *St. Louis Republic*, Friday, 18 August 1893, p. 1 (also Dreiser, *Newspaper Days*, p. 268). See also "Water Works Exten-

sion," *St. Louis Globe-Democrat,* 15 January 1892, pp. 31ff.; Bigelow, "Articles," pp. 150–75. On the construction of the St. Louis Union Depot, see "Greatest in the World," *St. Louis Globe-Democrat,* 11 December 1892, pp. 28ff.; Bigelow, "Articles," pp. 100–126.

14. See for example, from the *Pittsburgh Dispatch,* "And It Was Mighty Blue," "After the Rain Storm," "Odd Scraps of Music," "Some Dabbling in Books;" Bigelow, "Articles," pp. 840–94.

15. Bigelow, Introduction, "Articles," pp. liv–lvii; Dreiser, "Burned to Death," *St. Louis Globe-Democrat,* 22 January, p. 1–2; "Fever's Frenzy. John Finn Tries to Kill His Four Children," *St. Louis Republic* 9 August, pp. 1–2; Bigelow, "Articles," pp. 529–48.

16. Dreiser, "The Return of Genius," *Chicago Sunday Globe,* 23 October, p. 4; Bigelow, "Articles," pp. 90–95. Further references cited parenthetically.

17. Unsigned, "Heard in the Corridors," *St. Louis Globe-Democrat,* 29 December 1892, p. 7; Bigelow, "Articles," pp. 130–31. Further references cited parenthetically.

18. Bigelow, "Articles," pp. 134–35, no date or page.

19. "The Ball At Midnight," *St. Louis Republic,* 4 October 1893, pp. 1–2; Bigelow, "Articles," p. 732.

20. "Burned to Death," *St. Louis Globe-Democrat,* 22 January 1893, pp. 1–2; Bigelow, "Articles," pp. 183–214.

21. "Nigger Jeff," *Ainslee's,* 8 (November 1901): 366–75. Reprinted and revised in *Free and Other Stories* (New York: Boni and Liveright, 1918), p. 82. Further references cited parenthetically.

22. June Howard, *Form and History in American Literary Naturalism* (Chapel Hill: University of North Carolina Press, 1985), pp. 106–7. See chapter 4 on spectatorship and naturalism. On "Nigger Jeff," see also Donald Pizer, *The Novels of Theodore Dreiser: A Critical Study* (Minneapolis: University of Minnesota Press, 1976), pp. 21–25.

23. For the most complete accounts of Dreiser's association with *Ev'ry Month,* see Moers, *Two Dreisers,* pp. 32–43, and Joseph Katz, "Theodore Dreiser's *Ev'ry Month,*" *Library Chronicle of the University of Pennsylvania* 38 (Winter 1972): 46–66.

24. Lingeman, *Theodore Dreiser,* p. 165.

25. Dreiser, "Whence the Song," *The Color of a Great City* (New York: Boni and Liveright, 1923), pp. 138–55.

26. Katz, "Dreiser's *Ev'ry Month,*" p. 51.

27. Dreiser, "My Brother Paul," *Twelve Men* (New York: Boni and Liveright, 1919), p. 80.

28. Bigelow, "Articles," p. 130.

29. "Reflections," *Ev'ry Month* 3 (October 1896): 4; "The Literary Shower," *Ev'ry Month* 2 (June 1896): 21–22; reprinted in Donald Pizer, ed. *Theodore Dreiser: A Selection of Uncollected Prose* (Detroit: Wayne State University Press, 1977), p. 72. Subsequent references cited parenthetically in the text.

30. "Reflections," *Ev'ry Month* 3 (March 1897): 5. Arthur Henry, "It Is to

Laugh: A Little Talk on How to Write a Comic Opera," *Ev'ry Month* 3 (April 1897).

31. "Review of the Month," *Ev'ry Month* 1 (December 1895): 2–3 (signed "The Prophet"); Pizer, *Uncollected Prose*, pp. 36, 37. Subsequent references cited parenthetically.

32. "Reflections," *Ev'ry Month* 2 (May 1896): 2–6; Pizer, *Uncollected Prose*, pp. 52, 53, 54.

33. "Reflections," *Ev'ry Month* 3 (January 1897): 5–6; Pizer, *Uncollected Prose*, p. 100. Further references cited parenthetically in text.

34. "Reflections," *Ev'ry Month* 2 (September 1896): 2.

35. "Reflections," *Ev'ry Month* 1 (January 1896): 5; Pizer, *Uncollected Prose*, pp. 43–44. Further references cited parenthetically.

36. On window-shopping and the spectator in naturalism, see Rachel Bowlby, *Just Looking: Consumer Culture in Dreiser, Gissing, and Zola* (London: Methuen, 1985).

37. "Reflections," *Ev'ry Month* 4 (May 1897): 21; Pizer, *Uncollected Prose*, pp. 114–15.

38. "Reflections," *Ev'ry Month* 3 (October 1896): 6–7; Pizer, *Uncollected Prose*, p. 95.

39. "Decorative Notes," *Ev'ry Month* 2 (September 1896): 29–30.

40. Orison Swett Marden, ed., *Talks with Great Workers* (New York: Thomas Y. Crowell, 1901), p. iii.

41. Dorothy Dudley, *Dreiser and the Land of the Free* (New York, 1946), p. 142.

42. "Life Stories of Successful Men—No. 10," *Success* 1 (October 1898): 3–4; reprinted in Yoshinobu Hakutani, ed., *Selected Magazine Articles of Theodore Dreiser: Life and Art in the American 1890s* (Rutherford, N.J.: Fairleigh Dickinson University Press, 1985), pp. 120–29.

43. "A Photographic Talk with Edison," *Success* 1 (February 1898): 8–9; Hakutani, *Articles*, pp. 111–19 (citations on pp. 116, 118).

44. "A Monarch of Metal Workers," *Success* 2 (June 1899): 453–54; Hakutani, *Articles*, pp. 158–69. Further references cited parenthetically.

45. "Life Stories of Successful Men—No. 11, Chauncy Mitchell Depew," *Success* 1 (November 1898): 3–4; reprinted in Marden, *Talks with Great Workers*, p. 2.

46. "A Master of Photography," *Success* 2 (June 1899): 471; Hakutani, *Articles*, p. 251.

47. "The Story of a Song-Queen's Triumph," *Success* 3 (January 1900): 6–8; reprinted in Orison Swett Marden, ed., *How They Succeeded: Life Stories of Successful Men Told by Themselves* (Boston: Lathrop, Lee, and Shepard, 1901).

48. "He Became Famous in a Day," *Success* 2 (January 1899): 143–44; Hakutani, *Articles*, pp. 242–47.

49. Pizer, *Uncollected Prose*, p. 276.

50. "A Talk with America's Leading Lawyer," *Success* 1 (January 1898): 40–41; Pizer, *Uncollected Prose*, pp. 119–23.

51. Warren I. Susman, "'Personality' and the Making of Twentieth-Century Culture," in *Culture as History: The Transformation of American Society in the Twentieth Century* (New York: Pantheon, 1984), pp. 271–85.

52. "The Real Choate," *Ainslee's* 3 (April 1899): 324–33; Hakutani, *Articles*, p. 156.

53. "A Leader of Young Manhood," *Success* 2 (December 1899): 23–24; reprinted in Marden, *Talks With Great Workers*, pp. 323–30.

54. The figure of the orator seems to have interested Dreiser throughout his career. Eugene Witla of *The Genius* expresses his desire to be an orator, and Dreiser in *Newspaper Days* described his own ambitions to write by imagining himself as a "great orator with thousands of people before me" (p. 3).

55. "The Color of To-day," *Harper's Weekly* 45 (14 December 1901): 1272–73; Hakutani, *Articles*, pp. 267–78.

56. For the publication history of *Sister Carrie*, see Jack Saltzman, "The Publication of *Sister Carrie:* Fact and Fiction," *Library Chronicle of the University of Pennsylvania* 33 (1967): 119–33; and the letters and documents collected by Donald Pizer in the Norton Critical Edition of *Sister Carrie* (New York: W. W. Norton, 1970).

57. Christopher Wilson, "*Sister Carrie* Again," *American Literature* 55 (May 1981): 287–90.

58. Theodore Dreiser, *An Amateur Laborer*, ed. Richard W. Dowell (Philadelphia: University of Pennsylvania Press, 1983), p. 11. Subsequent references will be cited parenthetically in the text.

59. T. J. Jackson Lears, *No Place of Grace: Antimodernism and the Transformation of American Culture: 1880–1920* (New York: Pantheon, 1981), chaps. 1, 2.

60. Dreiser to H. L. Mencken, 27 March 1943. Quoted in Richard Dowell's Introduction to *An Amateur Laborer.*

61. This confidence, curiously, must stem from having written about Hurstwood, not only from the work being physically undemanding. In fact the narrative of *Amateur Laborer* in many ways reenacts the separate stories of Hurstwood and Carrie as one character—Theodore Dreiser.

62. In another blurring of fact and fiction, this dream became the story that Dreiser would tell of his experience to friends and biographers.

63. Dreiser was known as a powerful and autocratic editor among his staff, a position which can be seen in his relation to his readers as well. For a different view of Dreiser's editorship of *The Delineator*, one that stresses his identification with and aid to his female audience coping with a bewildering modern world, see Janice Radway, "Theodore Dreiser at *The Delineator:* Ideology, Readers, and Early Twentieth-Century Magazines" (unpublished paper, December 1984).

64. Theodore Dreiser, "True Art Speaks Plainly," *Booklovers Magazine* 1 (February 1903): 129; Pizer, *Uncollected Prose*, p. 156.

65. The pamphlet has been reprinted in Neda Westlake, "The *Sister Carrie* Scrapbook," *Library Chronicle of the University of Pennsylvania* 45 (Spring 1979): 78–83. Westlake also establishes that for this pamphlet, Dreiser wrote a

five-page "elaborate piece of propaganda"—previously attributed to Arthur Henry in 1901—in which he defended the novel against Doubleday's "suppression." According to Lingeman, Dodge chose not to include it, either because of its length or because of his fear of antagonizing a prominent publisher (Lingeman, *Dreiser,* p. 415).

CHAPTER SIX

1. Theodore Dreiser, *Sister Carrie,* ed. Donald Pizer (1900; rpt., New York: Norton, 1970), p. 1. All further references will be cited parenthetically in the text. For the choice of this edition over the new Pennsylvania edition, see n. 5 below.

2. Leslie Fiedler, *Love and Death in the American Novel* (New York: Criterion Books, 1960), pp. 241–48.

3. Alfred Kazin, Introduction to *The Stature of Theodore Dreiser: A Critical Survey of the Man and His Work,* ed. Alfred Kazin and Charles Shapiro (Bloomington: Indiana University Press, 1965), p. 5.

4. Early reviewers tended to single out Hurstwood's downfall for special praise and treated Carrie's story as a secondary theme. See Jack Saltzman, ed. *Theodore Dreiser: The Critical Reception* (New York: D. Lewis, 1972), pp. 1–52. For more recent examples of critics who privilege Dreiser's realistic qualities, see F. O. Matthiessen, *Theodore Dreiser* (New York: Sloan, 1951) pp. 52–92; Richard Lehan, *Theodore Dreiser: His World and His Novels* (Carbondale: Southern Illinois University Press, 1969), pp. 53–79; Mary Burgen, "*Sister Carrie* and the Pathos of Naturalism," *Criticism* 15 (1973): 336–49; Donald Pizer, *The Novels of Theodore Dreiser: A Critical Study* (Minneapolis: University of Minnesota Press, 1976), pp. 36–40.

5. Theodore Dreiser, *Sister Carrie,* The Pennsylvania Edition (Philadelphia: University of Pennsylvania Press, 1981), p. 579. Although this edition is an invaluable source for scholars, I have chosen to use the edition which was published by Dreiser in 1900 and has been read by readers since then, because I believe that the revisions either made by or authorized by Dreiser are as much a part of Dreiser's final product as is his "original" draft. As this argument suggests, I think that the deletions show that more is at stake in the "new edition" than accuracy, but it reflects a longstanding critical desire to recuperate the great American realist, without his embarrassing sentimentality.

6. Sandy Petrey, "The Language of Realism, the Language of False Consciousness: A Reading of *Sister Carrie,*" *Novel* 10 (1977): 104.

7. Cathy N. Davidson and Arnold E. Davidson, "Carrie's Sisters: the Popular Prototypes for Dreiser's Heroines," *Modern Fiction Studies* 23 (1977): 407; Daryl Dance, "Sentimentalism in Dreiser's Heroines, Carrie and Jennie," *CLA Journal* 14 (1970): 127–42.

8. Walter Benn Michaels, *The Gold Standard and the Logic of Naturalism* (Berkeley: University of California Press, 1987), pp. 29–58.

9. Philip Fisher, *Hard Facts: Setting and Form in the American Novel* (New York: Oxford University Press, 1985), pp. 14–21, 128–58.

10. Davidson and Davidson argue that Dreiser exposes the failure of domesticity, as does June Howard in *Form and History in American Literary Naturalism* (Chapel Hill: University of North Carolina Press, 1985), p. 178.

11. Theodore Dreiser, *An Amateur Laborer*, ed. Richard W. Dowell (Philadelphia: University of Pennsylvania Press, 1983), p. 45. See the discussion of *Amateur Laborer* in chapter 5.

12. Jane Tompkins, *Sensational Designs: The Cultural Work of American Fiction, 1790–1860* (New York: Oxford University Press, 1985), pp. 141–42.

13. Fisher, *Hard Facts*, pp. 154–55.

14. On this trope, see Alan Trachtenberg, *The Incorporation of America: Culture and Society in the Gilded Age* (Hill and Wang: New York, 1982), chap. 4.

15. For the notion of utopian desire in mass culture I am drawing on Fredric Jameson's "Reification and Utopia in Mass Culture," *Social Text* 1 (Winter 1979): 130–48.

16. Michaels, *The Gold Standard*, p. 383.

17. On the importance of atmosphere in Dreiser's novels see Fisher, *Hard Facts*, p. 141.

18. Ibid., p. 132.

19. Ibid., p. 147.

20. Ibid., pp. 141, 142. A similar argument about the absence of society in Dreiser is made by Richard Poirier in *A World Elsewhere: The Place of Style in American Literature* (New York: Oxford University Press, 1966), pp. 235–50.

21. Michaels, *The Gold Standard*, pp. 41–58. For an analysis of Dreiser's relation to the culture of consumption that is closer to mine, see Rachel Bowlby, *Just Looking: Consumer Culture in Dreiser, Gissing, and Zola* (London: Methuen, 1985), chap. 4.

22. Petrey, "The Language of Realism," p. 104.

23. Howard, *Form and History*, pp. 146–65.

24. On the lack of connection between details and narrative in naturalist writing, see Georg Lukács, "Narrate or Describe?" in *Writer and Critic, and Other Essays*, trans. and ed. Arthur D. Kahn (New York: Grosset and Dunlap, 1971), pp. 127–34.

25. Poirier, *A World Elsewhere*, p. 237.

26. Walter Benjamin, *Illuminations* (New York: Schocken Books, 1969), pp. 83–85, 88–90, 157–59.

27. Ibid., p. 158.

28. Michael Schudson, *Discovering the News: A Social History of American Newspapers* (New York: Basic Books, 1978), chap. 3.

29. On the lack of contact between people in *Sister Carrie*, see Poirier, *A World Elsewhere*, pp. 245–46.

INDEX